Argumentation in Highe

Argumentation in Higher Education offers professors, lecturers, and researchers informative guidance for teaching effective argumentation skills to their undergraduate and graduate students. This professional guide aims to make the complex topic of argumentation open and transparent. Grounded in empirical research and theory but with student voices heard strongly throughout, this book fills the gap of argumentation instruction for the undergraduate and graduate level.

Written to enlighten even the most experienced professor, this text contributes to a better understanding of the demands of spoken, written, and visual argumentation in higher education and will undoubtedly inform and enhance course design. The book argues for a more explicit treatment of argument (the product) and argumentation (the process) in higher education so that the ground rules of the academic discipline in question are made clear. Each chapter concludes with practical exercises for staff development use.

Topics discussed include the following:

- The importance of argument
- The current state of argumentation in higher education
- Generic skills in argumentation
- The balance between generic and discipline-specific skills
- Information communication technologies and visual argumentation

How can we best teach argumentation so that students feel fully empowered in their academic composition? Professors (new and experienced), lecturers, researchers, professional developers, and writing coaches worldwide grappling with this question will find this accessible text to be an extremely valuable resource.

Richard Andrews is Professor in English at the Institute of Education, University of London.

Argumentation in Higher Education

Improving Practice Through Theory and Research

Richard Andrews

Routledge
Taylor & Francis Group
NEW YORK AND LONDON

First published 2010
by Routledge
711 Third Avenue, New York, NY 10017

Simultaneously published in the UK
by Routledge
2 Park Square, Milton Park, Abingdon, Oxfordshire, OX14 4RN

Routledge is an imprint of the Taylor & Francis Group, an informa business

Typeset in Minion by

HWA Text and Data Management, London

Library of Congress Cataloging in Publication Data
Andrews, Richard, 1953 Apr. 1-
Argumentation in higher education : improving practice through theory and research / Richard Andrews.
p. cm.
Includes bibliographical references and index.
Academic disputations. 2. Debates and debating – Study and teaching (Higher) 3. Communication in education. I. Title.
PN4181.A59 2009
808.53–dc22 2009009259

ISBN 10: 0-415-99500-0 (hbk)
ISBN 10: 0-415-99501-9 (pbk)
ISBN 10: 0-203-87271-1 (ebk)

ISBN 13: 978-0-415-99500-9 (hbk)
ISBN 13: 978-0-415-99501-6 (pbk)
ISBN 13: 978-0-203-87271-0 (ebk)

Contents

Illustrations

Figures

Tables

Acknowledgements

I am grateful to Taylor & Francis, Mouton de Gruyter, and Routledge, and to the editors of *Teaching in Higher Education* ('The end of the essay?', 8:1, 117–128); *Text* ('Models of argumentation in educational discourse', 25:1, 107–28); and *Educational Review* ('Argument, critical thinking and the postgraduate dissertation', 59:1, 1–18; DOI: 10.1080/00131910600796777) for allowing me to include updated and revised versions of articles that first appeared in their journals in 2003, 2005, and 2007, respectively. In particular, I acknowledge the co-authors of the research reports that emerged from the Higher Education Academy research of 2005 in the United Kingdom and United States and form the basis of Chapter 4 (Carole Torgerson, Sally Mitchell, Paul Prior, Kelly Peake, Rebecca Bilbro, Beng Huat See, Samantha Looker) and those of the systematic research review that is referred to in Chapter 7 (Carole Torgerson, Graham Low, Nick McGuinn, and Alison Robinson). Part of Chapter 11 was first prepared for the Editorial and Commissioning Advisory Board of the Teacher Training Resource Bank, an initiative of the United Kingdom's Training and Development Agency, and was published online in July 2008. I am grateful to Paul Jenkins at the TDA and Mike Blamires at TTRB for their help.

Parts of Chapter 12 appeared in earlier versions as papers given at the Multimodality and Learning conference in London in June 2008 and in a public lecture given in the Graduate School of Library and Information Science, the University of Illinois at Urbana-Champaign (UIUC) in September 2008. I am grateful to the conference organizers (Jeff Bezemer, Sophia Diamantopoulou, Gunther Kress, and Diane Mavers) and to Caroline Haythornthwaite at the UIUC for the opportunity to include these as-yet-unpublished papers. We are grateful to Donna Al-Bu-Saidi at Magimix United Kingdom for permission to use the advertisement "Anyone for green tea?" and to Gillian Hilton for permission to use excerpts from essays from Middlesex University.

I am indebted to Henrice Altink, Gillian Anderson, Rebecca Bilbro, Andrew Burn, Caroline Coffin, Caroline Daly, Frans van Eemeren, Anton Franks, David Gough, John Hardcastle, Frøydis Hertzberg, Ann Hewings, Carey Jewitt, Petr Kaderka, Peter Keeley, Morlette Lindsay, Lia Litosseliti, Terry Locke, Samantha Looker, Graham Low, Nick McGuinn, Kieran O'Halloran, Kelly Peake, Andrew Ravenscroft, Chris Reed, Alison Robinson, Mark Roodhouse, Mary Scott, Chris Tindale, Carole Torgerson, Anne Turvey, Dominic Wyse, and John

Yandell, all of whom as colleagues over the years have provided me with just the kind of support that is most prized in academic life: integrity, critique, and intellectual verve, delivered in a spirit of collaboration and joint exploration in the field of argument and research methodologies. I owe a particular debt to Stephen Clarke, Gunther Kress, Peter Medway, Sally Mitchell, and Paul Prior for discussions over two decades that have helped me to change (and always to improve) my own views on argument and argumentation.

I am grateful to undergraduate and masters students at Middlesex University, The University of York, and New York University, especially those on the undergraduate course at York – 'Argumentation in Education' – where many of the ideas in this book were tried out. Specifically, I acknowledge Donna Sims, Rosie Abbotts, Rachel Brenkley, Lucy Todman, Sarah Watts, Hannah McGimpsey, Sarah Pycroft, Jennifer Michael, Joanna Wilde, Hannah Rees, Hannah Sylvester, and Laura Purdy, all of whose work is cited and who rose to the occasion when argumentation was introduced as part of a first-year introductory course in a multidisciplinary setting at the University of York, and Andrea Stratford and Peter Keeley, who was interviewed by one of the first-year students. The author of the dissertation on a five-year-old's marks on paper, Julia Stead, deserves special recognition. At the masters level, Lei Chen, Beatrice Lok, and Yu Ge's work has been cited. I also acknowledge the contribution to my thinking of doctoral students and faculty staff at the UIUC

Sarah Burrows, Alex Sharp, and Meg Savin at Routledge, New York, and John Hodgson in London, were a constant source of support and expertise throughout the commissioning, editing, and production of the book.

My wife, Dodi Beardshaw, and children David, Zoë, and Grace have long suffered my interest in academic argumentation. Some of their work is included in the book. Thanks also to Sam Strickland for his inspirational work, quoted in Chapter 6.

I continue to debate argumentational matters with research students and colleagues at the Institute of Education, University of London and in the Steinhardt School of Culture, Education and Human Development at New York University; it is to students in both these institutions that the book is dedicated.

1
Why Argument?

It is important to determine, at the outset of the book, why 'argument' (the product) and 'argumentation' (the process) are significant categories. There are different perspectives that need to be addressed here, some of which suggest that argument is too 'high' or abstract a category to be useful to student writers. This chapter argues the case for argument, providing a theoretical basis for the rest of the book based on the work of Bakhtin, Habermas, and Vygotsky.

The Importance of Argument

Why is argument important in higher education? In many ways, the answers seem obvious. It is important to be able to argue rationally in a civilized society, and students in higher education will be expected to be able to do so – both within their courses and in the wider world. Second, advancement in knowledge often comes via argument. A case is proved; a dispute is opened up and then solved; a new hypothesis is posited; academics, students, and everyone else are asked to look at an old problem in a new way. Third, argument is about clarification as well as persuasion. Well-argued speeches, essays, position papers, or research papers bring a sharper sense of meaning and significance to an issue. Fourth, argument can be enjoyable – and universities and colleges are spaces in which argument is encouraged and where it can flourish.

The foregoing reasons may seem obvious, but they are often taken for granted or neglected. Part of the purpose of this book is to look at these justifications afresh and to help professionals in the academic world think hard about how to bring the best from students with regard to argument.

There are other, less obvious reasons for taking a close look at argument. One is that argument and argumentation are so deeply embedded in subjects and disciplines, in different ways, that it is essential for teachers and students to know how the processes operate to be successful in that subject or discipline. Another is that good argument in speech, conversation, discussion, or debate does not always transfer to good argument in writing, and vice versa. Yet another is that it is sometimes difficult to teach argument well: some courses provide surface guidance about how to set out writing assignments. Others see argument as outside their field of reference or responsibility ('something the Writing Centre will deal with') because, for these lecturers and professors, argument is a transparent element in the business of teaching and learning the subject/discipline. One further reason is that despite the fact that there has been more attention on generic academic ('transferable') study skills, specific skills in argument are often left out of the equation. Furthermore, insufficient attention has been paid to argument in each of the disciplines: whereas there are some generic skills that can be used across the board, each discipline will have its own distinctive ways of constructing and validating arguments.

Finally, argument helps to bring together theory and models of learning in a particular field on the one hand and evidence, data, or real-world experience on the other. It is the essential mechanism and social practice for addressing and possibly resolving difference.

Argument and/or Argumentation

'Argument' and 'argumentation' are sometimes used interchangeably. In this book, a distinction is made between argument as an overarching, more general, everyday term that refers largely to the products or manifestations of argumentation, like debates, essays, position papers, research papers, and dissertations. It is also used to embrace a wider range of forms in spoken, written, and other (e.g., visual, spatial) modes. Argumentation is seen as part of argument and suggests a sequence or exchange of arguments. It refers to something more technical. It is the process of arguing in educational, political, business, legal, and other contexts. Argumentation in higher education, therefore, will refer to how argument takes place in colleges and universities, how it operates in subjects and disciplines, and how best to nurture it. Although it is a longer, more technical term than argument, it is the main focus of the book and, to avoid confusion and aid clarity, it is the term that will be used throughout. Alongside this term, and another subsidiary of argument in general, is the present participle and gerund arguing, which will be used where appropriate. Indeed, the verb to argue will be used in its various forms, as the action of arguing is central to the book as a whole and to the practices it aims to shed light on.

The root term argue is from the Latin *arguere*, meaning to show or accuse; its derivative, *argumentum*, means proof, accusation and, significantly, a summary of contents. Elsewhere I have tracked the etymology of the term (Andrews 1995), revealing its association with navigation and mathematics (finding a third point from two given points); with vernacular rows, disputes, tiffs, and spats; with summaries of narratives (the 'argument' of a chapter in *Gulliver's Travels*, for example); and with proof and evidence (as opposed to claims and propositions). All these dimensions of argument are important to this book. If asked for a simple working definition of argumentation that will act as a rudder for the book as a whole and that will guide us through the tributaries, creeks, and rivers of argumentation to the sea of argument, we can use 'a logical or quasi-logical sequence of ideas that is supported by evidence', though we will want to maintain the critical aspect of argument that distinguishes it from discussion or conversation. Argument, whether in speech, writing, or other modes, is 'discussion with edge'.

As a footnote to this section, I should add that I have used the adjective 'argumentational' to refer to the processes examined in the book, rather than the more commonly used 'argumentative'. The latter term carries too much of the everyday associations of tetchy, disputational, testy interaction – which are closely related to, but not synonymous with, the argumentational interactions in higher education. 'Argumentative' carries with it a disapproving tone, whereas 'argumentational' is, hopefully, more neutral. So, for example, there would be a clear difference between writing or speech that was argumentational on the one hand, and writing or speech that was argumentative on the other – though both may draw on the same dialogic energies.

Argumentation in Higher Education

The subtitle of the book is 'Improving Practice Through Theory and Research'. The main audience for the book is lecturers and professors in colleges and universities, and the main aims, to support such teachers by raising awareness of argumentation in the processes of teaching and learning, to provide theoretical and research foundations for the improvement of practice, and to supply some practical suggestions and guidance as to how this might be done. The book does not pretend to know the specific disciplines as well as specialists know them. However, there are examples from pre-disciplinary (in the American context), disciplinary, and interdisciplinary work in the book. Much of the disciplinary application of ideas contained herein will be in the hands of the lecturers and professors themselves. However, one of the key arguments of the book – and which makes it distinctive – is that a balance is required between what is known generically about argument and argumentation in higher education and how this can be applied variously in specific disciplines. The relationship between generic knowledge and discipline-specific knowledge is depicted simply in Figure 1.1.

The first point to note about the figure is that the student is at the head of it: he or she needs to gain command of the discipline or find his or her way within it. If the field in which he or she is working is interdisciplinary, like education, there will be added and more complex issues about how argument operates in that field of enquiry (for example, see the discussion, later in this book, on what counts as evidence in education).

However, the teacher, lecturer, or professor mediates between the student and the disciplines. His or her job is not only to induct the student into the discourses of the discipline but to act as gatekeeper, determining what

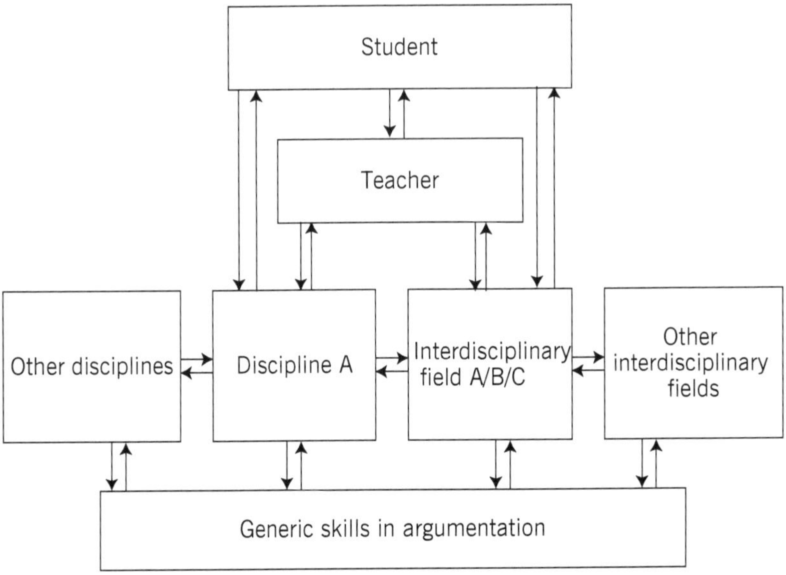

Figure 1.1 The relationship between generic and discipline-specific skills of argumentation

is and what is not 'allowed' as knowledge and in terms of the presentation of knowledge. Such gatekeeping happens during a taught course but most tellingly in the marking of coursework assignments and of examination papers.

Whether the teacher and student are working in a single discipline or in a multi- or interdisciplinary field of inquiry and/or practice, it is part of the thesis of this book that is it is essential that the discourses of that discipline or field are made explicit. Part of the problem with student assignments often results from the fact that the rules of the game have not been made explicit, so the parties operate from their own assumptions about what is required. These are not matters of surface compliance, nor are they matters of content. They are matters of the ways in which knowledge has been and is validated in the various disciplines.

It thus follows that feedback to the student is as important as the initial mapping out of the discipline's modi operandi. Feedback is often a bone of contention in university practice. Students appreciate it when it is detailed, when it points out how they can improve their grade, when it is positive and critical. In some institutions, there are agreements that a tutor will read one draft of an assignment before it is handed in. This is a civilized practice, because it allows the tutor to redirect the student if the draft is off course. Depending on the degree of detailed attention given to the draft, the feedback to the finally submitted assignment can be less or more detailed. As in many practices within school and higher education, however, feedback after submission (after the event) is less likely to have an impact than when it is provided formatively, during the course of the creation of the assignment.

The foot of the diagram shows the generic skills that will be brought to the process of learning and writing by the student and also (possibly) taught by the institution. These might come under the headings of 'critical thinking', 'essay-writing skills', or 'using sources to build your argument' and might be supplied at institutional level. The general feeling seems to be that the more abstract such courses are from the day-to-day working of the chosen disciplines themselves, the less motivation students have for attending them. Conversely, if the generic skills are taught by the disciplinary or interdisciplinary departments, there is often confusion between the generic and the specific.

An Example

To give a flavour of what is to come in this book and to focus initially on a common problem in the assessment of students' writing, let us concentrate on two openings of essays written by third-year students as part of an undergraduate course in educational studies. Education or educational studies is an interdisciplinary practice-based field of enquiry; there is, however, no practice dimension in the particular course from which these essays are taken. The title for the assignment was 'Choose one of the approaches to educational research that we have covered during the course. Give a full account of its procedures, the situations in which you might use it, and its strengths and weaknesses.'

Example 1

> Every year, newspaper headlines greet results from the latest educational research project (e.g., the *Times Educational Supplement*). Results are important, according to those in authority, and are even absolute – however parents and teachers do not seem to think so. Doubts soon follow by 'experts in the field' about methods, statistics and interpretations. The original researcher, sometimes, also announces that they were wrong all along. However, research is necessary in all fields of learning in order to bring new facts and information to light. Without medical research we would not be able to find the causes and cures of diseases; without educational research we could not diagnose and help backwardness. However, it must not be assumed that research is done only in order to seek causes and cures – it is also essential in devising new techniques and improving old ones. In this present study one shall be discussing the procedures of case studies, the situations in which this method can be used to its advantage and its strengths and weaknesses…

...In clinical work, the benefits of case studies accrue primarily to the patient in that the individual is the subject. This is known as the idiographic approach in that behaviour and attitudes are attempted to be understood without generalizing the results to other people or to groups. In contrast, most studies attempt to develop principles and theories having a wider applicability, whereby findings can be applied to large numbers of people, institutions or events...This is known as the nomethotic approach ...

Example 2

The approach to educational research chosen for close examination and analysis is action research; a notably controversial approach. Definitions vary, indicative of implicit tension between ideologies that lie behind the two words 'action' and 'research'. Its essence is succinctly expressed in '... action research is a small-scale intervention in the functioning of the real world, and a close examination of the effects of such intervention' (Halsey in Cohen and Manion, 1994, p. 186). Positioned within the qualitative boundaries of research, it specifically relies on the reflective action of the practitioner. The intention is not confined to illuminating problems but is extended to addressing the need to resolve issues as the research develops. Further, action research is concerned with discovering hypotheses as well as attempting to test them. Where conventional research seeks to minimize subjectivity, action research seeks to utilize it and give it a degree of credibility. Consequently, to what extent does this approach raise issues concerned with both subjective and objective concepts of knowledge and truth? Although the answer to this question is not within the remit of this essay it is useful to discuss action research within this framework. The approach would appear to cause unease within certain quarters of the academic fraternity whilst it is met with acclaim and enthusiasm within sections of the teaching profession. Why is this? In order to give a full account of action research and set it in some context, it would seem necessary to first briefly discuss the history and political implications of this method of discovery and action.

First impressions of a student's writing are important and often lead to early conceptions of the quality of a piece of writing – sometimes to a provisional grade in the lecturer's/professor's head. Your own first impressions, too, as reader of these pieces will be important: what criteria were you bringing to bear on your reading of them as student essays? Which do you think was the better of the two? Why?

My own view is that the second of these holds more promise for the rest of the essay than the first. I will explain why and hope that my explanation is taken as a starting point for argument rather than as an authoritative (and therefore closed-book) account of their relative worth.

The first essay opens with a bland generalization and gives an arbitrary example. It then follows with another generalization ('results are important') and betrays its own uncritical deference to authority with the qualification 'according to those in authority'. The problematic opening is compounded by the notion that results are 'absolute' (a strange idea), and then the first counterpoint is introduced: 'however parents and teachers do not seem to think so'. The first half of the first paragraph, then, is a succession of generalizations with some attempt to arrange them into argumentational alignment to provide the basis for the rest of the essay. Educational research is compared to medical research, but each new point undermines rather than builds on the previous one. The impression left of the main bulk of that first paragraph is one of shifting screens but of no clearly framed rhetorical and/or argumentational space for the essay or of an emerging problem or question that will be addressed. In its final sentence, the main focus of the essay – case study – is identified but introduced with an over-formal and awkward pronoun 'one' for 'I' or the often-occurring 'we'.

In its second paragraph, the first essay moves into a classificatory account of research approaches in clinical work, with technical terms such as idiographic and nomethotic revealing an expositional, non-argumentational style. Such list-like exposition is common in students' work and often reflects a parade of prepackaged knowledge rather than an argument. It's a textbook approach: you learn the information, then reproduce it. Or worse: you find the information on the Internet and reproduce it. In both cases, you might paraphrase to disguise the source. And in both cases, though there is a danger of plagiarism, the more likely outcome is a diluted representation of what has been found elsewhere, reflective of an assumption that knowledge is transferred from textbook and/or Internet and/or teacher to student.

The second essay, conversely, starts more promisingly. It may be rhetorically slick, but such fluency and manufacturing of the space in which to argue is a necessary prerequisite to a good essay. Right from the start, we are clear about the main focus of the essay: action research. What is clever about this opening sentence is that action research is cast as 'a notably controversial approach'. So from the opening sentence, the student has indicated that he or she is going to focus on something controversial. Such an opening not only arouses interest; it gives the student a space for argument and a topic on which to argue. He or she continues with definitional work: 'Definitions vary, indicative of implicit tension between ideologies that lie behind the two words "action" and "research".' Already laid out is the prospect of a spectrum of definitions, the identification of ideologies, the splitting of the two terms in the type of research that is about to be explored, and the suggestion that the essay will go below the surface (the 'implicit' made explicit) of what is ordinarily apparent. The student has not only opened up the possibilities of argumentation; he or she has set up the essay for maximum criticality.

The paragraph continues with a neatly embedded definitional quotation and reference. Already, by halfway through this first paragraph, a good deal of information about various aspects of action research has been expounded. 'Further', for example, indicates that another point is being made along the same lines. However, a pivotal point in reached with the next sentence: 'Where conventional research seeks to minimize subjectivity, action research seeks to utilize it and give it a degree of credibility'. This sentence is an important one in the paragraph (and in the essay as a whole) in a number of ways: first, the very act of pivoting is part of the articulation (joining together) of parts of an argument. Second, the essay pitches itself in opposition to the conventional orthodoxy, thus opening the space for debate, difference, and change. Third, the identification of at least two functions for action research (using subjectivity and creating a degree of credibility) begins to set out the stall for the argument, and the nuance of 'a degree of credibility means that there might be scope, further on in the essay, for some more distinctions of degree – and thus more scope for argumentation. In this way, notions of a degree of x are like the classic essay or dissertation title that begins 'to what extent…'.

Furthermore, the essay is clear about its limitations. Wisely, it steps back from a consideration of 'subjective and objective concepts of knowledge and truth' (at least four possible areas for exploration in philosophy classes) with the classic qualification that such a matter is 'not within the remit of this essay'. However, the very mention of such a framework means that, as readers of the essay, we are aware that the student knows his or her work can be framed in this way. By identifying that there is 'unease within certain quarters of the academic fraternity' (the hyperbole may be ironic), the student has identified an area wherein he or she can drill down at the point of dispute. The final sentence opens up again the possibility of criticality while, at the same time, giving the necessary momentum to start the main body of the essay via the historical and political implications of the method in question. Throughout, there is an tendency to problematization, to opening up spaces for argumentation, and to recognizing complexity.

Neither essay is perfect, and you could argue that the first essay is the better one. However, at least the discussion of these two openings of essays has raised some key questions for argumentation in higher education.

Is Argumentation Too 'High' a Term?

There are several objections to a focus on argumentation that need to be addressed before we can move on to the main body of the book. Addressing such objections is a classic practice in argument, as reassertions, qualifications, and acceptance of limitations in the light of such objections can strengthen an argument. Most of these objections have come from within the camp and present the first and, in many ways, most difficult challenge for proponents of argumentation in higher education.

Both Giltrow (2000) and Mitchell et al. (2008) think argument may be too 'high' a term to be of much practical use in the business of helping apprentice writers in higher education.

To Giltrow (2000, p. 129), argument is 'a term circulating among the professoriate, in classrooms, and institutional corridors, saturated with the ideologies of those places'. Her chapter in *Learning to Argue in Higher Education* (Mitchell and Andrews, 2000) focuses on the situatedness of argument 'by reflecting on pedagogical consequences of the use of the term 'argument' itself' (ibid.). She suggests that 'argument' is too high a term because writing centres in universities and other higher education institutions, at least in the United States and Canada, tend to focus on identifiable genres or text-types that are one level down from argument: abstract proposals, research papers, masters theses or dissertations, and the like. As writing centres work at the centre (or the margins) of a university, they are also sensitive to the differences between disciplines. Indeed, it is the differences between particular text types that Giltrow argues are the principal focus of such centres; they help students to navigate and negotiate these differences. To posit a meta-level category like 'argument', therefore, obfuscates and blurs these differences, producing in students a concern about how best to argue. In short, it produces a deficit situation in which students are constantly falling short of the mark of 'a good argument'. There are further sources of resistance to the widespread use of the term 'argument' for Giltrow: as a Canadian, she finds the term and its associated assumptions and practices too closely allied to the U.S.-based convention of 'freshman composition', deriving, as it appears to do so, from classical rhetorical models (see elsewhere in this chapter and in Chapters 2 and 3) and carrying with it all the anxieties and top-down insistence of the deficit assumption.

From the point of view of the present book, Giltrow makes a compelling challenge. The aim of the book, however, is not to provide yet another system or guidebook for a universal approach to argument and argumentation that can be applied in all contexts. Rather, it is to seek a balance between discipline-specific contexts for argument, and generic knowledge about argument, that can help the student navigate the demands of higher education. In the end, the teacher/lecturer has to be aware of how the generic aspects of argument can inform his or her field and what the particular demands of his or her field are. From the student's point of view, he or she needs to be able to draw down generic knowledge about how to argue and apply it to particular demands in the field, subject, or discipline in which he or she is working. There may well be, within any one field or discipline, a number of different text-types that are used and expected. These may differ in the degree of explicit argumentation that they require. Getting to know what these text types are and becoming adept at using them (while at the same time preserving the energy and expressiveness of the individual) is at the heart of learning to write well in higher education.

Mitchell et al. (2008) point out that the term 'argument' is laden with associations, making it difficult to distil the salient points that will help apprentice writers make sense of their academic practices. Like many such terms (and this is true of language in general), the different senses of each of the terms argument, arguing, and argumentation can make for confusion among students who are grappling with the right ways of couching their emergent knowledge and tentative data. Argument is seen at one end of the spectrum as the highest form of discourse within an academic subject or discipline and at the other as an everyday form of communication, often passionate, disputatious, and nonproductive and merely a matter of claim and counter-claim. Working out which type of argument is being discussed and how it applies to the business of discussion in classes and assignment-writing is a difficult game.

It is thus helpful to repeat the distinction made earlier in this chapter, between 'argument' and 'arguing' on the one hand and 'argumentation' on the other. Although it remains in the interests of this book to keep open the connection between the practice of argument in everyday life and the demands of argumentation in academia, it has to be said that the focus of the book is on argumentation. Argumentation is at once a more technical, specific term denoting the process of argument in thought and in academic contexts. Nevertheless, argumentation becomes a dry, narrowly academic pursuit if it is not linked to the everyday use of argument in domestic, social, political, and business contexts.

Argumentation, then, is not too high a term to be of practical use in the day-to-day practices of higher education: in discussions, debates, and speeches in the oral genres; and in essays, position papers, research papers, dissertations, applications, multimodal presentations, and so on in the written mode. Its particular value lies in its mezzanine position between abstract thought and 'critical thinking' at a more nebulous level and the various forms it takes at a discourse level. The next section discusses the place of argumentation in more detail, and Chapter 11 returns to the question of whether argument is too high a term for practical use in the academy.

The Position of Argumentation

Figure 1.2 posits the place of argumentation within a set of practices in higher education.

It is important to note that argumentation (see Andrews, 1989) is meta-modal. That is, it sits above the instantiations of expression in the

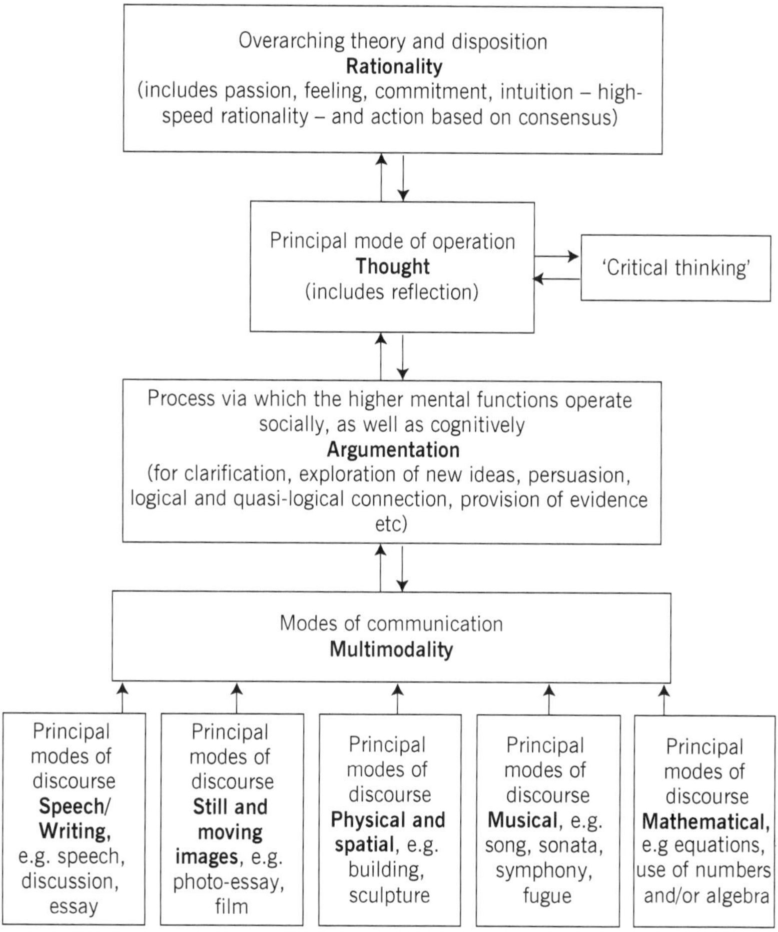

Figure 1.2 The place of argumentation

various modes of communication. It is not a genre in itself, nor a mode of communication. It is rather the result of a disposition toward the rational, toward exploring the nature of difference and, indeed, creating difference (Kress, 1989). Sometimes, but not always, argumentation helps to resolve difference. However, its territory clearly is one in which distinctions matter. More specifically, the argument of a student assignment – or of any exchange – can be represented diagrammatically. It is schematic, like a plan.

Following on from this point, argumentation (and arguments) can take many forms. All of these need to be seen in relation to a multimodal lens, because although it is a theoretical possibility for communication to be realized in one mode, such communication is rarely the case. Most texts, most utterances, and most instances of communication are multimodal.

In the figure, neither multimodality nor argumentation are 'theories'. They are rather frameworks, lenses, perspectives from which examples of human interaction can be observed and understood. Perhaps the best word to describe what is presented in the figure, and where argumentation sits within it, is to say that this is a model for presenting how argumentation sits within the firmament that ranges from abstract rationality to actual instances of communication. The theories that inform the model are discussed later in this chapter.

The advantage of putting argumentation as the centre of the model, for the purposes of this book and for the improvement of professional and academic practice for teachers, is that from this mezzanine floor, as it were, you can move both up and down, linking the abstract and theoretical to the concrete and particular. Argumentation is not 'too high' in such a model, but it is high enough to be able to link with the more abstract levels – the higher mental functions, as Vygotsky (1991) puts it. It is also low enough to be able to connect with actual rhetorical and discoursal choices students make as they compose.

Theoretical Justifications for the Focus on Argumentation

There are three main theorists for whom argument and argumentation play a major part in the development of their ideas and whose work, in turn, provides a theoretical canopy for the study and practice of argumentation. In chronological order of dates of birth, these are Bakhtin (1895–1975), Vygotsky (1896–1934), and Habermas (1929–).

Bakhtin

Ostensibly, Bakhtin's work is not about argumentation. Rather, it focuses on other cultural forms: the novel, speech genres, the epic, and the like. However, it is Bakhtin's dialogic approach to these cultural forms that provides the bedrock upon which theories of argumentation can build.

Characteristically, Bakhtin's own argument for the dialogic nature of the novel begins from a reaction against the surface preoccupations of twentieth-century stylistics. Rejecting notions of a unified surface 'prose style' for the genre, Bakhtin (1981) sees the novel as follows:

> [These] distinctive links and interrelationships between utterances and languages, this movement of the theme through different languages and speech types, its dispersion into the rivulets and droplets of social heteroglossia, its *dialogization* – this is the basic distinguishing feature of the stylistics of the novel (p. 263; my italics).

Dialogization – the historical and cultural interplay between utterances, whether they are spoken and/or written – underpins argumentation, too. Whereas the novel orchestrates the various voices in a pattern that lives through particular instances, particular settings, particular characters, and plot, argumentation operates more deductively through linking concepts or propositions, underpinned at the concrete level by evidence. This does not mean to say that the novel is a purely inductive genre or that argument is purely deductive. Both play the inductive/deductive range, but the novel tends to work inductively and argument deductively.

Dialogization works both at the macro-level and at the micro-level in argumentation, both externally to the particular argument itself and internally within the argument.

Externally, we can consider how arguments are triggered. Usually it is the case that a state of affairs, or the particular position of someone on a particular issue, prompts a reaction on the part of the protagonist. The protagonist, or initiator of the argument, takes a position that is at odds with the original position: it might be directly opposed to the original position or tangentially different (differences of position can be anything from 1 degree to 180 degrees away from the existing point of view or state of affairs). Whether the new position or proposition is 1 degree or 180 degrees away from the status quo (or somewhere in between), a dialogue is set up between the two positions. This dialogue can be aggressive (as is more likely to be, though not necessarily the case where the positioning is conceived to be 180 degrees in difference) or not: argumentation does not necessarily have to be aggressive. It is, however, interesting to note that arguments are often depicted as, or take shape as concerning directly opposed positions. This is where a simplistic binarism or dualism replaces dialogic structure, often oversimplifying positions to set up a rhetorical battle of opposing forces. Where arguments are established that are overly dualistic, they tend to descend into rows or disputes that generate more heat than light.

Internally, the structure and movement of an argument reflects to an extent its outward genesis. One of the ways in which articulation – the joining of one element of the argument to another in a horizontal or forward-moving plane – can be effected is via the dialogic principle. A statement is made. Whether that statement is supported at that particular point by evidence or not is not the focus of our attention at present. However, how that statement relates to the next statement, and the next statement after that, is a matter of logic. To say that it is always a logical relationship, however, is to assume that arguments always operate in a mathematical and/or philosophical mode. They do not. More often than not, arguments move dialogically, taking their cue for the next statement or point from the previous one and positioning themselves differently from it. Again, the articulation can be at anywhere between 1 and 180 degrees. For example, a sentence that begins 'Furthermore…' may be arguing along the same lines as the previous sentence and may have hardly moved even one degree from the direction that the previous sentence was taking. Whereas (a typical joining word in argumentational discourse in itself!)

a following sentence that begins 'However…' or 'Nevertheless…' indicates a contrary point. The overall point I am making in relation to Bakhtin's work is that, in argumentation, as in the novel (though differently), there is always more than one voice at work, and it is in the interplay between these voices that the argument resides. However monologic an argument seems, it is always predicated externally in relation to other positions and arguments and always operates internally in dialogic or multi-voiced mode.

What is also the case, and often overlooked in the professional world of arguments in essays, position papers, debates, seminars, and the like, is that all these academic argumentational forms embody the real, interactive, dialogic nature of everyday discourse and the histories of those dialogic encounters.

Vygotsky

The most extraordinary and significant statement from Vygotsky's work with regard to argument is the connection he makes between reflection and argumentation. With characteristic (not always empirically founded) logical verve, he writes:

> …there is an indubitable genetic connection between the child's arguments and his reflections. This is confirmed by the child's logic itself. The proofs first arise in the arguments between children and are then transferred within the child…The child's logic develops only with the increasing socialization of the child's speech and all of the child's experience…Piaget has found that precisely the sudden transition from preschool age to school age leads to a change in the forms of collective activity and that on this basis the child's thinking also changes. 'Reflection,' says this author, 'may be regarded as inner argumentation…'
>
> If we consider this law, we will see very clearly why all that is internal in the higher mental functions was at one time external…In general we may say that the relations between the higher mental functions were at one time real relations between people…
>
> We might therefore designate the main result to which we are brought by the history of the child's cultural development as a sociogenesis of the higher forms of behaviour (Vygotsky 1991, pp. 32–41).

The excerpt is quoted at length to demonstrate the steps via which Vygotsky comes to the conclusion that argumentation was once external. Much of the thinking is informed by Vygotsky's well-known theory of the ways in which cultural and historical patterning informs cognitive and conceptual development. However, there are a number of striking connections made in the statement above that shed particular light on argumentation.

First is the connection between arguments and reflections. Putting aside whether the connection is indubitably genetic or not, the link suggests that reflection is more than a miasmic, static read-off from experience. Rather, it is seen as dynamic mental space informed by social arguments (the sociogenetic aspect) and, furthermore, is in itself a dialectical operation in which the dialogue is both with experience/the outside world on the one hand and with ideas themselves in the internal process of reflecting/thinking on the other.

Second is the connection with Piaget's work. Often Vygotsky is pitched against Piaget, largely on the basis of the emphasis on inductive, empirical thinking leading toward a biologically driven theory of the self encountering and adapting itself to society on Piaget's part and Vygotsky's often purely deductive theorising in which society is seen to inform the internal cognitive processes of the developing individual. Such simplistic accounts, though generally valid, miss some of the nuances of the relationship between their work. One of those nuances is their apparent agreement on the significance of the move from preschool (which we can take to mean 'no school' rather than kindergarten or nursery contexts) to school. Such a move puts the child in a context wherein institutional and curricular framing and new relations with peers and teachers shape thought and argumentation. Although the transition from preschool to school is not the focus of the present book, the transitions from pre-university to university are. As the book argues and explores, one of the most significant additional framings that comes into play in this latter transition is that of disciplines, subjects, and fields of enquiry. To come back to the connection between arguments and reflections for a moment, the statement that 'reflection may be regarded as inner argumentation' is Piaget's, not Vygotsky's – but it is corroborated by Vygotsky.

Third, Vygotsky's statement that 'all that is internal in the higher mental functions was at one time external' can be broken down into two propositions: one, that there are relations between the higher mental functions and, two, that these relations 'were at one time real relations between people'. We need not spend too much time on the notion that there are relations between the higher mental functions except to say that hierarchical ('vertical', 'synchronic', and 'paradigmatic') and relational ('horizontal', 'diachronic', and 'syntagmatic') thinking is fundamental to subject and disciplines in various combinations and with varying emphases. Not all these higher mental functions are grounded in verbal language; some are based on other languages, like dance, the visual arts, architecture, music. Most are multimodal in their actual operation in the world. Nevertheless, these hierarchical and relational connections are central to and critical to the operation of learning and teaching in disciplines in higher education. Learning your way across a grid of such relations is learning to become competent (and thus worthy of the award of academic degrees) in the various disciplines, subjects, and fields. The development of the higher mental functions is associated with the entry to and success within higher education.

The proposition that such interconnections 'were at one time real relations between people' is the truly astonishing idea in the logical chain we are considering. The logic follows from earlier propositions in the quotation above and in Vygotsky's work more generally about the formation of thinking in young children. At the higher education level, let us consider the implications of the statement. Part of the underlying justification for the statement is that the development of disciplinary practices, historically, is the result of 'real relations between people'. The birth of English literature as a university subject in England, for example, arose from a dialectical need expressed, over a number of years, by workers' educational associations and particularly by women studying within and beyond those associations, for an alternative to classics as a central (but male-only) humanities discipline at the University of Oxford and subsequently elsewhere. The history of that evolution is well documented in Dixon (1991b). As the emergent subject established itself in the university repertoire, discussions between academics, students, and others would determine its development. Specifically, patterns of expectation and convention – what counts as a good argument in the discipline, the nature of the canon, the modus operandi in seminars, the journals created, the discourses and discourse of the discipline – all these would establish themselves and be adapted further. Thus, the lines and conduits along which thought and argumentation take place are determined, distinguishing the discipline from others. When these conduits for thought and argumentation become too over-prescribed, a reaction sets in that changes, with Hegelian dialectic, the nature of discourses that are 'allowed' within the disciplinary framework that has been established. Such 'real relations between people' are largely mediated by speech.

A case like the emergence and development of English literature in England has 150 years of history, and Vygotsky's phrase 'at one time' can refer to far-distant history (too far to be evidentially researched and validated) or to a more compressed time scale. In a much more specific way, Bazerman (1988) charts the development of the experimental article in science, demonstrating how a vehicle for argumentation in a meta-discipline like science emerged from social interactions between people, and relations between people and the material world.

To give a much more contemporary example, consider the relations between a student on an undergraduate course and his or her lecturer/teacher. The student submits a piece of writing. Explicitly and/or implicitly, the lecturer proves feedback in spoken or written form that suggests to the student how he or she might 'improve' (i.e., might get closer to and exceed the expected discourses of the discipline at undergraduate level). Such interaction, at its best, is specific, extensive, formative, and positively critical. Whatever its quality, it is always part of a set of institutional and personal power relations. Thus 'real relations between people', different in nature from the previous two examples of the birth of a discipline or the creation of the scientific article, determine the operation of the higher mental functions.

The topic of lecturer/student approaches to argumentation is addressed later in the book.

Given the three steps outlined above on the connection between argumentation and thought ('the higher mental functions'), it is but a small step to the final proposition in the quoted passage: the sociogenesis of the higher forms of behaviour. Behaviour in the academy is determined by the engines of inquiry and the sociology of teaching and learning within institutions and disciplines and, in due course, it informs and shapes further reflection/thought. Within a rational paradigm, argumentation plays a key part in the development of such social relations.

Habermas

At the core of Habermas's work is that communicative competence is more than being able to generate and understand utterances and sentences. He suggests that we are constantly making claims. These claims are often implicit, and often they are not backed up by evidence, but the exchange of claims appears to be part of the fabric of human interaction. As McCarthy puts it in the introduction to his translated edition of Habermas' major work on rationality and communication, *The Theory of Communicative Action*,

> we are constantly making claims, even if usually only implicitly, concerning the validity of what we are saying, implying or presupposing – claims, for instance, regarding the truth of what we say in relation to the objective world; or claims concerning the rightness, appropriateness, or legitimacy of our speech acts in relation to the shared values and norms of our social lifeworld; or claims to sincerity or authenticity in regard to the manifest expressions of our intentions and feelings (1984, p. x).

Claims do require evidence – or at least they need a degree of validation that might come from logical consistency, the character of the speaker, the nature of the context, or via methodological support – and they are more likely to be accepted if they are supported in a number of these ways. At the same time, they can be challenged, defended, and qualified. As suggested above, claims might be strengthened by being subjected to challenge. Indeed, the very nature of making claims (one ingredient in the making of an argument) is that they invite counter-claim. Habermas's particular contribution to the thinking about communication is his insistence that mutual understanding without coercion is the basis of rationality and of human consensus and social action.

Within Habermas' view of societies reaching consensus and thus being able to 'get on' with the business of the everyday world, argumentation has a particularly significant function:

> The rationality proper to the communicative practice of everyday life points to the practice of argumentation as a court of appeal that makes it possible to continue communicative action with other means when disagreement can no longer be headed off by everyday routines and yet is not to be settled by the direct or strategic use of force (1984, 1:17–18).

Thus, to varying degrees and in contexts ranging from the everyday and seemingly mundane/local at one end of the spectrum to high politics at the other end, argumentation is part of the fabric of human existence. Its status as a 'court of appeal' suggests that it can be made explicit and raised to a level of social consciousness whereby the best way forward can be debated. However, it is also implicit in the conduct of human interaction, even when it is not acknowledged as such. Such a fundamental and central role for argumentation is important for the thesis of the present book, which argues that tacit and implicit practices in higher education often need to be made more explicit to help teachers understand what they are asking students to do and, in turn, for students to understand what they are being asked to do.

Perhaps the most telling statement from Habermas with regard to the purposes of the present book is his assertion that argumentation is closely linked to learning:

> Argumentation plays an important role in learning processes as well. Thus we call a person rational who, in the cognitive-instrumental sphere, expresses reasonable opinions and acts efficiently; but this rationality remains accidental if it is not coupled with the ability to learn from mistakes, from the refutation of hypotheses and from the failure of interventions (p. 18).

Like Vygotsky's statement on the genesis of the higher mental functions, Habermas's insight into the centrality of a process, argumentation, which is at the heart of higher education, is a crucial one. Being rational means being able to learn from mistakes, from critiquing half-formed hypotheses, and from the failure of interventions in experimental and non-experimental situations. Such openness to learning via the process of argumentation is one to which teachers, lecturers, and professors, at their very best, are amenable and one that students have to learn to develop if they are to progress within their chosen subjects, disciplines, or fields of enquiry.

Is Argument a New Preoccupation?

Finally, in this opening chapter, we address the question of whether the exploration of argument and argumentation in higher education is a new preoccupation or whether we are returning to an old topic of interest in a different guise. Purely rhetorically, it is advantageous to claim that there is 'growing attention' in the field or that the exploration of argument in education is somehow 'new'. Such claims can be seen as the manufacturing of rhetorical space in which to create something different and to justify the need for a book or a new research project, for example.

Rather than suggest that a focus on argument and education is new, it is better to say that there are indeed specific gaps in the field of argumentation, and – more important for the purposes of the present book – specific gaps in the literature on induction into the practices of higher education that the books tries to address. This is not to say that the issue is being addressed for the very first time. On the contrary, classical Greece and Rome dealt directly with argumentation in the public domain; and renaissance rhetoric dealt with argumentation in relation to university and school curricula, particularly the relationship with grammar and logic, and the centrality of argumentation to humanistic thought. In a different way, argumentation resurfaced in the Enlightenment as a means by which scientific thought could progress; and then again, in Hegelian philosophy, via the formula of thesis-antithesis-synthesis. In each of these cases, and in many others, broad educational principles were revisited or the implications for education were, at the very least, hinted at.

It appears to be because argument lies at the interstices of psychology (especially cognitive development), philosophy, linguistics, discourse studies, education, and the operation of democracies that it is such a powerful and compelling area to explore. It is a complex and multi-levelled crossroads, like a 'spaghetti junction' of intersecting motorways, main roads, and minor roads. The list of disciplines is not simply a list of easily comparable and evenly distributed fields. Some are tightly framed disciplines; others are interdisciplinary fields of enquiry; yet others are ways of operating in the world. For a historian to say that 'argumentation is the discipline' is to take the influence of argument and argumentation too far, perhaps, but this historian is making a point about the epistemological division of knowledge. That point appears to be that however we chart and define the boundaries of disciplines, and however those boundaries are further reified into 'departments' in universities, there remains an irrepressible interlinking of the abstract to the particular, of one way of looking at phenomena as compared to another, and of competing claims and debates about evidence to support them, that are the lifeblood of rational exchange and argumentation.

The Structure of the Book

The rest of the book is structured as follows. Chapter 2 establishes a historical and policy-based context. Historically, in traditions that have eschewed rhetoric (like the English higher education tradition), argumentation has been thought to be less worthy of attention than the substance of the discipline. In other traditions – for example, the Scottish/American tradition – rhetoric thrives, and thus argumentation is seen to be a skill to be taught. The transferable skills agenda in the United Kingdom and elsewhere tends to neglect argument. In the United States, the emphasis has been on generic rhetoric and composition, with many courses (except in the most enlightened of writing centres) divorced from the actual business of writing in the disciplines. The chapter thus provides a context that will help readers in different countries and cultures to position argumentation within their own professional practice.

The third chapter asks, 'What are the generic skills in argumentation at higher education level?' That chapter looks at a number of models that attempt to map such skills and discusses how they might be applied in a range of contexts. The advantage of a core set of skills and practices is that they can be used not only to bring unity to studies in argumentation but to point out where particular practices diverge from the norm. It also looks at rhetoric and composition courses wherein such generic skills are assumed to have value. However, the chapter also addresses one of the main points of the present book: that there needs to be a balance between generic and discipline-specific approaches to argumentation if interventions are to be successful.

Most studies to date that have addressed the issue agree that discipline-specific argumentation is more useful and more apposite than generic approaches. Accordingly, the fourth chapter looks at a range of disciplines to determine how argumentation differs and at what can be done in these particular contexts to help students understand the rules of the game in becoming not only competent but excellent in their chosen field of study.

There is new analysis of some data from the Higher Education Academy project in Chapter 4. The balanced approach to generic and discipline-specific skills development in argumentation at institutional level in higher education is addressed in Chapter 5. Which elements can be approached generically, and which specifically, is at the heart of that chapter. Guidance on such balance will make for much improved policies and practices with regard to students' study skills across the sector.

In Chapter 6, we turn to the potential of information communication technologies (ICT) to help teach and/or research argumentation. Using information and communication technologies to undertake argument is not the same as multimodal approaches to argument. Much ICT work in argument is highly textual, but there is the possibility of a more multimodal approach, afforded by the use of images and sound on computer screens. Examples of such work by students will be included. That chapter, then, looks at both ICT and multimodal questions, charting where they overlap and where they are distinct from each other.

Chapter 7 refers to research previously completed by the author as part of a systematic review with colleagues at the University of York, United Kingdom. It refers to a systematic research review, undertaken in 2006, of work in the 7- to 14-year age range, and looks at implications of that review for undergraduate education, including a look at transitions that are made from one education phase to another.

Undergraduate students have their own views on argumentation and its place in their discipline and in higher education more widely. Chapter 8, accordingly, reports on an empirical study in which education studies–undergraduates interviewed other undergraduates in a range of disciplines. There is remarkable commitment to understanding the function of argument, but also a strong sense among students that argument is not addressed, or made explicit, by lecturers. It is a hidden 'rule of the game' that students need to know more about. Furthermore, the reemerging issue of 'student voice' in further and higher education is one that needs to be borne in mind in negotiating how, where, and why argumentation takes place. That chapter focuses on spoken argumentation.

Chapter 9 examines a number of essays (and other forms of written assignment) in a range of disciplines and lecturer feedback to student assignments. The author has taught a cross-disciplinary course in Argumentation in Education to undergraduate students. He also looks at the range of topics chosen, from theoretical discussions through standard academic essays on primary, second, or tertiary education, to studies of visual argumentation. Furthermore, the chapter looks at student feedback to the course and how it has helped improve the content and delivery over the years.

In Chapter 10, the question of feedback is considered. The principal focus of this chapter is on how professors and lecturers negotiate and establish the parameters of argumentation through their feedback to students; how they encourage and 'police' these; and how alternative forms of argumentation can be accepted into academic practice.

In Chapter 11, methodological issues in researching argumentation are addressed. Part of the problem in argumentation research is that it is informed by a number of disciplines, including sociology, linguistics, discourse studies, philosophy, and literature. Such a range of disciplines means that the underlying ideological assumptions and value systems are not stable or paradigmatic; the field is interdisciplinary. An added difficulty is that the phenomenon of argumentation is evident only in texts, images, codes, and so on; determining the nature of argued thought needs a range of approaches. That chapter draws on cutting-edge thinking on the questions of how to research the field.

The book closes with a chapter that asks, 'What don't we yet know about argumentation in higher education, and therefore what needs to be researched? Are there cross-cultural issues that need to be addressed, and if so, how are such studies to be conducted? What are the implications for research, policy and practice – and the way they interrelate – from the present study?'

The Practical Dimension

Each chapter closes with two proposed activities. Lecturers/professors can choose one or both of these – or choose not to use them – in staff development and/or academic development sessions. They can also be adapted for use with students. The aim of the activities is to raise awareness, and to develop capabilities regarding the use and function of argumentation in higher education.

Activity 1.1: What is Argument?

Write down your own definitions of 'argument' and 'argumentation'. Then compare notes in pairs or small groups with a colleague or colleagues. What are the key features of argument that you have in common? And how are your definitions different?

Aim for a comprehensive picture of argumentation in higher education, showing how you think argument in the academy is related to argument outside the academy. For example, what elements of argument in the everyday world are also present in academic argument? How do they manifest themselves in the academy?

Activity 1.2: Argumentation and Other Related Terms

Some lecturers/professors and students find the terms argument and argumentation do not describe exactly what goes on in their subjects and disciplines. Develop the definitions worked out above in Activity 1.1 to include a wider range of terms and practices, including some of the following:

Spoken forms:
discussion
debate
seminar
conversation
dialogue.

Written forms:
essay
assignment
position paper
research paper
dissertation
thesis.

What other terms are used in the broad area of spoken and written interchange in your college or university? Can you map these in relation to your working definitions of argument and argumentation?

2
The Current State of Argumentation in Higher Education

This chapter charts the establishment of a historical and policy-based context for the book. Historically, in traditions that have eschewed rhetoric (like the English higher education tradition), argumentation has been thought to be less worthy of attention that the substance of the discipline. In other traditions – for example, the Scottish/American tradition – rhetoric thrives, and thus argumentation is seen to be a skill to be taught. The transferable skills agenda in England and elsewhere tends to neglect argument. In the United States, the emphasis has been on generic rhetoric and composition, with many courses (except in the most enlightened of writing centres) divorced from the actual business of writing in the disciplines.

There is thus a difference between the traditions of rhetoric and argumentation in the United States on the one hand and in England on the other. These differences are reflected, to varying degrees, in the traditions in other countries and in the particular ways they interpret the rhetorical and argumentational traditions.

For example, Corbett and Connors' edition (1999) of *Classical Rhetoric for the Modern Student*, first published as Corbett (1965), reinterprets Aristotelian classical rhetoric for students in higher education in the United States. There is a basic premise to the book: that Aristotelian rhetoric and argumentation theory, conceived for use in Athenian democracy, is applicable to students' spoken and written needs in contemporary higher education. The other principle to bear in mind in consideration of Corbett and Connors' work is that the book is intended for the mass higher education audience of students at undergraduate levels in the United States. Such an approach to rhetorical (specifically writing) skills in undergraduate education has not been a priority for England where, as late as the 1970s, only 8 per cent of 18-year-olds went on to higher education. And such an elitist higher education system did not require its students to train in rhetorical or argumentational discourse, as it was assumed they had such skills.

Classical Rhetoric for the Modern Student, after an Introduction devoted to a brief explanation of classical rhetoric and some classificatory work on canons and kinds of persuasive discourse, is divided into sections. The first of these deals with the discovery of arguments: the modes of persuasion and the topics for argument. The next deals with arrangement, adopting the five-part structure which I discuss in more detail in the following chapter. Then there is a section on style, covering grammar, diction, sentence structure, figures of speech, and paragraphing. A new section in the fourth edition is one on *progymnasmata*, or examples of classical and Renaissance pedagogy in which the basic approach is rule, example, imitation. Finally, there is a section on the history of rhetoric. The book as a whole, illustrated with examples of rhetorical language from the past to the present, is a comprehensive compendium.

Despite its quality and range, there are three main problems with the premises of making classical rhetoric available to the modern student. First, the contexts are different. Classical rhetoric was developed over a long period (pre-Athenian, Athenian, and Roman) to serve the needs of orators and others in public discourse. It was primarily designed for oral delivery, hence the emphasis on emotion, feeling, the characters of the speaker, and other aspects that do not translate readily into the written mode. Second, its complex categorization makes for an unwieldy manual for contemporary spoken or writing practice. It is comprehensive, but too much so. The machinery of rhetorical guidance needs, in the contemporary world, to be light and transferable. Third, the inclusion of *progymnasmata* may be interesting historically, but the pedagogy is primitive. The sequence of rule-example-imitation may form part of a contemporary pedagogy, but it is not sufficient, nor is it wise, to use one simple transmission-like approach in current teaching.

In fact, all three limitations above derive from a change of emphasis from the teacher to the learner. A teacher must ask: how will the learner make sense of the knowledge that is presented and is discoverable? What kinds of pedagogical variation are best suited to the learner? What memorable structures and other guidance are manageable for the learner? How can the approach be varied in terms of the particular contexts and disciplines that the teacher and learner share?

Probably the most comprehensive book to date on the teaching of writing, composition, and rhetoric at the college level in the United States is Lindeman's *A Rhetoric for Writing Teachers* (1982/2001), now in its fourth edition. It breaks into three main sections: the composing process, rhetorical theory and practice, and teaching as rhetoric. By the latter category, it means developing writing assignments, responding to student writing, designing writing courses, and teaching writing with computers. There are three striking aspects of the book as far as argumentation is concerned. One of these is the absence of much on argument and argumentation: references to argument are sprinkled through the first half of the book, but there is no sustained treatment of argumentational writing. Another is the *implied* reference to argumentational writing under the broader canopy of material on *writing*. In this case, it is interesting that argumentation is subsumed under the heading of writing, confirming the assumption that argument is taken for granted (and thus rendered invisible) in writing and assessment practices in higher education. These implied references are largely concerned with the practical business of writing. Last, there is a new chapter on cognition in the fourth edition (2001) that is classified as more theoretical. However, it does not address questions of argumentation.

Argument, for Lindeman, is placed rhetorically within categories of writing in which the addressee is the principal focus. In this sense, she follows Kinneavy (1971/1980), suggesting that argument is best seen as having a conative function and a persuasive aim. Typical examples of such writing would be propaganda, debates, editorials, and sermons. Though Lindeman is at pains to point out that categorization of this kind can be reductive, she does not explore the fact that argumentation also needs to address the needs of the writer(s) and the facts of the case in a range of real world contexts. Furthermore, there is no recognition that argumentational texts may be hybrid in form, function, and mode.

Lindeman does, however, in her survey chapter on 'What do teachers need to know about rhetoric?', not only explicate well the history and relevance of the complex traditions of rhetoric to writing but distinguish Aristotelian definitions of rhetoric as the art of persuasion from a broader, twentieth-century and Burkean (see Burke, 1969) position. This latter position sees rhetoric as more than the art of persuasion. It sees it as an integrating theory for understanding the human need to communicate, to work toward consensus via the exploration of difference, to represent feeling, intellect, and physical movement. As such, it is more of a return to an inclusive theory of the motivation for human action. One could say that Lindeman's own approach is within the Burkean tradition, which is perhaps why argument is subsumed within writing and rhetoric and why it is not particularly foregrounded. Lindeman's book works at the level of the theory of rhetoric, linking it closely to the practices of writing and composition wherever possible. It is therefore operating, theoretically, at a level one floor up from argumentation.

Interestingly, the most extensive reference to argumentation in the book is the recitation of Quintilian's version of the Aristotelian division or arrangement of argument. Whereas for Aristotle the primary division was between statement and proof, Quintilian develops Aristotle's schema into a five-part model. This model is discussed elsewhere in the present book. For now, it is worth noting that Corbett, Lindeman, and Fulkerson – all three American theorists and practitioners on composition and rhetoric – return to classical models when discussing argumentation.

Fulkerson's *Teaching the Argument in Writing* (1996) embraces a broad conception of argument: one in which 'mutual dialectical interchange' (p. ix) can lead to decisions that are 'always subject to revision as better arguments and better evidence become available' (ibid.). The book is aimed at high school and college teachers of writing, but Fulkerson's experience in teaching a seminar on argumentation to doctoral students extends the application to the graduate/

postgraduate level. Avowedly non-postmodernist, the author establishes the theoretical basis of his approach in the work of Habermas, Heidegger, Perelman, Dewey, Burke, and Toulmin: broadly speaking, rationalists and neo-classicists.

Interestingly, Fulkerson's starting point is in many ways similar to that of this book. He points out that Lindeman's *A Rhetoric for Writing Teachers* fails to include a chapter on argument in an otherwise extensive and comprehensive manual for writing teachers at the college level. The lacuna is puzzling: if academic argumentational writing is so central to higher education, why is it so patently absent from many books of contemporary rhetoric? There are a number of possible reasons. First, the likelihood is that the ability to argue in writing – for example, in the default genre in higher education in the humanities and social sciences, the essay – is taken for granted (cf. the previous point that, in the United Kingdom at least, only a small proportion of 18-year-olds went on to higher education, and it was assumed they already had argumentational skills). Second, there is perhaps an assumption that argumentation is the province of thinking and thus cognitive training, rather than of language and discourse. Third, it might be the case that some authors of books for writing teachers at advanced levels think that argumentation is too difficult, too impersonal, too abstracted from everyday experience to justify attention. Fourth – and an assumption we will explore more fully later in the book – it might be thought that epistemological thinking, as enshrined in each of the subjects at the school level and in each of disciplines in higher education, is sufficient; in other words, that argument is so deeply embedded in the various subjects and disciplines that it cannot, and does not, need to be explicated.

Fulkerson's solution is to draw on (a mix of formal and informal) logic, to sidestep post-modernism, Toulmin, and the Amsterdam school of pragma-dialectics, and instead to reinterpret the classical approach to argumentation as represented in Aristotle. He neatly distills various schemes from classical rhetoric to generate three categories of thesis statement: substantiation (basically, claims that do not involve value judgments), evaluation (claims that *do* involve value judgments), and recommendations (claims that something should be done). He also includes a chapter on fallacies, which concludes that it is teachers rather than students who need to know about fallacies in argumentation to be able to identify weaknesses in compositional argument. His last main point is drawn from Govier (1988) and identifies nine characteristics of 'a good argument':

1. The language used is relatively neutral and unbiased.
2. Facts that would tend to support an interpretation different from that of the arguer are acknowledged.

3. The point is acknowledged whereby expert opinion is cited, though relevant experts may differ from each other in position.
4. Controversial interpretations are acknowledged; reasons for them are given.
5. The arguer does not introduce their own special point of view as being one the audience would naturally adopt.
6. Sources are given so that they may be checked, if necessary.
7. Arguments are careful and well-reasoned, not fallacious.
8. Alternative positions are stated, explained, and considered.
9. The point is acknowledged whereby evidence and reasons are less than rationally compelling. An explanation is given as to why the position taken nevertheless seems the most appropriate in the context.

It will be seen from the foregoing list that the Govier/Fulkerson position is one of reasonableness in a democratic, tolerant society (and in which argumentation plays a key part in maintaining such a civilized *status quo*).

Perhaps the most comprehensive textbook and reader on argumentation for higher education students is Fahnestock and Secor's *A Rhetoric of Argument*, originally published in 1982 and now it its third edition (2004). The title suggests a rhetorical analysis of argument, but the book is more like an extensive exposition on argumentation for students – a 'rhetoric' in the sense of a rhetorical handbook or textbook. The handbook would be an excellent complement to the present volume, which is aimed at lecturers and professors rather than students (though it has implications for students) and is based on research.

The present book has much in common with Fahnestock and Secor, however, in that it claims to inhabit 'a space halfway between the highly abstract identification of formal features, which is difficult to translate into specific instruction for writing, and the wholly concrete discussion of particular instances, which is difficult to generalize' (2004, p. xviii). We also share a common approach that argumentation needs not be adversarial, that there are alternative models of argumentation that are consensual and driven by metaphors of dance, construction, or journey, rather than by war. Where the two books differ is in terms of their procedural approach. Fahnestock and Secor ground their approach in the identification of 'fixed types of questions that an argument can address' (ibid., p. xvii) by helping students to address questions concerning 'facts, definitions, causes, values and actions' (ibid.). Their book and its model are structured along these lines, in sequence. The derivation of the model is Aristotelian in that the appeals from his *Rhetoric* – to *logos*, *pathos*, and *ethos* – are used. Like all the American theorists discussed earlier, the classical models provide a foundation for work in contemporary academic rhetoric for students. The basic locus of their approach is that is it generic and that the generic focus for courses on writing and composition is that of statis theory. Statis theory derives from Ciceronian judicial rhetoric and is concerned with identification and definition (framing, in the broad rhetorical sense) of the topic in question. What is impressive about Fahnestock and Secor's book, in particular, are the breadth of reference to contemporary texts and the added dimension of an online resource on which lecturers and students can draw.

Where I would like to make a distinction between Fahnestock and Secor's excellent handbook and the present book rests in four areas: first, the present book is research-based and for lecturers' own professional development, rather than for students; second, it discusses a range of models, placing these on a spectrum as to their function and usefulness in thinking about responses to students' work; and third, the present book operates with a slightly narrower conception of argument and argumentation. In respect of the third difference, Fahnestock and Secor suggest that 'every discussion you have in the classroom is an argument, as people articulate and test their interpretations of what they are learning' (p. xxv). I would want to qualify that statement by saying that all interactions in classrooms are potentially dialogic but that such dialogue (one hopes it happens!) is not always argumentational. In cases wherein there is no dialogue, there is no space for argumentation. These are classrooms wherein there is an excessive transmission model at work. However, even in cases wherein there is ostensible dialogism, it may not go as far as argumentational exchange if (a) there is not an acceptance of the possibility of critical edge or challenge in the discussion and (b) the ideological positions of those engaged in the argument are not made clear or acknowledged in some way. The reason for a focus on professional practice in the area of argumentation in higher education in the present book is that, all too often, either the possibilities for argumentation are not made explicit for students or they are positively discouraged by (rarely) authoritarian pedagogic approaches or (more commonly) a sublimation of the rhetorical and argumentational lineaments of the subject, discipline, or field.

The fourth area of difference between the present book and *A Rhetoric of Argument* is that Fahnestock and Secor's book is based on the premise of a generic approach to argumentation, whereas the present book's position is that of continually working toward a balance between generic and discipline-specific approaches.

In the first chapter of the present book, the justification for a focus on argumentation was made, drawing support from three major theorists: Bakhtin, Vygotsky and Habermas. In this chapter, the relationship between rhetoric and argumentation is explored. It has already been suggested that argumentation inhabits a 'mezzanine' floor between theory and practice. If the practices of composing – in speech, writing, and in other modes – operate at the ground or first floor, then rhetoric theory's position is at the second or upper floor, above the mezzanine wherein argumentation operates.

A key distinction to make, however, before we explore the relationship between the upper floor of rhetoric and the mezzanine of argumentation, is that rhetoric and argumentation are considered as more than Aristotle's 'art of persuasion'; rather, the present book sees rhetoric as the 'arts of discourse', a broader and less functional category. This distinction might help to explain why applications of Aristotle to contemporary rhetorical demands are less than satisfactory: not only because the contexts are different but because Aristotle's conception of rhetoric is a narrower one than we need.

By the 'arts of discourse', I mean the craft and design of communication. Discourse can range from everyday conversation in speech to the composition of formal written documents, from simple mono-modal utterances to multimodal compositions. Throughout, the emphasis is on *composition*: the putting together of elements to communicate something to someone or to a group of people.

Rhetoric, then, is a highly pragmatic body of theory as well as having a long history of drawing on linguistics, politics, social sciences, the arts, and other disciplines. It is essentially about who is communicating to whom about what, with what purpose (why?) and how? The five elements – who, what, to whom, why, and how? – are ostensibly simple. They contain within them the complexities of real communication in real situations. As far as higher education goes, we can characterize them in more detail as follows.

Who?

The so-called 'rhetor' or speaker/writer/composer can range from a single individual to a group (a pressure group, a committee, an authority, a corporate entity). Whichever the composer is, he or she will have a certain degree of power invested in the role. For a teacher or lecturer or professor in higher education, the power is considerable. You are in a position to design curricula; to design the learning platform; to feed back to students on their compositions; to speak to them not only about the topic of mutual interest itself but how to compose in relation to that topic; and, crucially, to mark and assess their work, hopefully providing detailed feedback to help them improve on future assignments. Ultimately, the power rests with such assessment of student offerings and with the examination boards that recommend the final grades that students take forward as part of their academic profile. Such grades can include decisions about the pass/fail borderline.

For the students, conversely, there is little power. They speak/write/compose within certain constraints and in response to certain assignments. Although there is a good deal of freedom in the articulation of thought within these disciplinary and pedagogic/assessment constraints, that freedom is used to demonstrate competence and prowess within the discipline. Students are very dependent on their tutors to interpret what the rules of the game are. If those tutors are unconscious of the rules they operate by or are unwilling, for whatever reason, to make these explicit to students and to mediate for them, the student is at a disadvantage. Furthermore, if feedback to the student is always after the event (that is, after a completed piece of work has been submitted), it is likely to have less impact than if it were given during the process of composition. Sometimes, students get no feedback at all and are left guessing why they received a particular grade for a particular piece of work. All too often, a student thinks he or she has done a good piece of work, only to find out that the markers do not think the same. If there is no feedback or explanation, the student remains in the dark, and the act of handing in work for assessment is not a learning process; it can, indeed, be a disincentive to future learning in the field.

What?

What is to be conveyed – the subject-matter of the communication – isn't always as straightforward as the notion of 'content' implies. There are situations and contexts in which there is a clear body of incontrovertible content that is to be conveyed. In these cases, the rhetorical and argumentational parameters are tight. There are usually set ways in which to convey such content, and the emphasis is on clarity. The value of rhetorical and argumentational considerations in cases like these is that clarity is not always evident; the act of rewriting can aid clarity and, therefore, communication.

In the social sciences, arts, and humanities, it is usually the case that the 'content' of the assignment is closely tied into the means by which that content is conveyed. One of the reasons for this close association of form and content is that assignments are means by which thought, feeling, and 'position' are conveyed. The content, then, is a set of ideas or propositions that are critiqued or laid out by the speaker/writer/composer. The very setting out of a set of propositions brings the utterance close to argumentation, especially if a position is consciously and clearly articulated. If evidence is supplied, of whatever kind, the assignment positions itself squarely within the field of argumentation.

To Whom?

Often the audience of a piece of academic composition is not clear. If a student is preparing a presentation for an audience of fellow students and the teacher/professor/lecturer, the audience is fairly clear (as it usually is with spoken compositions). However, if the student is writing or composing something multimodally, the very fact of the tangible product that is created can obscure the fact that the product is a means by which to communicate with an audience. In the 'real world', again, the audience is usually clear: you write a letter to a particular person; you compose a website for whoever wishes to access it; you write a set of guidelines to be followed or discussed by co-workers, and so on.

In academia, the audience for writing is rarely specified, with the emphasis being on the substance of the piece and on the critical/creative faculties and capabilities of the composer. In fact, the audience is usually the lecturer or lecturers who are marking the assignment, any other examiners who might be brought in to ensure reliability in the marking process, and external examiners who are brought in to verify and validate the marking process. Rarely does a piece of student work, even at the masters level, go much beyond that. Students may read each other's work at the drafting and pre-submission stages; occasionally, a piece of writing may be so good (or so bad) that it is held up as an exemplar; and very occasionally, a piece is developed further for publication (especially the case at the doctoral level). However, the audiences for academic work are small, self-referential, and not clearly specified (you don't necessarily know who the second marker is, or who the external examiner will be).

Rhetorically, then, the student is at a disadvantage. He or she does not know for whom the writing is being produced, nor what their particular predilections are. The work is submitted for consideration, and then a mark (and sometimes the work, with annotations and/or feedback) is returned.

Why?

Why is such a large amount of oral, written, and/or multimodal presentation needed from the student to arrive at an overall and summative grade? The principal function of such presentation by students is demonstration, rather than real argumentation for a persuasive purpose. Essays, assignments, artworks, talks, and other productions are submitted. They are considered, graded, annotated, and returned. These productions are part of the currency of academia: they are exchanged for grades and ultimately for a passage out of the academy with a certain class of degree. So the student has to *demonstrate* to the academy that he or she *can* argue, *can* make a clear exposition of an aspect of knowledge, and can communicate thought clearly. All this communication is within the academy and has no or little bearing outside the academy – except at the doctoral level, and then only rarely. In most cases, even the doctoral thesis is a *rite de passage*. Such a scenario might seem self-defining, self-perpetuating and, indeed, depressing, and some students think so and act accordingly, or do not even start the process. However, such is the scale of the operation worldwide that higher education seems not only a means to an end (higher salaries, better economic prospects, more satisfying jobs, and the like) but an end it itself. Idealistically, that end-in-itself is the pursuit of knowledge and learning for its own sake. More pragmatically, it is the contribution to a community of enquiries or to communities of enquiry that reach beyond the particular department and university you are studying in to electronic communities, global communities, and other such communities that operate via study groups, seminars, conferences, and others with a common interest.

Though the education system can seem pointless from certain perspectives, it does create spaces for reflection, abstraction, and the reformulation of problems and solutions that are important in the real world. Such a separate space is a real space in real time and also a rhetorical space in which all the aspects of rhetoric that have been set out earlier and in the current exposition are at play. Inevitably, such a space generates its own *modi operandi* and its own rules, regulations, and procedures: in fact, academia is particularly good at this governance side of learning. Part of the point of this book, however, is to suggest that though these qualities may be evident and explicitly articulated, the discourses of particular subject areas are less exposed to scrutiny and discussion. It is these discourses – particularly those of an argumentational nature that are key to the success of a student – that are the subject of this book.

The question of how such principles are taken forward can be evidenced through an example: an analysis of Storey's *Writing History: A Guide for Students.*

A Case Study: Argumentation in History

Storey (2009) is the third edition of a book, *Writing History: A Guide for Students*, that was first published in 1999. In its 10 chapters, it probably provides the most comprehensive guide to writing in a discipline for undergraduate students or 'beginning historians' (p. ix). These chapters are 'Getting started', 'Interpreting source materials', 'Writing history faithfully', 'Use sources to make inferences', 'Get writing!', 'Build an argument', 'Narrative techniques for historians', 'Writing sentences in history', 'Choose precise words', and 'Revising and editing'. Although this is a practice-based rather than research-based guidebook, its various sections provide much for the development of argumentation in history and much that is relevant to the present book.

The first piece of advice in *Writing History* is 'find a historical conflict'. This advice can be squared with that of the history lecturer interviewed and quoted elsewhere in this book: 'Drill down at the point of dispute'. This first step is a crucial one. If it is not taken, students are likely to find themselves in uncontroversial, 'accepted' territory and outside the interest area of the academic study of history. Too many students believe that retelling the existing narratives of history, or engaging in expository writing – like arraying the various views of secondary academic texts – is the way to study and to submit assignments. If they do so, they are likely to gain marks and grades at the lower end of the spectrum.

A further part of the introductory work in the study of history – apart from identifying sources – is the forming of a 'hypothesis' that will guide the evolving research. This hypothesis will, in turn, help move the research toward the forming of an argument. The hypothesis appears to evolve from the generation of questions (see Andrews, 2003b), one of which is selected as the most promising, and the right scale for answering in an undergraduate assignment. However, the hypothesis used in history, as identified in Storey's book, looks a little less defined than the hypothesis that might generate a scientific research project. Hypotheses are more than inverted questions: they are proposals, projections of what might happen or might be the case.

It is my own view that hypotheses are not necessary for the development of arguments. It is possible to argue from a proposition or a question, as in the following examples: 'The Blair years were a time of radical social reform in the UK. Discuss.' and 'To what extent did Bill Clinton succeed in bringing about social form in healthcare?' The discussion of terms such as *proposition*, *hypothesis*, and (research) *question* may be academic, and it could be argued that the first example given is a proto-hypothesis. However, it is important to establish what the *starting points* for an argumentational essay or assignment are. More important, what do these different starting points imply for the development of the piece of writing?

As work continues on the preparation for the assignment, Storey refers to *inferences* that historians make from the evidence they have gathered. Inferential argument is the gradual building up of an argument through inferences, and these inferences are generated through thoughtful comparisons of the evidence that is discovered. There are spaces that open up as reading takes place: in the internal consistency of primary sources, between primary sources, between primary and secondary accounts, and so on. These gaps need to be exploited by students and scholars, because that is where critical contributions can be made to the subject, however small. Further, it is not just the identification of gaps that opens up the possibilities for new inferences and potential arguments. They are also generated from the juxtaposition (Storey's term) and tension generated between apparently conflicting sources and interpretations.

How to build arguments from inferences? Storey (ibid., p. 63) suggests:

> Small inferences must be built into larger arguments, and arguments must be made persuasively. When you read your sources, start thinking about ways to compose your essay. How can you move from asking questions about events and sources to composing a story and argument of your own?

He goes on to discuss how both deductive and inductive reasoning are used by historians to build arguments from inferences. It is important to note that the reasoning is both from ideas and concepts 'down' toward evidence and from evidence 'up' toward ideas. Elsewhere in this book, I have suggested that different disciplines may have a predilection for one direction over the other (for example, those that favour the generation and use of hypotheses may be seen to be deductive in their operation); but it important to remember that inductive and deductive reasoning are two sides of the same coin, and one is dependent on the other. We cannot generate ideas from data and evidence without stopping to consider whether those ideas are valid; and to test this, we need to move from the idea back to the evidence. Equally, deductive thinkers must, once they have made their deductions, revisit their ideas to test whether the evidence supports them.

Let us look in particular at the sixth chapter, 'Build an argument'. It, in turn, builds on the previous chapter, which is concerned with planning and large-scale structuration. The main point of that previous chapter is that the direction and significance of the argument must be made clear in the skeletal framework or plan and that, indeed, plans can be developed to ensure that they are relevant and detailed enough to provide the basis for a good argument in the fully fledged essay. It is obvious that there comes a point at which planning must stop and the real business of writing the actual essay begins. Because the nature of writing is that ideas come as the writing takes place, it is inevitable that there will be straying from the original plan. Once the first draft is finished, or even during the act of composing it, it will make sense to check back with the finished plan to make sure that there is unity and a clear argument and that the main points of the plan are embodied in the essay.

However, too tight a plan can make for a wooden essay. The characteristic formula of the five-paragraph essay with, in each paragraph, its topic sentence, evidence to support the claim, and transitions from the previous and to the next paragraphs is sound but can lead to a dull read. The formula seems to suggest that the paragraph is an organizing unit in an argument – helpful in some cases but restrictive in others. Storey himself recognizes that there is more than one way to construct a paragraph and does not subscribe to the five-paragraph essay orthodoxy.

As well as reinforcing the importance of defining terms, especially if they are contentious, the chapter is concerned with counterarguments. This is a characteristically weak area for undergraduates, who tend to devote most energy to constructing the main line of their argument. Even though this main line – if it emerges, which is encouraging – is crucially important, it will have derived as a counter-position to existing bodies of thought and to particular arguments. It is not just American students who are sometimes poor at identifying counterarguments in their reading and in their writing (see Larson, Britt, & Larson, 2004); the same is probably true of students worldwide who are not prepared to question the texts they are reading or who find it difficult to imagine the counter-position to the one they are developing.

Finally, there is a point on which Storey and I might disagree: the nature of concluding paragraphs in history essays. His line is that, although there is no formula for an introduction or conclusion, part of the purpose of the concluding paragraph of an essay will be 'to put your ideas back in a broader context' (p. 86). I think this is sometimes appropriate, and much will depend on the specific context in which the essay in being written and examined. However, it is reasonable to say that concluding paragraphs do not always have to refer to the broader context, whether in history of other disciplines. They can range from paragraphs in which the focus remains specific, seeing an argument through to its tight and convincing conclusion; in which a counterargument (rather than a more specific counter-point) is raised, thus suggesting an occasion for further debate beyond the confines of the present essay; in which a new direction is offered for further research; or in which the significance of the argument in the body of the essay is explored. In other words, conclusions need not frame the arguments of essays in a wooden, fixed way, and they certainly need not repeat what has already been said. They can be challenging, interesting, even oblique and seductive at times, leading the reader on and giving him or her the impression that there is more that could be said if only the writer had more time and space to say it.

In general, Storey's excellent guide is more about argumentation than it suggests. Discussion of argument pervades the chapters, spilling over from the ostensible chapter about the topic to others on narrative techniques and on planning. The weakness of the book is that it embeds argumentation into the processes of composition, leaving little space for the generation of arguments outside the writing process (e.g., in thought and in speech prior to, during, and after the writing act). It also draws thinly on theories of logical and/or rhetorical argumentation and does not discuss the use of images as evidence, nor does it consider, as part of its most recent edition, multimodal issues both in terms of evidence and with regard to composition.

Issues of multimodality in relation to argumentation are addressed in Chapter 6, then again in a look at the future of argumentation in higher education in Chapter 12. In those chapters, there is consideration of whether we can assume that the burden of argumentation is carried largely by spoken and written verbal language or whether it can be carried entirely visually or aurally. The debate about these matters is being carried on a website devoted to the influence of e-learning and multimodality on the nature and form of the doctoral thesis, on www.newdoctorates.blogspot.com. There is no reason that such debates might not also apply to the masters or undergraduate dissertation in a range of subjects and disciplines.

The Practical Dimension

Activity 2.1

Accounts of the history of rhetoric and/or argumentation in particular subjects and disciplines are rare. Apart from Storey's book, referred to earlier in the case of history, a notable example is Bazerman's (1988) book on the genesis of the scientific article, *Shaping Written Knowledge: the Genre and Activity of the Experimental Article in Science*. Each of these books is instructive, in its different ways, about any discipline's development (in Bazerman's case, of a genre within a set of disciplines) in that there is a degree of transferability between disciplines and their genres. It is also the case that histories of rhetoric and/or argumentation in academic disciplines take on an epistemological dimension, because the nature of the shaping of knowledge is addressed in each case.

Consider the history of rhetoric and/or argumentation in your own subject or discipline. What research is there? You might have to extend the search beyond your library collection to online databases, records of dissertations, and other sources.

Activity 2.2

Visit the website www.newdoctorates.blogspot.com and contribute to the blog. In particular, consider the implications of some of the material there for the presentation and assessment of work on your undergraduate or masters levels courses.

3
Generic Skills in Argumentation

What are the generic skills in argumentation at the higher education level? This chapter looks at a number of models that attempt to map such skills and discusses how they might be applied in a range of contexts. The advantage of a core set of skills and practices is that they can be used not only to bring unity to studies in argumentation but to point out where particular practices diverge from the norm. It also looks at rhetoric and composition courses wherein such generic skills are assumed to have value.

By reviewing the different available models of argumentation, we can understand more clearly how argument is charted/mapped and also gauge the applicability of such models to different aspects of the composing process in higher education.

The previous chapter contained reference to Quintilian, the Roman rhetorician, and his five-part arrangement for argument. Lindeman (2001: 134–136) adapts it for the needs of contemporary writers and readers and notes that it derives from Aristotle. Although the classical rhetoricians proposed everything from a two-part to a seven-part structure, Quintilian's formulation may have provided a distant model for the American 'five-paragraph essay' that is a staple of school education. In Quintilian's version, an argument consists of five parts: the *exordium*, the *narratio*, the proof or *confirmatio*, the *refutatio*, and the *peroratio*.

The *exordium* is an introduction that explains to the audience what the argument is about and why it is important. The *narratio* is a narrative of events and/or a statement of facts. Although such a statement may, in itself, be selective, it needs to state as clearly as possible what the facts of the situation are. It could also serve to state a thesis or proposition that the rest of the argument hangs on. The third part, the *confirmatio*, provides the core of the argument: it might consist of a combination of claims/propositions and evidence, or it might proceed logically through a series of propositions. The weakest part of this section is usually contained in the middle, so that the strength of the argument is evident at the beginning and end of the section. This part can often be the longest in the argument overall. The *refutatio* is the refutation: this part deals with real or hypothetical objections to the argument. In a powerful argument, handling the refutation can be used to strengthen further the main argument by the deft use of the elements of the opposing argument(s). It is possible to accept some of the opposing points of view without diminishing one's own main argument or, indeed, to demolish counter-arguments and thus strengthen your own. Finally, the *peroratio* is the conclusion in which the argument can be summarized. There can be a return to the introduction, a recitation of the main points of the argument, a look forward to how the argument can be applied or built upon, an emotional appeal to the audience, and the use of any other device that will wrap up and make more effective an argument in hand.

Quintilian's model is essentially rhetorical and compositional: it applies equally well to speech and writing. Although it was conceived as a guide to arguing in the public fora of Rome, it can be used at school and college level as a sound structure for organizing arguments. Its critical inclusion of a section on refutation fills the gap that was identified by Larson et al. (2004) and mentioned previously.

Recent Models of Argumentation in Education

The premises behind the use of models of argumentation is that 'argument' is a mode of thinking and composition or 'meta-genre', and 'argumentation' is the process of operating within that mode. That is to say, argumentation is not a specific text-type (like the research paper in the United States or the conventional doctoral thesis in a particular discipline), nor is it a socially situated set of discourse conventions, as in the definition of genre as social action (see Bazerman, 1988; Freedman and Medway, 1994; Miller, 1984; Swales, 1990). Rather, argument and argumentation are like the noun and verb of a grammar in which rationality is the overriding semantic.

What is so attractive about argumentation is that it is so closely connected to the operation of the mind, to social interaction, to politics, and also to change and the exploration and resolution of difference or controversies.

Furthermore, the relationship among logic, dialectic, and rhetoric as informing theories in argument and argumentation has recently resurfaced as a topic of interest to philosophers, discourse analysts, and rhetoricians. Blair (2002) maps out clearly the nature of each of the perspectives in a contemporary context and also draws the complex interrelationships among the three. Following Wenzel (1980), he suggests that in any act of argumentation, all three perspectives are at play: logic is concerned with the *product* of argumentation, dialectic with the *procedures*, and rhetoric with the communicative *process*. However, he differs from Wenzel in suggesting that it is difficult to separate one perspective from another and that 'there is more than one type of relationship among them' (2002: 130).

In this chapter, I start with a discussion of the spectrum of argument studies, with reference to theoretical underpinning, and then look at some of the models that have emerged in the wake of Toulmin's seminal work in the

1950s. Consideration will be given to the recent updated edition of *The Uses of Argument* (Toulmin, 2003).

Definitions

Let us revisit what is meant by 'argument' and argumentation'. Argument can be said to refer, variously, to a claim or proposition, to the evidence cited in support of a proposition, or to the phenomenon of arguing itself. It is seen by logicians as the enthymemic moves made to establish proof. According to Honderich (1995) in *The Oxford Companion to Philosophy*, its most important sense for philosophy is as 'a set of propositions (called its premisses) and a proposition (called its conclusion)'. This kind of enthymemic compression gives rise to examples like 'Souls are incorporeal; therefore they have no location', but that very formulaic compression has given rise to antithetical ways of describing argument, as in Toulmin's *The Uses of Argument*. From a 'conventional', pre-Toulmin perspective,

> an argument is valid when its conclusion follows from its premisses (other descriptions are 'is deducible from' or 'is entailed by'). It can be a good argument even when not valid, if its premisses support its conclusion in some non-deductive way, for example inductively.
>
> (Honderich, 1995: 48)

In demotic terms, it is characterized as 'row', 'quarrel', or altercation, with or without resolution. From a communications point of view, it is a phenomenon broadly conceived by rhetoricians and discourse analysts as 'a connected series of statements intended to establish a position'. To complicate matters yet further, the term *argument* is used as an umbrella term to include both the observable activity or *thing* – which we have earlier called 'argument', and the process of arguing: 'argumentation'. *Argumentation*, then, is the process of developing arguments, the exchange of views, the seeking and provision of good evidence to support claims and propositions - the *choreography* of argument. As such, it is argumentation that is of principal interest to education, because it is about transformation, clarifying, and changing ideas, personal growth, identity formation, and other dynamic aspects of learning. Argument can be considered the noun; argumentation the process *in verb*.

Most argument would hope to be persuasive, but not all persuasion is argumentative. Although Aristotle characterized rhetoric as 'the art of persuasion' in a general sense, persuasion describes the effect or effectiveness of an approach from one person or a number of persons to another/others. Argument and argumentation, on the other hand, describe the interventions and dialogues that make up human transactions. It is a category error to conflate the two.

Rather than continue to pursue definitional nuances here, the reader is referred to previous explorations of the meaning of 'argument' and 'argumentation' in Mitchell (1994a: 4–6); Andrews (1995: 2–4); Andrews and Mitchell (2001: 1–44); Andrews (2000: 1–11); and to Honderich (1995) and Toulmin (1958, 2003).

Literature Review

The books and articles on the topic of argumentation cover a wide and fascinating range. Those by George Myerson, like his *The Argumentative Imagination* (1992) – which studies dialogic and dialectical imagination in Wordsworth, Dryden, *The Book of Job*, and *The Bhagavad Gita* – emphasize the literary, rhetorical dimension of argument. That position is more clearly set out in *Rhetoric, Reason and Society* (1994) with its sub-title, *Rationality as Dialogue*, or in his book with Dick Leith, *The Power of Address* (1989), which positions argument at the rhetorical end of a spectrum that has at its other end logic. At the logic end of the spectrum of argument and argumentation are works such as Jane Grimshaw's *Argument Structure* (1990), a highly technical monograph on argument within the sentence and working within the discipline of linguistic enquiry; many of these studies see argument as sealed off from the world and operating behind the closed doors of fabricated and made-up sentences and propositions: their tools are the enthymeme, logical relations; their *bête noire*, the fallacy. Their weakness, from where I have positioned myself in the middle of such a spectrum, is that their own fundamental fallacy is an attempt to make verbal language do the job of mathematical language. The propositional formulae do not translate readily above the level of the sentence.

If those are the two ends of the spectrum, what lies in between?

The work of Deanna Kuhn in, for example, *The Skills of Argument* (1991), is situated in the middle of the spectrum. This is a study of argument for high school and college students and also for older participants in YMCA job reentry schemes in New York City. It takes as its conception of argument a distinction between two main kinds: *rhetorical*, by which it means the restricted sense of an assertion with accompanying justification, and *dialogic*, which it takes to mean the juxtaposition of two opposing assertions. This distinction can be confusing, because the very essence of a rhetorical view of argument and argumentation is its dialogic nature (and thus the dialogic nature of thought, if you scale up to the cognitive level). The problem with Kuhn's formulation is the pejorative use of 'rhetorical' argument and the sentimental use of 'dialogic'.

Part of the conceit of the spectrum I've been mapping – with a logical, structural view of argument at one end and a rhetorical, choreographic view at the other – is that I'm positioning the work that Sally Mitchell, others, and I have done right in the middle of the spectrum. That might be seen as a compromise, but I'd argue it's a strong one and a necessary one for educational purposes. It is also strategically appropriate in that it allows me to weigh up the pros and cons of the various studies (including our own) and to make some kind of triangulation – in the sense of navigational positioning on the sea – in relation to studies that have already been completed. Thinking reflexively, it might also be a superficially rhetorical ploy to convince you (persuade you) of my argument. We see such even-handedness deployed cynically by politicians and employers and by those in positions of power to sell a particular policy. Conversely, a balanced position is often a strong one. Personally, I tend more toward the rhetorical side of the central point because I'm interested in argument in its applications in democratic processes; in contingency; and in rhetorical moves; and in its various manifestations and versions in different disciplinary settings, both at high school and college levels. At the same time, I accept that there must be generic models of argument and argumentation to allow the measurement and discussion of difference: for example, different conceptions and practices of argumentation in different disciplines or contexts. It is to these generic models that the present chapter now turns.

The 'Toulmin Model'

There has been a great deal of work, in the last 50 years or so, on what might be called 'applications of Toulmin', including by Toulmin and his associates (Toulmin, 1958; Toulmin, Rieke, & Janik, 1984). What inspired Toulmin was partly a dissatisfaction with the strictures of formal logic. His model moves us along the spectrum, away from the extreme of formal logic, and has been developed by Douglas Walton (1989) and others in the informal logic movement. Between the informal logicians and the 2000 model of Mitchell and Riddle (I'll come on to these models diagrammatically in the next section) is a vast shoal of studies on how Toulmin might be adapted for the classroom – and specifically for the writing classroom. One of the best of these is Hegelund and Kock (2000). Another is by Lunsford (2002), who problematizes the notion of context in work deriving from Toulmin. She acknowledges that Toulmin warns, in his original edition, that the 'model' must be interpreted with particular contexts in mind – that gauging the soundness of argument is, in Toulmin's terms, a 'field-dependent' matter. What Lunsford adds to this caveat is an exploration of the notion of context, suggesting that it is a complex, multi-faceted phenomenon. In writing and composition terms, she also describes problems faced in creating a 'projected context' (i.e., an imaginary audience and environment to motivate students' writing). Lunsford therefore puts her finger on a key dilemma in the application of 'Toulmin's model'; on the one hand, the model is attractive because it provides a framework within which students and teachers from different fields and disciplines can compare and contrast their argumentative practices. On the other, it achieves full application only when it is grounded in particular contexts. One could argue, then, that its function as a model for the composing of argument is both inviting and dangerous.

The updated edition of *The Uses of Argument* (Toulmin, 2003) provides an interesting commentary on how the original aim of the book has been adapted by communication theorists, discourse analysts, and lecturers/teachers. 'When I wrote it', says Toulmin in the preface,

> my aim was strictly philosophical: to criticize the assumption, made by most Anglo-American academic philosophers, that any significant argument can be put in formal terms: not just as a *syllogism*, since for Aristotle himself any inference can be called a 'syllogism' or 'linking of statements', but a rigidly demonstrative deduction of the kind to be found in Euclidean geometry.
>
> (2003: vii)

The disavowal of any application to rhetoric or argumentation is, on the one hand, a clarification and a positioning within the discipline of philosophy; on the other, a distancing from what the Platonic philosophical tradition would see as the lesser arts of rhetoric and (as a sub-field of rhetoric) argumentation. Toulmin goes on to say:

> my concern was with twentieth-century epistemology, not informal logic. Still less had I in mind an analytical model like that which, along scholars of Communication, came to be called 'the Toulmin model'.
>
> (2003: vii)

Nevertheless, the publication by Toulmin et al. (1984) of *An Introduction to Reasoning* – essentially an undergraduate textbook in rhetoric and composition – reinforced the applicability of the model to communication practice and research and, as Toulmin himself admits, 'it would be churlish of me to disown the notion of "the Toulmin model", which was one of the unforeseen by-products of *The Uses of Argument*' (2003: viii). It is taken for granted, in the present chapter, that the Toulmin model has an important presence in late twentieth-century thinking in communication and composition studies, but Toulmin's caveats are a timely reminder that the 'model' has its origins in epistemological thinking, and that, as Toulmin points out,

> If I were rewriting this book today, I would point to Aristotle's contrast between 'general' and 'special' topics as a way of throwing clearer light on the varied kinds of 'backing' relied on in different fields of practice and argument.
>
> (2003: viii)

Most of the studies mentioned in this book operate within the Western rationalist, dualistic paradigm. That is to say, they take it as given that argument operates at both micro-, mezzo- and macro-levels in a Hegelian dialectical pattern of development: thesis, antithesis, synthesis. It would be useful to explore other paradigms in which argument had a different function within education. Deborah Tannen's work on conversational discourse (e.g., *You Just Don't Understand: Women and Men in Conversation* [1991] on differences in gender conceptions of argumentative discourse, or *The Argument Culture* [1999]) point the way to what could be done in the educational context. Tannen writes in the preface to the British edition of *The Argument Culture*:

> The concept underlying the argument culture is the notion of ritualized opposition, in contrast to the literal opposition of genuine disagreement. It is the Western tendency to view everything through the template of a battle metaphor, and to glorify conflict and aggression, in contrast to the Eastern emphasis on harmony as a way to defuse inevitable conflict. (1999, p. 4)

Although it is fair to say that the battle metaphor pervades ideas of argument and argumentation in the West – reflecting adversarial notions of argument deriving from classical rhetoric and Hegelian dialectic – Berrill (1996) and others have pointed out that there are a number of metaphors describing argument, including those of 'journey', 'construction', and 'dance'. The latter, in particular, expresses a more consensual, dialogic view of argument. See Costello and Mitchell's (1995) *Competing and Consensual Voices: the theory and practice of argument* for a more nuanced view of argument, and Berrill (1996); and Mitchell and Andrews's (2000) *Learning to Argue in Higher Education* for a more subtle international view of diversity in argument and argumentative styles in different disciplines and cultures.

There is also a need for studies of the choreography of argument: how do arguments start, how are they taken up, how do they develop, and how do they end?

Models of Argument

Mike Riddle (in Mitchell and Riddle, 2000) has written on the role of models in identifying the key elements of theoretical systems; ultimately they can be seen in terms of metaphorical frameworks for distilling the salient from the residual. As far as argumentation and its applications in education are concerned, there are a number of models that can be discussed.

Of seminal importance is Toulmin's (1958) model, referred to in the previous section. The particular function of this model is to provide a test for the soundness of arguments. The key axes of the model are, first, the relationship between claims ('propositions') and grounds ('evidence') and,

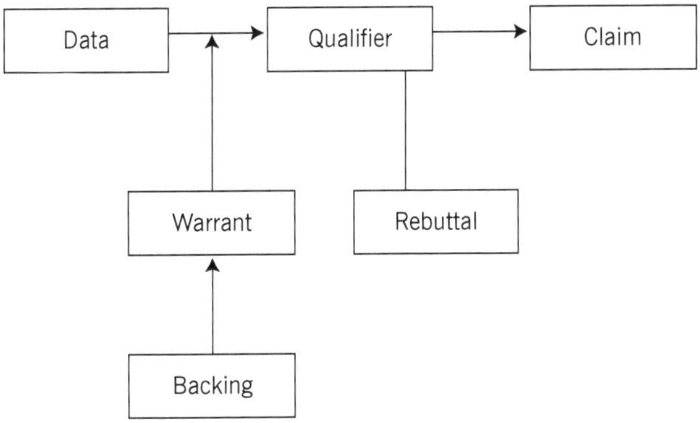

Figure 3.1 Toulmin's model (1)

second, the relationship between the warrant ('means by which the claims are related to the grounds') and its backing (justification for the warrant within disciplinary or other contexts; Figure 3.1).

Mediating between the claim and grounds is the possibility of a qualifier, so that 'in certain circumstances' or 'under certain conditions', the relationship between the claim and its grounds can be adjusted. Furthermore, a rebuttal might be included to challenge the relationship between the grounds and the claim, either helping to reinforce the relationship or challenging it to change (and, for example, be qualified). It can be noticed, from the figures, that the direction of the arrows in the model are all toward the substantiation of the claim. The various elements of the model are there to support the claim and to test its 'soundness' (Figure 3.2).

In a reorientation of the model, we can see its archaeological nature more clearly. The metaphor driving it is one of unearthing and discovering the basis to a claim. As such, it is a relatively static model, more suited to testing the strength of existing arguments than to generating new ones, as

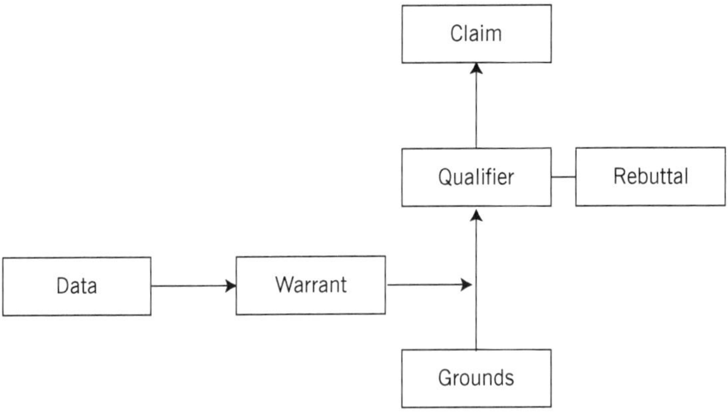

Figure 3.2 Toulmin's model (2) (1984)

Toulmin suggested. In education contexts, it might best be used to gauge the soundness of a draft argument before the submission of a final version for assessment or debate. Such reorientation helps us to see that the model might be used for compositional ends – again, not as it was originally intended but adapted for the purposes of students at undergraduate and postgraduate levels who are grappling with the problems of how to gather and marshal evidence in support of their arguments. Students are often asked in their assignments to be 'more critical' without clear explication of how to be more critical. It is clear, from the examination of the marking of student scripts, that criticality is highly prized and rewarded. In practical terms, it can be enhanced in a number of ways: by the weighing up of one source against another; by the adoption of a sceptical 'vow of suspicion' (Ricoeur) toward existing published knowledge, rather than by a 'vow of obedience'; by the development of a point of view; and with the use of surface markers such as 'however', 'nevertheless', 'on the one hand.../on the other', and other devices that enable the student to articulate an argument.

Problems with the application of Toulmin's model to learning contexts are not only that the model itself seems not to be dynamic and thus not open to rhetorical variation but that it is technically difficult to understand and apply. For example, the distinction between the warrant and its backing can be hard to maintain. If a 'warrant' is the means by which the evidence counts in support of a claim or proposition, the backing is the set of values or ideological context in which the warrant, proposition, and evidence are validated or given significance. The first is operational; the second substantial. What is difficult is trying to separate these two elements in some fields, especially where it is not clear that the field is informed by a set of (competing) theories. In pre-paradigmatic fields of enquiry, such as educational research, it is often hard to explicate what the backing is and therefore hard to distinguish it from the operational modes of linking propositions to evidence in the field. Educational research draws on a number of bodies of theory: sociological, psychological, political, philosophical. It does not always make clear (either to itself or to its audience) what body of theory or range of theories it draws on.

Nor does it allow for the evolution of grounds into a claim via a process of testing and concept formation (as in the inductive processes of scientific reasoning and experimentation). These problems have been addressed in a model developed by Mitchell and Riddle as part of the Leverhulme-funded research project on 'Improving the Quality of Argument in Higher Education' (Mitchell, 1997; Mitchell and Riddle, 2000; see also Riddle, 2000). Their model is a simplification of Toulmin for written text in education contexts. It justifies itself thus:

> The core model...with its use of the everyday language terms SINCE, THEN, BECAUSE to express the three-part relationship within argument, is motivated by exigencies reflected in current pedagogical

> debates about argument. There is a need to meet the objections of disciplinary staff who find proliferation of argumentative terminology [problematic]. There is a matching need to reiterate the inescapable 'connectedness' (Gage, 1996) between argument's core elements, when the concept of argument is introduced into discussion in academic situations. From this flows the motivation to choose terms from language use which occurs naturally when discussing relations between parts of argument, such as *since, and, so, therefore, because, if,* and *then.*
>
> (Mitchell & Riddle, 2000)

One of the helpful aspects of the Mitchell/Riddle model is that it can serve not only as an analytical tool for assessing the structure, nature, and quality of arguments but as a generative tool for planning and composing arguments. This is because the arrows that join the various components are dynamic rather than static or one-way; they signify two-way, dialogic movement. Its problem, however, is that the terms used to denote the agents in the act of argumentation – SINCE, THEN, and BECAUSE – are syntactic conjunctions. Their function in conjoining phrases and clauses in sentences is not the same as their function in articulating argumentation. They have, for example, both narrative functions and argumentational ones – as in the sentence 'I have been waiting here *since* six o'clock; *then* a bus finally came' where the conjunctions have a principally narrative but also a quasi-argumentative function (*post hoc, ergo propter hoc*). In other words, 'since', 'then', and 'because' do not always operate as SINCE, THEN, and BECAUSE. It could be said that a certain degree of precision has been sacrificed to make a model that is more accessible and more generative.

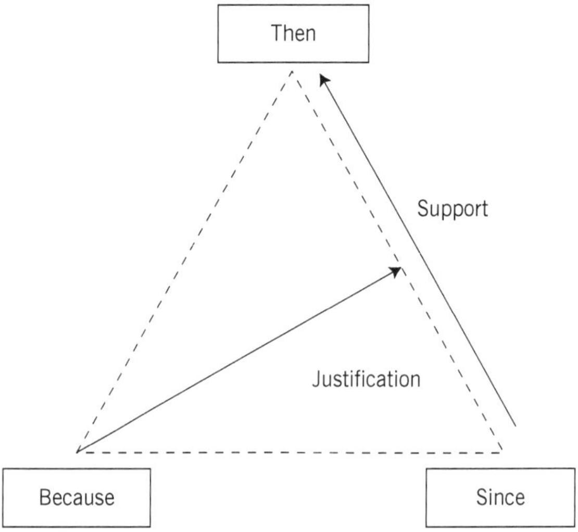

Figure 3.3 Mitchell and Riddle's triangle model

The relationship between the micro-, mezzo- and macro-levels of potential discourse in argumentation needs to be developed.

As we move along the spectrum from the logical to the rhetorical, generic properties of argument *per se* are reduced, and rhetorical contingency increases. The next two models are decidedly on the rhetorical side of the spectrum; indeed, their function is not so much as models of argument as of composition, though each is concerned with the composition of argument.

The first of these is based on Vygotsky's theory of concept development (Vygotsky, 1986), which moves from 'heaps' through 'complexes' to 'concepts'. Vygotsky's notion is that 'thoughts' develop from uncollected heaps of associations that begin to cluster into a unity when a unifying idea brings them together. Such 'complexes' can be of two kinds, as depicted in the second and fourth stages in Figure 3.4, the second kind being unfocused chains of association. At each stage, the first word in the caption to the depictions of concept development are Vygtosky's, the second is Applebee's, and the third is mine. The intention is to map narrative (Applebee) and argumentational (Andrews) development onto the Vygotskian theory of concept development.

Stage one represents 'heaps' of unconnected elements. At the conceptual level, these could be objects piled in a heap, with no obvious connection. At the narrative and argumentational levels, they are the iron filings of a story or

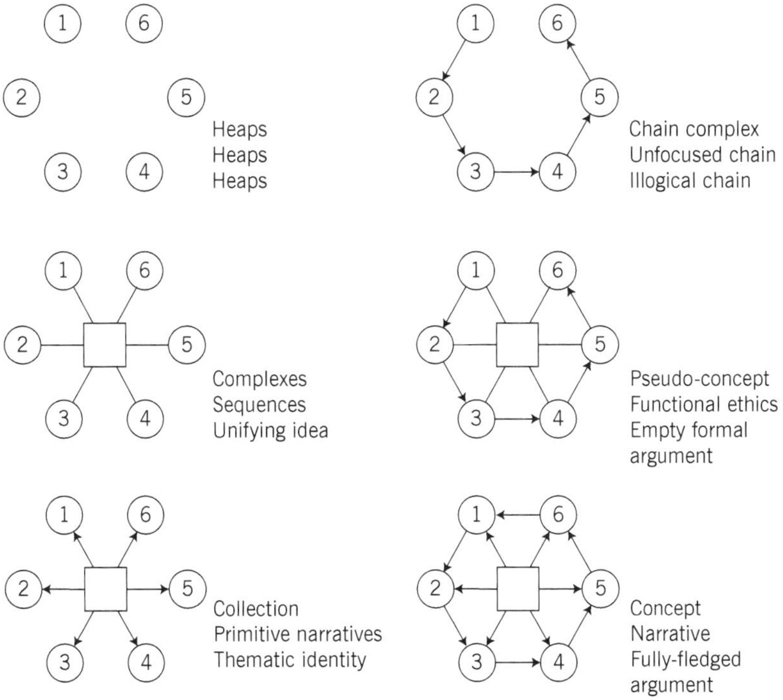

Figure 3.4 The evolution of concepts in relation to narrative and argumentational structure

an argument that has yet to take shape. Stage two (moving down the left-hand column) represents 'complexes' or clusters of preconceptual elements, wherein the previously unconnected phenomena have a nominal unity emerging between them. At the argumentational level, this stage corresponds to the emergence of a topic. Stage three represents a move on from the complex in that, at the preconceptual level, it is the unifying idea that begins to give meaning and significance to the constituent elements (hence the direction of the arrows), rather than the other way around. Such is the structure of episodic, primitive narratives and, in argumentational mode, thematic identity is fully established.

The 'fourth' stage of development at the preconceptual level is that of the chain complex. Actually, it is not so much a fourth stage as a parallel third stage but with the connections taking place between the constituent elements rather than from a central unifying node. There can be no logic to the set of elements at the argumentative level, because (as in stage one) there is no unifying topic or theme; there is, therefore, no way to bring meaning to the chain of connections.

Fully fledged concepts (stage six) have both thematic unity and a logical 'chain' holding them together, each dependent on the other: every element in the concept is related to every other element, either thematically or logically. 'Pseudo-concepts' (stage five) appear to have such unities but are incomplete chains, and the various elements do not link dynamically to a central unifying idea. The model of concept development – highly verbal in its genesis – was built on by Applebee (1978) to show that narrative development (at a macro- or modal level) reflected the pattern of concept development (at a verbal, lexical level). The second term in each of the stages in Figure 3.4 refers to Applebee's notion of how narratives develop: from heaps of unconnected phenomena, through sequences, primitive narratives or unfocused chains (e.g., inexplicable dream sequences), to focused chains and thence to fully fledged narratives, with thematic and sequential unity. Applebee's grafting of narrative structure and development on to a concept development model was an important theoretical move in its time, as it placed narrative centrally in terms not only of cognitive and cultural development of individuals and societies but provided a foundation for educational practice and progression. For example, the third stage of narrative development would be instanced by episodic, 'primitive' narratives; the fourth stage by dream-like sequences or by the archetypal additive construction of stories that are connected by 'and' conjunctions but that have no direction or point (they could go on endlessly adding elements to themselves, but without ever reaching significance). At the fifth and sixth stages, the narratives would be, respectively, suggestive (but somehow incomplete) and suggestive and complete.

In turn, I have built on the work of Vygotsky and Applebee to graft a model of argumentational development onto the conceptual and narrative patterns. Arguments can begin with unconnected heaps of associations. They attain the beginnings of unity when a central unifying idea is generated to hold them together. Such a cluster achieves thematic unity when the central unifying idea is linked to its satellite 'points'; at the same time, an illogical chain might be made to link the various points together. These later two stages combine to form an 'empty formal argument' or 'pseudo-argument' wherein the thematic and logical unities are almost complete but lack the dynamism and completeness of the fully fledged argument. In this last stage, each point is linked to all the other points, not only through thematic coherence but through logical and sequential connection. One striking aspect of such a visual representation of the relations in concept, narrative and argumentative development is that, in my doctoral research (Andrews, 1992), I noticed that 11- to 13-year-olds, when they were planning to write arguments, went through exactly these same stages – and spontaneously, without direct input from a teacher.

The value of such a model is that it might help in the planning and design of arguments, building on what students already (subconsciously or intuitively) know about structuring discourse; it should not be seen, however, as a prescriptive model for composition, as many students might miss one or more of the stages – if indeed they commit any of them to paper – in the formation of arguments. Like Mitchell and Riddle's model, it might also be used to test the unity of arguments – though it has to be remembered that this model does not have the generic logical coherence of the first two models discussed in this section.

Perhaps the model with most immediate appeal – in that it reflects compositional processes for many of us – is that of Kaufer and Geisler (1991). This is a purely compositional model and does not claim to act as a model of argumentation. Nevertheless, it embodies much of what happens in the construction of academic written arguments. Kaufer and Geisler suggest that in creating the rhetorical space for a new line of argument, writers often position themselves in opposition to an existing assumption of argument (Figure 3.5). Such an oppositional point is used as a navigational device to determine the main path of the writer's argument.

While following this 'faulty path', it might seem that the writer is straying from his or her 'main path', but a way is found back to the main path, and we are clearer, as a result, of the nature and direction of that main path. Subsequent faulty paths tend to be less extreme, each coming closer to the main path and lending weight to the main direction that is being taken. By the end of the composition, the writer and reader are clear that a number of paths could have been taken, but a particular one *has* been taken. That particular one has direction (from A to B) and is strengthened by reference to a number of other points on the way. For example, a student wishes to argue that bilingualism is advantageous rather than disadvantageous. She might, however, begin an

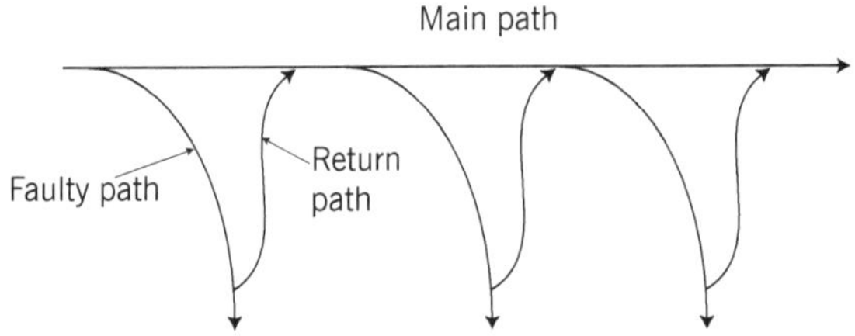

Figure 3.5 Kaufer and Geisler's main path/faulty path model (1991)

essay by summarizing or making reference to research (largely undertaken in the 1960s) that suggested bilingualism was disadvantageous to the learner. The initial faulty path provides a counterpoint to the main thrust of the argument. The 'return path' is often signalled by pivotal words and phrases such as 'however', 'despite the fact that…', 'nevertheless', 'in contrast to these views', and so on.

For yet another model of argumentation – not discussed fully here but in Driver, Newton, and Osborne (2000) and as one particularly relevant to the interaction among reasoning, theory, and argument in the development of scientific ideas - see Giere (1991). This appears to be a derivative of Toulmin's model in that the elements are distilled to data (grounds, evidence), claims (hypotheses), and warrants. The strength of this model is that it provides an eminently pedagogic frame for understanding the operation of argument in carrying out science. Like Riddle and Mitchell's 'since-then-because' model, it is dynamic and descriptive of the learning process in a way that Toulmin's seems not to be (and was not intended to be). However, like Toulmin, there is the potential for the original claim or hypothesis – for example, 'light travels in straight lines' – to be transformed into common knowledge through the process of scientific testing and retesting and thus to provide part of the new foundation or backing for the play of new claims and grounds, as linked by warrants.

Visual Argumentation

The models previously discussed are inherently *verbal* in their conception of argument and argumentation, even though the genre of the 'model' invites diagrammatic representation to simplify and communicate its key elements and the relationship between them (see Mitchell and Riddle, 2000, for a discussion of the function of models *per se*). To get verbal notions of argumentation into perspective, it is necessary to discuss briefly another form of argumentation: visual argumentation. This is the first of three takes in the book on the topic: we return to it in Chapter 6 with regard to multimodality and again in the last chapter on the future of argumentation.

It could be said that a single image can *persuade* – think of advertisements in magazines, on billboards – but it would be harder to convince someone that such an image can argue. For argument to be implicitly present, there must either be some tension within the image (for example, a contrast between poverty and affluence) or there must be at least two images juxtaposed so that tensions can be explored and a 'point' can be inferred. Such juxtaposition does not spell out its argument (indeed, it might be coincidental); rather it offers the opportunity for inference and inductive argument through comparison. It is as though we are presented with evidence but without the propositions; we are asked to provide these for ourselves.

If tension within a single image, or between two images, is the minimal form of visual argumentation, a sequence of images can develop and secure the argument further. A photo-essay is an example of such an argued visual sequence. The stage of development beyond the photo-essay is the sequence of images that make up a film: arguing in and through moving image as opposed to still images.

Tarnay (2002), in a paper on the conceptual basis of visual argumentation, discusses the indirect propositionality of images, asking 'whether we can still do argumentation without the requirement of propositionality?' (2002: 1001). Typically, verbal explication of a visual argument is seen as an act of hermeneutic reconstruction:

> Propositionality is not a property of the images, but of the meta-language in which the arguments associated with, or elicited by them are made explicit. More loosely put, it is 'instantiated' visually.
>
> (2002: 1002)

Tarnay goes on to identify three modes of visual argumentation: the purely textual mode, in which images are nothing but the visualization of verbal arguments; the mixed mode, in which visual and other elements are co-constituents in an argument (in, for example, political cartoons, wherein the verbal and visual combine to make a point and where the reader/viewer has to contribute his or her own knowledge of the contemporary political scene to complete the intended communication); and the third, or genuinely visual mode. Tarnay argues, 'We have a clear case which appears to be a kind of visual argumentation based especially on the persuasive (ethos) and emotional (pathos) elements' (2002: 1004), for example, in narrative and/or documentary film. However, Tarnay ends with a caveat. Films are meant to achieve their effects by means of juxtaposition and editing, so it is not surprising that this technique has been seen as the visual counterpart of verbal argumentation. However, he argues,

> we should be cautious in taking mise-en-scène, editing [and] disposition to be the counterpart of logos (speech) in visual art. For one reason, because we have seen that they are the very means by which continuity (suture) is realized in classical film. For another, if they are revealed as conveyors of thought, they are dependent on conceptual integration

> or blending. In other words, topology is always already tropology in visual art.
>
> (2002: 1005)

Tarnay's argument rests, it seems to me, on a premise that argument and argumentation are inextricably associated with – indeed, informed by – a rationalist, deductive view. Argument as the servant or vehicle of rationality assumes a Platonic commitment to the abstract, with dialectic and rhetoric seen as procedural and process-based dimensions of the drive toward consensus and action. From this point of view, the visual must be seen as subsidiary to the verbal, relegating the purely visual to having emotionally (viscerally) persuasive power but not argumentational capacity. In educational terms, at least, I would wish to counter this point of view with a claim that purely visual argument can operate inductively, not just as evidence for a verbally conceived set of propositions but as a set of propositions in its own right.

A Spectrum of Models

In summary, there are a number of ways of representing aspects of argument along the spectrum I suggested earlier. Toulmin's model and its adaptation in Riddle and Mitchell's version offer us both a means for testing the soundness of arguments and a mechanism for generating arguments. They take propositions as their building blocks or units of argument. These propositions are rooted in logical conceptions of argument and both use micro-propositions on which to build and/or project mezzo- and macro-structures. The development of narrative structures based on Vygotskian notions of concept development offers us another basis for the development of argumentational writing, this time focusing more on the processes of working toward a fully fledged argument in which its constituent parts gradually form to make a whole. Finally, a more purely rhetorical model is offered by Kaufer and Geisler, who provide a description of what happens in the course of writing essays. Mitchell has suggested a number of developments of this model, one of them refining it to depict the movement from 'oppositional' faulty paths at the beginning of an essay toward finer distinctions as the essay moves toward its conclusion and another incorporating the Riddle/Mitchell model as part of the movement and generation of arguments within an essay.

These models are more flexible than the formulaic structures derived from classical rhetoric – which are often reduced to a tripartite 'beginning, middle, end' banality in the teaching of essay writing: 'First say what you are going to say, then say it, then say what you've said'. They try to look beneath the surface of argument as manifested in verbal form to the deeper structures that underpin the movement of ideas in an essay (or other form of argumentational writing). Not all of these models have been tried and tested pedagogically to the same degree. What would be useful at this point are descriptions, in the anthropological tradition, of arguments taking place in educational and ostensibly non-formal educational settings to see how much space is given to the various participants to engage in argument (see Prior, 2005, for an excellent critique of the 'models' approach from an anthropological viewpoint). We know from studies going back to *Language, The Learner and the School* (Barnes, Britton, & Rosen, 1969) that schools and colleges can be places wherein argument is stifled because of the dominance of teacher discourse; that some speech genres in education are more argument-friendly than others; and that essential elements in the encouragement of argument are an acceptance of the contingency of knowledge, a receptive classroom open to different interpretations and positions, and enough space for learners to hypothesize and test ideas. It is ironic that some educational institutions, even in their very layout and architecture, militate against the very higher-order thinking that they are supposed to encourage.

The Practical Dimension

Activity 3.1

Discuss the various models as set out in this chapter. Use them as a basis for a staff/faculty development session and/or discuss them with your students. Do you agree with the point of view expressed in this chapter that they all have advantages and can be arrayed in a sequence that makes sense in the process of composing argument in your discipline? Or do you have a preferred single model?

Activity 3.2

Take six picture postcards. Arrange them in different ways: a horizontal line of six; a set of five with one outsider; a pyramid; an inverted pyramid; two sets of three; three sets of two; and so on. What does each structural arrangement offer in terms of (a) generic approaches to written argument and (b) purely visual argumentation?

4
Discipline-Specific Skills in Argumentation

RICHARD ANDREWS, CAROLE TORGERSON
AND BENG-HUAT SEE

Most studies that have addressed the issue agree that discipline-specific argumentation is more useful and more apposite than generic approaches. Students, too – when given the choice between generic programs in rhetoric, composition, and/or argumentation on the one hand and discipline-specific discourse training on the other – prefer the latter. Accordingly, this chapter looks at a range of disciplines to determine how argumentation differs and at what can be done in these particular contexts to help students understand the rules of the game in becoming not only competent but excellent in their chosen field of study.

We draw in this chapter on a report (Andrews et al., 2006b) of a pilot study undertaken at universities in the United States and the United Kingdom in collaboration with Sally Mitchell, Kelly Peake, Paul Prior, and Rebecca Bilbro. This report looked at argumentational skills of first-year undergraduates in three disciplines: history, biology, and electrical engineering/electronics. First we summarize what we discovered in the course of the research; then we go on to reinterpret what the students said in response to a questionnaire and in focus groups and in interviews with lecturers. The pilot study was undertaken alongside a systematic review of the research literature on the teaching of argumentational skills in undergraduates (Torgerson, Andrews, Low, McGuinn, & Robinson, 2006).

1 Joint principal investigators for the project, which took place from 2004 to 2006, were Richard Andrews and Carole Torgerson. Co-applicants were Sally Mitchell and Paul Prior. The design of the questionnaire was undertaken by Beng Huat See in collaboration with Richard Andrews, Rebecca Bilbro, Sally Mitchell, Kelly Peake, Paul Prior, and Carole Torgerson. Beng Huat See undertook the initial analysis of the questionnaire data for all three disciplines at two universities in the United Kingdom, but the interpretation was the work of the team as a whole. The interview protocol was principally designed by Paul Prior, Sally Mitchell, Kelly Peake, Samantha Looker, and Rebecca Bilbro. Fieldwork for the particular university discussed in this chapter was undertaken by Beng Huat See. Beng Huat See administered interviews with staff in the biology and electronics departments and document collection in those departments; Carole Torgerson assisted with interviews with students and staff in biology; Richard Andrews undertook the interviews and document collection in history. For the interviews, transcription was undertaken by Beng Huat See for biology and electronics data and for student interviews in history; Richard Andrews transcribed the history staff interviews. The chapter also draws on interview data collected by Sally Mitchell, Kelly Peake, and David Russell and reported by Kelly Peake and Sally Mitchell in Andrews et al. (2006b).

A mixed-methods approach was used in the pilot study, which included a questionnaire survey of freshman students, focus groups with students in each discipline, interviews with lecturers and students, and document collection and analysis.

Pilot studies are merely preliminary studies whose principal function is to test methodology and methods and open up questions about the substance of the research. Their 'results' must be taken as tentative. Discussion of the pilot study project must therefore come with a caveat. The particular pilot study we undertook was, however, a large-scale one over a year, so we can come to some initial conclusions from it, of both a substantive and a methodological kind.

The results of the study suggested that first-year students believed argument to be important in their disciplines, though there was some confusion as to what the term meant and how it applied to particular disciplines. Students expressed the need for more explicit instruction *in* or discussion *of* disciplinary argumentation, so that the 'rules of the game' were made clear. Rather than learn a new set of skills quickly, they tended to draw on argumentation skills learnt in the previous stage of formal education. Most students, for example in biology and electrical engineering, were not sceptical in their academic reading and thus tended to accept what they read: they did not approach academic reading with a critical frame of mind. The study also suggested that differences among institutions, disciplines, and individual lecturers were significant when it came to argumentational practices and assumptions and that there was sometimes a mismatch between the way lecturers and students saw argument and its place in learning. Finally, whether argument was formally assessed or not appeared to be key to how highly it was valued by students.

We discuss each of the tentative results next, then go on later in this chapter to look at each of the disciplines in turn.

First-Year Students Believe Argument to be Important in Their Disciplines

One suggestion from the research was that first-year students in all three disciplines were aware of the importance of argument. Such 'belief' or 'awareness' varied from discipline to discipline, with historians being made more aware of its centrality to the discipline than biology students or electrical engineering students. The awareness was often reinforced by lecturers who would use the terms *argument* and (less so) *argumentation* in discussing the demands of oral engagement and/or written assignments. Typically of educational courses or stages, there was an assumption that students would learn to argue well by the end of the program; those who could do so at the start were at an advantage.

The problem associated with such belief or growing awareness is that it can remain nebulous. Such cloudy conceptions of the phenomenon, gathered under the term *argument*, can lead to a vague notion of what it means to argue well in a discussion or essay. Furthermore, such vagueness, if it goes unchecked and remains implicit, can lead to anxiety on the part of students who are not sure what sort of contribution they are supposed to make to academic exchange.

Those students for whom argumentation remains a too-distant goal would not be able to process feedback from lecturers who were urging them to be more argumentational, more critical. Such students remain at descriptive or expositional levels in their written work or at a weak consensual level in their oral discussions. Interestingly, some students in biology suggested that argumentation was too high a goal for their undergraduate studies and that they would not be expected to argue until they were much further along in the discipline. In other words, they saw argument as important but beyond what they were capable of, given their limited knowledge of the content of the discipline. Electrical engineering and history students were more willing to engage in argument, as they were aware it was either central to their discipline (history) or was an important element in presentations when they were defending or justifying their designs (electrical engineering).

Students Feel the Need for More Explicit Instruction

In all three disciplines that we studied, students felt the need for more explicit instruction or discussion about what was expected of them in terms of argumentation and what such argumentation would look like. The conclusion is that too much of the discourses of disciplines is left implicit and unexplained. From a lecturer's point of view, assumptions are often made that either students will know what the discourses of the discipline are or that they will intuit the ways to communicate. There is certainly a hidden criterion for success in a subject or discipline: that students will, by the end of the course, demonstrate such communicative competence that they will seem like 'biologists', 'historians'. or 'electrical engineers'. A degree in any one of these subjects, then, is like a passport to the territory of that subject.

From a student's point of view, the revealing of the rules of the game can come (if at all) in a number of forms: via guidance on how essays should be composed and submitted; via exemplary good essays or bad examples of how not to write an essay; via feedback from the lecturer on work submitted early in the program; and/or via discussion with the lecturer or tutor about the 'rules'. Of these possibilities, the second and fourth approaches are likely to be most productive. The first option – guidance – is in the abstract and yet often takes the form of hints or requirements as to how an essay should be composed. Of the examples we have seen, most tend to deal with surface features of composition in particular disciplines. Very few grapple with the conceptual, structural, and evidential (what counts as evidence) issues that are at the heart of argumentation; they tend to address matters of format, style, and accuracy. The fourth approach – feedback – is hugely variable. Sometimes it comes after the event, when it is least useful; sometimes it is minimal and takes the form of a grade or score that (hopefully) is based on grade descriptors that can be referred to. It is most useful when it is extensive, delivered during the process of composition (e.g., in response to a draft), and in oral form so that the student can ask questions of the lecturer to clarify any points that seem unclear. Further discussion of feedback occurs in Chapter 10.

The two most useful approaches, then, are examples and discussion with the tutor. This book includes a number of examples from a range of disciplines, analyzed in various ways with regard to argumentation. The act of discussion with a tutor or lecturer about work submitted or work about to be submitted is an underplayed element in helping students to argue well. Students often declare that they wished they had more one-to-one interaction with their tutors, especially where the massification of higher education has meant that they get little such contact. One-to-one tutorials are a chance to discuss ideas and approaches to topics and to exchange ideas on the structure and arrangement of these ideas in spoken, written, or other forms. Because such encounters can be student-led, there is a chance for students to ask about particular aspects of the process of learning in higher education and to receive direct feedback. There is also an opportunity for students to link the personal with the demands of the discipline, thus making the learning process more significant.

Students Tend to Draw on Argumentation Skills Learned in the Previous Stage of Formal Education

In any stage of education, consolidation and advancement take place. Indeed, some consolidation is necessary for advancement to happen. In the case of submitting assignments in higher education – especially if there is little in the way of advice or guidance on the content, structure and format of what is expected – students are likely to fall back upon genres and practices that they know from the previous stage of education and in which, in all probability, they were successful.

In the study of literature, for example, 16- to 18-year-olds in the United Kingdom tend to get used to writing 'essays'. Such essays in the field of literature are, at best, finely textured appreciations of works of literature. They are not necessarily noted for their grasp of literary theory nor for their critical purchase on literature. Mitchell (1994b) gives a fascinating account of the transition from the study of English literature at school level (called 'sixth form' in England) to university level, in which students struggle to find the degree of critical stance that is expected in a literature course at their chosen university. They draw on their experience of the sixth-form literature essay. Such consolidation often occurs when a student is being challenged on other fronts: theoretically, by a new text or author and/or by a new approach.

There is danger in such consolidation, however. It can lead to conservative thinking or to a misunderstanding between the expectations of the lecturer and the intentions of the student. Essentially, at least in the field of literature study, the difference between appreciation, which tends to tease out the nuances of the text within accepted boundaries on the one hand, and critical argumentation, which tends to challenge the text with theories and/or by altering the frameworks via which it is read on the other, is significant. If that distinction is not understood by students and lecturers, misunderstanding and disappointment can ensue.

Most Students are not Sceptical in their Academic Reading

The report of the pilot study showed that most students are insufficiently sceptical in their reading, and such critical awareness is closely allied to argumentational understanding and competence. From the questionnaire that was administered, with a sample of 236, the following results were generated:

> The questionnaire showed that first year undergraduates in our sample generally do not appear to display scepticism in academic reading (according to self-report). Many seem to accept the findings of articles or reports that are peer reviewed (79%) or recently published (63%). The majority of students (85%) are willing to accept a piece of research as good if it is substantiated by statistical or numerical data. However, more than three-quarters of the students (77%) are aware that the conclusions need not be true even if the argument is convincing.
>
> (Andrews et al., 2006b, p. 19)

Those are interesting, albeit provisional findings. The high proportion of students accepting the findings of articles or reports that are *peer-reviewed* suggests a deference to authority: the assumption here is that if other experts in the field have accepted results, those results must be true. Such an assumption is unsurprising: students are candidates for initiation in their respective fields. However, it is somewhat surprising to note that 63 per cent of the sample would accept findings if recently published, and 85 per cent would accept them if substantiated by statistical or numerical data. In these latter cases, there are uncritical, almost naïve assumptions that recent, numerically supported research must be true. Behind these assumptions is perhaps a belief that recent research (especially in science wherein there is more of an accretion of knowledge than in the humanities or arts) is more telling and, on the part of students who do not have high numerate confidence, that numbers are more reliable than words when it comes to evidence.

There was differentiation between disciplines with regard to criticality. History students in the sample appeared to be the more critically aware, perhaps because argumentation is seen as central to the study of history and because the method of drilling down from tertiary (textbook) through secondary (academic synthesized research) to primary sources and evidence is an accepted part of undergraduate practice in history.

In a different study carried out at the University of Northern Illinois with 79 native, English-speaking, introductory-level psychology students, Larson et al. (2004) found that students were 'not proficient comprehenders of natural, written arguments. They identified only about one-third of the main claims and reasons, they selected reasons that could not possibly support their stated claim, and they often identified a stated counter-claim as the main claim' (p. 220). The results revealed that students were aided by a brief tutorial that explained the process of argument comprehension 'as long as they were not given the task of reading to rebut' (ibid.). Furthermore, students did not always know that an argument can begin with a counter-argument.

The results from the Larson et al. study suggest that these particular students were not equipped with the radar to read arguments critically. Not only were they incapable of distinguishing a main claim from a counter-claim (and thus could not be aware of the whole general direction of an argument); they also seemed unable to separate reasons from claims and evidence from either of these elements. It is interesting that a brief tutorial could help them begin to make sense of arguments and read them with understanding (not necessarily *critical* understanding) but that such tutorials were effective only if the students were not asked to identify a rebuttal. In short, these students seemed unable to read against the grain nor to provide any kind of critical perspective on the arguments they were reading.

Why do students from these two separate studies find critical, sceptical reading so difficult? There are a number of possible explanations. First, they pursue their studies in deference to the texts (and teachers) they encounter, learning passively rather than actively. Second, their reading is driven by a need to make sense of it, not to criticize it. The stages of making sense ('comprehending') require sufficient energy to disable their critical faculties. Third, it is possible that many students do not put sufficient effort into making *critical* sense of their reading; that is, comparing it to other accounts, weighing up claims and propositions from different articles against each other; testing the relationship between claims and evidence; and reading articles carefully to make sure the results are valid and reliable and that the conclusions drawn from them by the writers are sustainable.

Differences Among Institutions, Disciplines and Individual Lecturers are Highly Significant

It cannot be said that all institutions, disciplines, and individual lecturers are the same when it comes to the demands they make on students and the ways in which they mediate argumentation for their students.

At the institutional level, argumentation may be more prized, more a part of the fabric of intellectual inquiry at some universities than at others. At universities where there is an umbrella term – exposition – that covers research papers, position papers, essays, and other academic genres, it is more likely for there to be some conflation between exposition and argument. Such conflation can dull the edge of argument. In such a situation, students may not be aware that the synthesis and re-presentation of other people's thoughts and ideas is valued less highly than the development of an original position through logical, quasi-logical thinking and the provision of evidence. There is a particular problem in this regard with the reflective journal. There is no reason that journal entries could not be as critical, argumentational, and richly referenced as any other academic genre. Indeed, when they are well written, the marrying of the personal and the academic is impressive. However, the personal and reflective nature of the journal tends toward a more informal, less intellectually demanding style, which, in turn, makes for descriptive and expositional writing where the degree of reflection can be slight.

At a disciplinary level, differences are explored at length in this book. In general, it can be said that the differences in argumentational approach between the disciplines is a result of epistemological variation. What constitutes knowledge and how that knowledge is framed in the various disciplines is highly significant. If we translate the discussion to Toulminian terms, the *warrants* that enable us to connect claims (propositions) and grounds (evidence) vary from discipline to discipline. Furthermore, the *backing* can vary too, so that values and social and political framing can determine the context within which the argument takes place. What is also interesting is that, as students move through the educational system from high/secondary school to university, subjects become disciplines. Though that process is delayed in the United States and Scotland, for example, by the broader choice of topics in the first two years of a university education, by the time the major is selected, the disciplinary discourses are determining the kinds of argument that are accepted. In the English system, the focus on the discipline (and therefore a sharper sense of what counts as argument) happens earlier.

There is also no legislating for the variation between individual lecturers. Some will make the ground rules explicit from the start; others will not even be aware that there are ground rules. Some lecturers will be open to discussion of work in progress and talk with their students about the processes of learning, providing help with drafts, and deconstructing the assessment process. Others will wish to keep the processes of learning and assessment something of a mystery. It has to be said that the latter position is increasingly anachronous when students are made aware of the terms of their study and also feel they have rights to explicit criteria for success. They will also hope to have lecturers who are open to the processes that both lecturer and student are engaged in and are willing to discuss and negotiate those terms. It is particularly on the matter of drafts that lecturers tend to disagree. Some think that reading of and commentary on a draft is the best time to intervene in a student's developing work; others feel that no time should be spent on a student's draft and that the only time to 'intervene' is after the work has been submitted, without help, by the student. To make the position more equitable, some academic departments have drawn up policies on when a lecturer will look at a student's draft, on how many occasions (usually one), and with what degree of attention.

There is a Mismatch between the Way Lecturers and Students see Argument

If there is a mismatch between the way lecturers and students see argument, what is its exact nature? Lecturers and students both have their focus on the content of what they want to say/expect to see and on the way it is said. In disciplines wherein the epistemological base is assumed to be more fact-oriented, there might be less emphasis from lecturers on the way the knowledge is conveyed. However, in disciplines wherein the expression of knowledge is inextricably related to its formulation, as in the humanities and social sciences, the way ideas are expressed is crucial. It therefore follows that humanities, arts, and social sciences lecturers (though there is great variation between these clusters of disciplines) set a high store by the structure, style, and expression of the student's writing. Whether these lecturers are or are not aware of the argumentational dimension, there will be, at the very least, subliminal attention devoted to the way argument manifests itself in students' work.

The more subconscious the attention is, the less likely are students to be able to work out what is in the lecturer's mind. It is common to hear students talking about lecturers' teaching styles and the different expectations that such lecturers have. The less communication there is between lecturers and students, the higher the chance that misunderstanding will occur as to what is expected from each party. Such misunderstanding can be compounded if all the feedback that the student gets is in the form of an unexplained grade. Furthermore, if the norm for that work is an 'A' and there is little feedback, the possibilities for real intellectual improvement are slim; students are unlikely to want to question such a grade too deeply.

Finally, another possible source of misunderstanding is that students tend to see argument in its vernacular forms – personal disputes, rows, quarrels, fights – rather than in the more academic sense of a series of propositions underpinned by evidence. To use the diction of argument and argumentation is to use a technical vocabulary that needs to be explained, so that misunderstanding can be kept to a minimum.

If Argument is Formally Assessed, it is More Highly Valued by Students

Biology students in one of the universities in the pilot study (Andrews et al., 2006b) suggested that they valued argument more highly in their discipline when it was part of the assessment for their learning. If they were required to argue by the course, they would. The implication is that, for most of the time, they were *not* required to argue. The formal assessment of argument and argumentation in disciplines in higher education varies; it is more likely to take place in course work or portfolio work, largely because there is time to piece together something approaching an argument. However, it is also evident in formal examinations when students are asked to argue under pressure. There are other occasions in higher education, too, when argumentation occurs in formal assessment situations. Perhaps the most obvious and formal examples are defences or *viva voce* examinations, in which a candidate is asked to defend his or her dissertation or thesis. These occasions require high concentration and the answering of questions that are posed by examiners or in private or public forums. How to answer such questions, some of which might be extremely challenging, is part of the art of arguing orally in academic contexts; the art draws on classical and contemporary rhetoric, requiring both assertive defence and the acceptance that some of the points being made might, in fact, be justified.

Let us now turn to the three disciplines in more detail.

Argument in Three Disciplines: History, Biology, Electronics

In the pilot study, we looked in depth at three disciplines: history, biology, and electronics (or electronic engineering). The reasons for choosing these disciplines were that some work had already been undertaken in the United Kingdom on these very subjects (Entwistle, Nisbet, & Bromage, 2004; Hounsell & McCune, 2004); they were disciplines that the three universities (two in the United Kingdom, one in the United States) involved had in common, and they represented a range from a pure science through an applied science and technology subject to a humanities discipline.

We will not repeat the findings of the project here; the full report is available online. We *will* attempt a critical summary of our work, linking the work in the three disciplines to the theme of the present book. First, there appears a brief summary of what the data and analysis in the two UK institutions showed about the three disciplines (see Andrews et al., 2006b for a fuller account), followed by a more in-depth look at lecturers' views in each case from data collected at the northernmost of the UK institutions. The pool of data from which we are drawing, then, in the rest of the chapter is smaller than for the original research project as a whole.

History

Historians – at least lecturers and those students who read the rules of the game earlier enough to make a difference to their own studies – see argumentation as central to the discipline. One lecturer said, 'It *is* the discipline'. What they appear to mean by this is that the processes of sifting evidence; of distinguishing between the affordances of tertiary, secondary, and primary evidence; of putting together logical and quasi-logical narratives to explain particular aspects of history; of weighing competing theories of what happened and why it happened; and reading sceptically – all these contribute to the sense that studying history is intimately connected to practising argumentation. It is no coincidence that the more articulate and voluble historians are also engaged in public life, some as politicians. They are used to marshalling evidence in the service of a particular point of view.

History students at the university in question were used to hearing arguments in lectures and engaging in them in seminars. They read arguments in secondary source material, usually in the form of academic books on the subject. They engaged in oral argumentation in seminars and group tutorials and in writing extended papers in which argumentation had a high profile. Individual oral presentations were particularly conducive to argument, because they required students to put together a case, present it briefly (15 to 20 minutes), and then defend it against the challenges of other students and the lecturer. Such oral preparation did not always translate into success in written arguments. Indeed, one lecturer said that he noticed that those who were good at oral argumentation were not necessarily good at written argumentation, and vice versa. It is probably the case that the dialogic nature of oral argumentation is difficult to translate into the more monologic form of the written essay; there may be other reasons too, like a predilection for oral rather written expression.

Biology

In biology, the view of some lecturers is that students cannot know enough at undergraduate level to argue a position. The work of the undergraduate years is to build up knowledge of the field. The provision of evidence is more a matter of testing given concepts via the classic 'scientific method' rather than testing new ideas. So biology students are more concerned with fair tests, confirming existing truths, undertaking and getting used to empirical testing, building up content knowledge, and applying existing theory and concepts to practical situations. The practice of academic 'argument' is a distant prospect for most biology undergraduates; they still tend to see argument in terms of everyday disputes rather than academic development, so some of them are not sure they want to stray too far into the territory of argument. For biology majors, or those for whom biology is a main subject, the confidence that comes from feeling that this is *your* discipline (especially when combined with chemistry, say, in a biochemistry course) means that argumentation can begin to function. This increasing confidence is an interesting phenomenon, suggesting that the varying competence in two disciplines brings about a leap forward in argumentational confidence in the major of those two subjects.

Where argumentation does appear in biology, it is in the latter stages of the undergraduate years and takes the forms of essay writing or small group tutorials. It also varies according to the preferences of the particular lecturer; some are more open to debate about aspects of biology, wishing to relate the discipline to ethical, political, and other real-world issues. As suggested earlier in this chapter, students have to gauge the institutional, disciplinary, and *personal* predilections of their lecturers for argument.

Where biology programs have compulsory modules or courses in scientific and transferable skills or their equivalent, there is scope for exploring the demands of argument in the discipline. Furthermore, the discourses of science at undergraduate level are made explicit and are open to experimentation and discussion. Much will depend on whether students come to university with a wide range of discourse skills or whether they are straight-down-the-line scientists and/or mathematicians. Students mentioned that a background in history and biology trained them in essay writing, so they felt at ease with the construction of arguments in biology. The interesting distinction in this discipline is that lecturers tend to see the real intellectual business of the discipline – categorization, concept-forming, hypothesis-testing – as unconnected to the means of expression in argumentation. Where the two come together, for example, in debate and in the possible overturning of a hypothesis, there is a major shift in the discipline; it happens rarely, and undergraduates are unlikely to make such major shifts. Argument is, therefore, subjugated at undergraduate level to hypothesis testing and the rather looser exploration of the application of biological knowledge in society. Part of this situation stems from the fact that, although verbal language plays a major part in the formulation of biological thinking and expression, biologists tend not to see the part that language plays. Rather, their focus is on the concepts, procedures, and practices that make up the subject.

Electronics/Electrical Engineering

The core practices of electronics seem, on the surface, to have little to do with argumentation. Undergraduate students and lecturers were, however, very open to the part that argumentation played in their discipline, seeing it as largely to do with the communication of their designs and proposed solutions to problems posed by the field. They tend, therefore, not to see the business of the discipline – designing, problem-solving, analyzing circuits, writing programs, designing filter networks, theorizing, testing, and implementation – as having much to do with argument. Like biologists, there is much to learn about the content of the discipline; as an applied science/technology, the field is informed by scientific and mathematical knowledge that is taken as given. It is not problematized, on the whole, but seen as a foundation for work in the field of electronics.

Also as in biology, the scope for argument increases when the discipline is subjected to interface with real world problems, such as how to save energy, the impact of electronics on the environment, and the idea of 'best designs'. It is the third and last year of the undergraduate course in the United Kingdom, for example, wherein argument comes into play. By this point, electronics students know a sufficient amount about the field. They are asked to undertake a project in which they must justify their designs, persuade an audience of fellow students and lecturers that they have made reasonable choices in the process of design, and test their product and gauge its usefulness in the world. They also have to write up a report on the project. The process of argumentation, then, prepares the students for the professional dimension of their work in electronics; it is intimately connected to communication and persuasion.

When students are asked to weigh up a number of options and decide on one route over another, argument comes into play. They are then forced to make critical choices, and must justify those moves.

Let us look more closely at lecturers' views on argumentation in the three disciplines from just one of the universities.

History

Two in-depth interviews took place with history lecturers. These interviews were presented in summary in the final report of the project but not discussed in depth. Here the interviews are discussed to reflect upon the way two (pseudo-anonymized) lecturers saw the development of and importance of argument in their discipline.

Margaret taught mainly on the history of race, slavery (Caribbean, American slavery), women, and the post-emancipation period. These topics relate closely to her research. The teaching was based on 15 student seminars and some lectures to 200 students. She had been teaching in higher education since 2000 and since 1997 at the university level as a teaching assistant, plus to American students at a summer school in Maastricht. It is interesting to note at the outset that the topics she taught are rich with contention and ideology. They are topics that had been neglected in some earlier versions of history and had fought their way into the mainstream history curriculum; but they still carried with them the freight of opposition and resistance. Their very positioning as topics within a grand narrative of post-Enlightenment history made them contentious and of particular interest to contemporary students. In other words, there was argument at stake even in their place in the curriculum.

The term *argument* was certainly used in Margaret's field. By argument, she meant the main thesis: either confirming or disproving it with evidence. What is interesting here is that the conflation of the meaning of 'thesis' – both as an informing idea and as a tangible text-type/genre in academic communities – is revealed. Margaret means 'thesis as argument', thus preferring the notion of the thesis-as-an-idea corresponding to the argument. In this sense, the thesis *is* the argument and vice versa (as in the question 'What is your thesis here?' which could not be asked of a tangible text-type/academic genre). It is clear, however, that confusion could arise in students' minds as to what 'thesis' means, and also, as a result, what 'argument' means, too.

She saw a clear distinction, for instance, between an argument and a discussion: the argument *is* the thesis. The role of argument was 'to make the field go forward; to revisit particular arguments; to polish them up or reject them; and to progress in our interpretations'. It has a high priority in history.

Margaret saw evidence being selected and weighed according to the topic. With an economic or political issue, she looked primarily at numerical or statistical data; for social and other aspects of history, qualitative evidence became more important. She looked for good summaries by students to get to the heart of an argument. Indeed, the function of summary or précis writing was important in her teaching, as it required students to focus on the main points in a historical narrative or nexus of ideas and evidence. By distilling the main points, the students underwent a histiographic process of prioritization, selection, and representation. One of the weaknesses of students, however, was that 'they can't structure things in order of importance'. They were weak in horizontal (logical) connections and in vertical (drilling down, hierarchical) connections.

Margaret saw terms related to argument and argumentation as being assertion, claim, and thesis and, for evidence, accounts and sources. If we refer to Toulminian terms, she saw an argument as being equivalent to a proposition or claim rather than covering the whole model of claim, grounds, backing, and warrant. It is interesting that in history, understanding the nature of the grounds to support a claim (or proposition/thesis) are an essential part of learning to be a historian. These take the form of documentary and other kinds of primary evidence and sources. Perhaps it is only in the science subjects and law that there is a similarly high degree of focus on the nature and function of the evidence.

For history students, Margaret believed it was crucial to learn to argue. First-years, she thought – at least in her university – were not doing too badly. The students had the confidence to speak. Third- (or final)-year students drew more heavily on the scholars they had read, but some still did not get the main thesis of an argument. They had wider reading but did not always solve the structural problems in an argument. In her view, the ability to argue was central to a 'good' degree – which, in UK terms, means a 'first' or '2.1' on a five-point scale of 1/2.1/2.2/3/Pass. She noticed a difference between schools: some prepared students well in these regards; others did not. This point in particular confirmed the generally held perception that a student's cognitive and discourse training in one phase of education is taken forward to inform the kinds of thinking they do in the next phase(s).

History students engaged in oral argument with the lecturer and with one another. They were used to counter-argument. Quite often those who were good oral arguers could not get to the point on paper, however. This lack of transfer between oral and written argumentation was a concern. Both history lecturers who were interviewed commented on the fact that the transfer was not clear-cut and that, indeed, those who were good at oral argument were often not so good at written argument, and vice versa. However, one activity that helped bridge the gap between oral and written argument was 'forced debate': the students could not choose sides but were asked to argue according to a brief, and come up with three arguments to support a position. This appears to be a case of a formal speech genre being closer to the written forms than the less formal speech genres, wherein the gap was often insurmountable for students.

It is interesting to compare the views and practices of one lecturer with another in the same department. David is a modern historian who has taught in higher education since 2003. His teaching included modules on the 1960s; on poverty and charity (in collaboration with colleagues) and on issues in historical thought – the 'least popular but most important' module. In 2005–06, he taught a period topic to first-years, primarily through secondary source material. He had not taught outside the United Kingdom but had supervised as a postgraduate at Cambridge and at a summer school there.

According to David, the term *argument* was very much taught in the field and especially when giving feedback to students on their essays. For him, historical argument was based on an appeal to evidence about the interpretation of events in the past. It included criticism of primary and secondary sources. At first-year level, he suggested that 'we would only expect students to engage with secondary sources'; students were taught by 'drilling down' from tertiary to primary sources. 'I see what we do [in the first year] as questioning summaries, critiquing the bases of evidence, what are the limitations of the evidence, i.e. a critical reading of secondary works'. There is an interesting difference here between his views and that of Margaret's. Whereas she sees summaries as a means by which students distil what they know about a historical topic and also at the same time give a particular slant to it (the difference between summary and a more literal précis), David is asking students to critique any summaries they find appearing in the secondary literature. The two approaches are related: the first is concerned with writing summaries and the second with reading them.

By the third year, the students should understand how historians construct their arguments from primary and secondary sources, be able to critique these arguments, and make their own historical arguments. This ability is developed through the special topic, which is traditionally seen as the pinnacle of an undergraduate history degree in the United Kingdom and which usually takes the form of a longer essay or dissertation in the final year.

In discussing the different terms around the concept 'argument', David tended to talk about 'making a case' and making an analogy with a court of law. Students had to make a persuasive case. The best answers, he thought, admitted their own limitations. That approach seemed to clarify the requirement for students. David saw the role of argument as central to history: 'it's the discipline'. Students often saw history as narrative; but that is problematized for them at an early stage in the degree. There is dispute about 'what happened' in the past. According to David, historians need to drill down 'at the points of dispute'. The analogy with Greek *topoi* was made. David admits a tendency to get down to the epistemological level; he has to stop himself 'going too far down that well', to stop students from losing confidence.

There is much to unpack in the views expressed here. First, seeing the study of history as making cases, as in a court of law, brings the formal side of the oral genres of academic study closer to the written genres. It is not so much discussion in seminars or in the more informal discussion between students outside the seminar room that helps them shape their written offerings (though it must be admitted that these less formal opportunities are when the function of exploratory talk is to find one's own way through material). Second, being aware of the limitations of a particular viewpoint helps justify the taking of that viewpoint and inferring that there are other viewpoints that could be taken. Third, and perhaps most important in terms of the didactics of history as a discipline, the compressed statement 'it's the discipline' suggests that doing history is about thinking and operating historically and argumentatively rather than covering ('historical') periods in time. In other words, the banner title 'history' for the subject or discipline studied at university is really a cover for what actually happens, which is historiography. To put it another way (and more crudely), it is the process, not the content of history, that is the focus of attention.

To continue the analysis of the views expressed: it is clear that David saw the study of history as problematizing accounts of the past, especially those that cast history in simple and/or grand narratives. There is an interesting issue at stake here. The problematizing of issues is an activity that is typical of academia. Whereas other fields of activity, such as business or sport or the arts (wherein, even in the latter case, the handling of problematic issues tends to be distilled and presented in a form that simplifies, to an extent, in order to communicate) tend to simplify, academia tends to problematize. This means an 'unpacking' of variables and complexities, an abstraction from the everyday course of action, and the search for more general patterns of explanation. Such problematizing is not for its own sake; its function is to understand a phenomenon or situation by unravelling the threads of complexity. Those students who go on to be academics – by taking postgraduate degrees and even research degrees – enjoy the act of problematization. Those who prefer the world of action tend to move on, seeing their degree as a passport to influence in the world. It is as if there is a split, as was characterized in the Renaissance, between the *vita contempliva* and the *vita activa*, except that contemplation does not always lead to problematization. The problematizing spirit of academia arises from the use of the intellect to understand and ultimately solve problems; it is the product of a rational frame of mind and one in which argumentation flourishes. In essence, as far as history is concerned, argumentation provides the means whereby different accounts of what appear to be the same phenomena can be generated; these accounts are then subjected to comparison and 'argued out' until the best explanation for the phenomena or situation is reached.

The next point made in David's account of teaching history to undergraduates is that to open up the possibilities for argumentation, students should 'drill down at the points of dispute' in the discipline. In this respect, he made an analogy with ancient Greek *topoi*, or the 'places of argument'. Interestingly, in the light of the discussion of problematizing, the philosophy journal *Topoi* has the following description of its focus:

> *Topoi*'s main assumption is that philosophy is a lively, provocative, delightful activity, which constantly challenges our received views, relentlessly questions our inherited habits, painstakingly elaborates on how things could be different, in other stories, in counterfactual situations, in alternative possible worlds. Whatever its ideology, whether with the intent of uncovering a truer structure of reality or of soothing our anxiety, of exposing myths or of following them through, the outcome of philosophical activity is always the destabilizing, unsettling generation of doubts, of objections, of criticisms.
>
> (*Topoi*, 2008)

My interpretation of *topoi* in this context is that these are the places within a discipline that are both the time-honoured places and topics of dispute but also that may be the contemporary ('topical') places of dispute. The first problem for the student, then, is identifying these *topoi* before he or she begins to drill down. He or she can be helped to identify them through the actual curriculum of the course and/or by the tutor who will lead discussion toward these difficult and unresolved places. To give an example from another discipline, the core (compulsory) module/course at the MA in English Education at the Institute of Education in London is expressly focused on contemporary issues in English education. That is to say, its 10 taught sessions each focus on an area of dispute and contention within the field: the literary canon, issues of language and identity, how to teach sentence structure, and so on. These *topoi*, in whichever discipline, are interesting and engaging precisely because they are contentious. There is no right answer emerging from them, and thus they present a nexus of difficulty and irresolution. At the same time, such complexity makes them ripe for discussion, for alternative theses, and for possible resolution.

Once the *topoi* are identified, the art is to 'drill down'. As far as history goes as a discipline, drilling down means starting at tertiary sources (textbooks) and moving through secondary sources (academic and other titles that comment on aspects of history) to primary sources, which are then used to interrogate the assumptions made by secondary and tertiary texts. Drilling down as far as the secondary sources can also create a critical dimension and space by which the tertiary sources can be questioned. In other disciplines, 'drilling down' can also be used a metaphor for intellectual investigation. In the study of literature, for example, the level of sources would be that of the literary texts themselves. In science, it might be the generation of new data (or new ways of interpreting data). In social science, the exploration of secondary data analysis can be complemented and questioned by the collection and analysis of new data.

David's commitment to drilling down comes with a caveat. He admits that, on occasions, he drills down too far and breaks into the epistemological foundation strata of the discipline itself, thus causing confusion for undergraduate students of history for whom this is a level too far: they have come to study history at university, and too much disturbance of the foundational principles on which history is based can unsettle them. Nevertheless, the activity of drilling down to the epistemological basis of disciplines (as in philosophy of science courses, for example, or theory of literature courses) can be an enlightening activity that perhaps should be undertaken at some point during the degree, so that students can be aware of the parameters of the discipline. All too often, though, such theorizing and epistemological mining is undertaken too early in an academic programme when the students are finding their feet. It might come at a better point during, or towards the end of their programme of study.

In the first week of the course, David asks students to find a review of a book in a journal; the following week they are asked to write a review. They prepare a bibliography. Then they are asked to write an essay, with guidance from the course handbook. In tutorials, they tend to talk about the practicalities of essay writing rather than the content. The first essay is not marked. After that, there is tutorial feedback. For the next essay, an essay plan or plans are requested. Then tutorial notes are written by the students. Content is meshed with study skills. It would also seem to be a good place to introduce students, not necessarily to the epistemological bases of the discipline they are studying but to the modi operandi. These discourses – and argumentation plays a central role in history and a significant role in many other disciplines – are essential if students are to make headway in the subject and to feel at home in the diction, genres, and particular characteristics of communication (i.e., the discourses) that are expected and are at play.

David comments, 'I regularly use debates' (e.g., line-up debates wherein there is a spectrum of positions), and 'I sometimes take questions and dissect them with them…I use role-play – not directly for argument – [but] to empathize with others' point of view'. David hopes that essay writing and tutorials are the most helpful for developing argumentational skills. Debates are also as important in shaping ideas but perhaps not acknowledged as such by students. In this sense, he is close to Margaret in seeing the formal speech genres as helping students to gain command of and confidence in the written genres of the discipline.

In response to questions about the strengths and weaknesses in first years' argument, David mentioned a lack of specificity. He noticed a tendency to generalized statements such as 'some historians say…'. At the other end of the general-particular spectrum, he pointed out a tendency for students to get over-specific. 'Another thing I find frustrating is paragraph use, which reflects an inability of students to structure their thoughts clearly'. The problem is largely at sub-textual level, linking ideas and evidence from sentence to sentence (not so much within the sentence). The use of the personal pronoun leads students to express an opinion rather than to argue, but David encourages some students to use 'I' where students can compare their own view to less personal positions. The word 'however' and other connectives like 'therefore' seem to be over-used by students, who fail to make the distinction between *sounding* like they are making an argument and actually making an argument.

This last distinction is one with which we will finish the present section. Courses in school tend to make sure all student to have the apparatus for argument by teaching them *aide-memoires* and lists of key connectives, like 'however', 'nevertheless', 'on the one hand/on the other hand', and so on. Though these are useful points of articulation for the construction of spoken and written arguments, they can be used as mere scaffolds without the deeper structure of thinking through the nature of an argument to be expressed. It might, at this point, be worth returning to the examples of two beginnings of essays used in the first chapter of the book to determine whether the essay that appeared to be the better one in terms of argumentation *really did have the substance behind it to justify that claim.*

Biology

Andrew and Ralph are biology lecturers. Andrew worked to the position of biology lecturer via a research assistant post in which he also worked as a laboratory technician. He gained his doctorate part-time while doing his work as a research assistant – an unusual route to a lectureship in the United Kingdom, where more commonly, the move would be from a full-time doctorate into a junior teaching post. His teaching focus was largely on microbiology, though he had responsibility in his department for teaching the Scientific and Transferable Skills module. This module, in which it might be expected to find material on argumentation in science, was taken by students in the first and second years of their undergraduate degree in biology. It largely consisted of 'study skills' in the broad sense, namely computer skills, how to handle data, project management, how to use the library, basic learning skills, how to use Word, Powerpoint, and Excel, and how to prepare for a professional life as a biologist. It is interesting to look further into this list, because what is evident is the lack of any focus on argumentation.

It is important to note that such a course runs alongside the academic, disciplinary focus of the subject, which starts from the first week the undergraduate arrives at the university. This pattern of parallel disciplinary and transferable skills courses seems a good model, given what was discussed earlier in the book (and is discussed in the following chapter) about the balance between discipline-based and generic argumentation. After some of the elements described in the previous paragraph, students are exposed to statistics and experimental design. They learn how to collect and analyze data. Then they move on to simple group projects that enable them to develop team working and management skills. As the year progresses, the transferable skills become less general and more specialized, so that, for example, students learn to use powerful data processing techniques; they learn how to identify DNA fragments and to grow cells in tissue culture. All these skills might be generally described as tools for doing biology.

When it comes to writing, they follow a course in scientific writing. The terms *argument* and *argumentation* are not used much. Rather, the emphasis is on the ability to synthesize existing research and practice to identify gaps in the field. Once a gap is identified, an experiment is designed and conducted to begin to attempt to fill the gap. Tutorials are used to encourage students to be critical. For example, students appraise scientific papers and are taught to look for weaknesses: they might find that there is no control group in an experiment or that the data are suspect or minimal or that they are used to make claims that are too grand. Such training is helpful in *reading* argumentation, rather than in writing or composing it. However, we have to remember that the arguments are formulaic in that they follow a predictable pattern: gap, hypothesis, experiment, data/results, conclusion. The experiments that are conducted tend to lead to reports rather than arguments, and there is a good deal of description in the reports because the emphasis is on new empirical data. Hypotheses are, on the whole, tightly defined. As with electrical engineers, there is more scope in final-year reports and dissertations (project reports) wherein the writing is often accompanied by a presentation in which justification for the progress of the research is made. With a particular audience in mind (fellow students, lecturers, external examiners), the rhetorical dimension of the exercise is foregrounded, and argumentation comes to the fore.

It is in the final year, then, that argumentation comes into its own in biology. Lecturers differ in their emphasis, and Ralph tends to draw out the potential for evaluation, judgment, and critical decision making (choosing between two courses of action, for example, requires a weighing up of the options) rather than repeating the mantra that 'there are lots of facts to learn in Biology before you can begin to argue in the discipline' view. He suggests:

> We probably don't do as much [argumentation] as we should. We are a bit weak in that. What we do is develop that type of thinking in the tutorial system and the 3rd year projects. We're looking at whether we ought to develop that…we have a sort of balancing act in Biology. If you think of a traditional arts subject, it's very subjective, it's developing a feeling for something – that's how I see it as a scientist – whereas in science, it's very much [a case of] here are the facts and we are trying to develop something between the two. You need the facts, but you've also got to be able to appraise the facts, evaluate the facts so that you can then go on and do further research.

It can be said, then, that biologists do argue but that they don't use the term much and they don't see themselves, on the whole, as using the discourses of argument that they assume take place in the arts, humanities, and social sciences. When they debate and discuss issues about biology's interface with the 'real world' – for example in matters of ethics, biotechnology, climate change, pollution, and the like – they are forced to take positions and then find themselves in a more argumentational context. However, this is the field of politics, issues, and opinions and somewhat alien to the core practices of biology as a science. Even though the sociology of science would claim that there is no science without ideology and social construct of some sort, it appears to be the case that biologists like to create an epistemological, rhetorical, and discoursal space in which they can focus on what they see as the core elements of their discipline: the gathering and analysis of data, the weighing up of such data against hypotheses and other claims, and the pushing forward of the field of biological science via the identification and filling of gaps in research. They protect this 'space' with mantras such as 'there are lots of facts to learn in Biology', but these are defences against distraction rather than actual requirements for progress in (and initiation into) the subject. It might equally be said of history or medicine or literature as disciplines that there are a lot of facts to be learnt. However, these fields have learned to live with selection and put the emphasis instead on the interpretation of facts within the discipline. It may be the case that the development of knowledge and understanding in undergraduate biology is accretive and that certain facts need to be known before further development in the field is possible; such might also be the case in mathematics or in learning a foreign language.

However, as in history, the addressing of a topic such as pollution can be used as a starting point for drilling down to the epistemological foundation of the subject. It tends to happen in tutorials rather than in lectures or seminars: a topic such as the sinking of the *Exxon Valdez* and the resultant oil spill in 1989 might be used to consider pollution and its effect on the ecological balance of the nearby coastline. As students discover from the Web and other sources that the evidence is unreliable (dates and timings differing, accounts of the amounts of oil spilled differ, views on the extent and seriousness of the event differ), they are encouraged to first accept that sources can be unreliable; second, to use relatively reliable search engines and databases of scientific papers to determine the 'science' behind the stories. In other words, the act of doing science is an act of trying to determine the accuracy of a phenomenon and its causes and implications. Whether such investigations are couched as essays and/or presentations and whether these assignments 'count' in the buildup of credit toward the award of a degree in the subject are matters for each biology course and each university to determine. If, as in some cases, such essays are seen as 'tutorial' essays only and do not count in the final assessment, it is clear that any such argumentation embodied within them is downgraded in the students' eyes.

Such downgrading may be countered by the emphasis on building good arguments in tutorials. Andrew felt that it was critical that biology students learn to argue, but in practice that argumentation – called 'critical evaluation' in the subject – takes place orally in the tutorials through discussion rather than in writing.

From the biology lecturer's point of view, there is a big difference between undergraduate learning and school learning:

> When students come from school, they are very much focussed on just regurgitating information…but we question whether they can understand that information and the application of that information. The other thing is the acquisition of information; they are very reliant

on the web when they arrive and we think it's the way schools are encouraging them to do that to get through exams.

It is interesting that the lecturers we interviewed hold this view. It is not untypical of lecturers to feel that the schools and colleges that prepare students for entry to university do so in a reductive way and that students bring an unreformed, uncritical mind to the start of a university course. Such a view is held not only by lecturers. In every phase of education, particularly at the transitions between primary/elementary and secondary/high school; then again between what is called in England the end of compulsory schooling at the study of advanced level; again between 'sixth form' (16 to 18 years old) and university; and yet again between undergraduate and postgraduate: at every stage, the lecturers and teachers of a particular stage criticize the previous stage for its literal, basic approaches to educating its students. What is behind this assumption? We will need to understand the problem to shed light on how argumentation is seen at the various stages and particularly at the undergraduate and postgraduate stages – the focus of this book.

It appears that teachers at each stage of education feel that the students enter that stage with a *tabula rasa*. Perhaps more accurately, the feeling is that although the students may know something, they need to be *re-educated* for the new phase. It is not so much that the new students know nothing; it is more that what they do know can be considered only basic and sometimes misguided. This kicking away of the traces of previous stages of education is psychologically interesting, because it suggests that to make any impression in the phase that is about to start, there must be a clean start. If a clean start is established, it is possible to see progress during the stage. In each stage, too, there is a predictable rise in expectation so that whereas a student might start a stage with a basic, literal, descriptive knowledge, he or she will end it with interpretive, critical, abstracted knowledge and know-how. Most curricula and syllabi are based on this premise.

Such articulation through the stages, and idealized movement within the stages, is game-like and might be seen by a sceptic as self-justification in the extreme. Do teachers and lecturers really have to justify their existence by downplaying the achievements of the previous phase? Are they drawing on some quasi-Piagetian notion that all students will move through these stages, then consolidate their knowledge at the end of each key stage before moving on to the next one? The process probably has more to do with curriculum design than with the progress of learning, particularly if we see learning as an individually determined and measured phenomenon and a group-based and publicly accountable activity. (The issue of transition from one phase to another in education, and what it means for argumentation, is treated in more depth in Chapter 7.)

Ralph, a lecturer for 32 years at the same institution, noticed a change in students' approaches to learning and argumentation. Whereas a generation ago he was teaching small groups and the emphasis of the department was very much on teaching, now he felt that the university's attention had turned to research, that teaching groups were larger, and that the university and students were complicit in a game that involved true/false answers and short answers, rather than extended debate and inquiry. For lecturers such as Ralph, whose *raison d'être* is the quality of teaching and learning, such a situation (including increased accountability) must be depressing. He felt that the 'amount of assessment in a degree in biology to do with constructing an argument' had declined and that, perhaps, students who chose to do biology at university were, in general, not always the most articulate kind. They would have, in his view, more content knowledge but less verbal confidence than students in other subjects.

In one particularly illuminating part of the interview with Ralph, he expressed where he thought the core of argumentation was in the undergraduate biology degree:

> The ultimate [test] of their ability to construct an argument is in the written report of their third [final] year project. They are given a project to conduct by themselves…It normally involves a laboratory investigation but it can involve fieldwork, or it can involve no gathering of data but just constructing an argument. That piece of work is a bit like a scientific paper where you ask the question and you answer it, and you debate whether you got the answer right or not…But if you look at most scientific papers, they are not really much about arguments. They are one-sided cases…Very often they will not engage in any material that opposes that view. It's a very strange thing that they like to pretend that they like to debate. They don't. They just want to be right.

So, on the one hand students are led to expect that the final project is the capstone of their three years' undergraduate study (and it may carry more weight in the final reckoning that any other individual paper or course). On the other hand, they are not provided with models in the scientific literature, as most scientific articles tend to argue one side of an argument without providing any counter-argument or self- (or outside) rebuttal. In other words, the actual argumentational substructure of scientific advance is largely hidden from students. Much seems to depend on the individual lecturer and his or her preference for taking students (or not) to the epistemological arguments of science. Some prefer not to drill down that deep; others have a personal dislike of 'arguing' – a largely verbal or multimodal and discoursal activity – that may be one of the very reasons they opted for science rather than the humanities, arts or social sciences.

Electronics/Electrical Engineering

Lecturers in the electronics department of the university where interviews took place took a similar view to those in biology: at undergraduate level, 'we teach the very fundamental stuff'. A distinction was made between undergraduate and postgraduate levels. In the latter, there was more room 'for argument, discussions, agreement, disagreement'. In the former, the complexity of the fundamentals of electronics had to be taught, and that very complexity required total attention on the part of lecturers and students. It was a body of knowledge, according to one of the lecturer interviews, that had not changed much for 100 years but which needed to be known by students if they were to make any progress in the discipline. There is an interesting point here with regard to argumentation: 'There just is not any room for it in the undergraduate course, because the demands of understanding the basics are too great'.

The metaphor of learning that underpins the conception of the discipline, and therefore curriculum and its pedagogy, is one of building blocks. Students are kept away from higher theory or contentious areas of the discipline at undergraduate level and are provided with the blocks one at a time. They do not know what sort of building they are constructing. This approach is interesting, because it does not provide much space for criticality. To be more critical, a student needs to weigh what is observed/given at one level against ideas, theories, and assumptions at another level. Such a disciplinary approach – also called 'bottom-up' – does not eschew theory, however. It simply approaches theory from a pragmatic perspective.

When argument is encouraged, the lecturer knows what the answer is before he/she engages the students. The task for the students is, therefore, to find their way to the right answer. In a worst-case scenario, this is a matter of 'guessing what is inside the lecturer's head'. It is no surprise, then, that lecturers find the students shy about answering questions. As in a school context, there is much to lose for the student if he or she provides a wrong step, even if ultimately it helps the class to travel in the right direction. According to this lecturer, the transferable skills programme in electronics at undergraduate level is very basic and not to do with argumentational development.

Another lecturer (Duncan) had a very different view, confirming the sense that different lecturers within the same discipline and same department can have very different positions in relation to argumentation. Again, as in biology, the space for argumentation opens up when the lecturer is interested in the interface between the discipline itself and its applications. In this case, Duncan is interested in environmental aspects of electrical engineering: for example, power efficiency, power saving, and life cycle analysis. More concretely, he is interested in the latest in tungsten light bulbs or low-energy/high-efficiency devices. An issue that is at the heart of engineering design, for instance, is whether to use low-energy/high-efficiency light bulbs: they may last eight times longer and use a fifth of the power of a conventional light bulb, but they take a great deal more energy and resource to make, and to recycle or destroy them might also take more power and energy than it would do so for a conventional product.

In electronics, transferable skills modules or courses do not include much on argumentation. They tend to concern themselves with reports, posters, project design, creativity, system design, and business plans. In other words, the course deals with the tools that students need to complete the course. These tools are seen by the discipline as moulds (genres in the sense of text types) into which the knowledge will be poured and shaped. The emphasis is on the end product and presentation rather than on the intellectual processes that will help students learn and produce high quality products.

Perhaps there are three occasions when the students' argumentational skills are brought to the fore. One is when they are required to present their design solutions to their peers and to invited industrialists who come in to judge a competition on the best designs to engineering problems. Although these presentations are short (10 to 15 minutes for each small team), the challenges are to make the complex process of electronics design simple enough for the audience; to persuade the audience that the design process was logical and coherent; to convert the knowledge that has been gained through the design process into communicable language(s); and to win the competition.

Another occasion when students can argue is the laboratory report. Here, discussion takes place as to why the circuit did or did not work. There is little scope for defence or for considering alternative solutions. The emphasis tends to be on low-level argumentation, with reasons provided.

The third occasion is, as in biology, the final year project. Duncan describes the project not in terms of argument as such, but as a document describing a project. It consists of '...the project, the idea, the background to it, and what other work is being done. This is how the project works, how it evolves, these are the results, the conclusions and further possible work'. There is a good deal of discussion in some projects. Duncan comments, 'I guess the students who provide very clear arguments are the students who do better, a lot better'.

The discussion of a structural/mechanical engineering project, in Chapter 10 of this book, gives a good account of what project reports in engineering are like and the extent to which they incorporate argument.

Conclusion

What can we say about the differences between disciplines in terms of argumentation? There are a number of lessons to be learned.

One of them is that the differences do matter. Although certain skills in argumentation and generic and transferable, students and lecturers tend to see the particular demands of their own discipline as paramount. They can get very bored, very quickly, with generic knowledge that is not applied to their particular field, especially if the knowledge is expressed in a mode that is not seen as primary in the field (e.g., verbal expression rather than spatial and/or visual and/or conceptual design).

Some disciplines see argumentation as central to their operation from the start; others see it as an aspiration toward which students move over the course of their studies. In the latter case, we have a situation wherein knowledge is seen as developing from the factual and descriptive, through the explanatory and expository, toward the argumentational, disputed and justified. Whatever the discipline and whatever the mode of learning that is preferred on the way to argumentational competence, it is generally accepted that argument does play a significant role in successful completion of undergraduate courses. To be successful means to be able to argue in that field: to be aware of possible alternative explanations; to be comfortable with the discourses of the subject; and to generate difference and movement in the field. Argumentation tends to be seen by disciplines with a scientific or applied scientific bent as inhering in the verbal mode. It is thus – to begin with at least – alien and distant. Command of its nature comes with time and experience and crucially with the confidence that is built up over a number of years in thinking in the discipline. It is possible that argumentation could be seen as more central to these subjects if the range of modes in which it is seen to take place could expand to include the visual, spatial, conceptual, and aural as well as the verbal. (Addressing these questions is part of the focus of Chapters 6 and 12.)

The onus, then, is on individual departments or subject associations to work out how argumentation best fits within their discipline. Such discussion is often taken for granted or unexplored. One very practical way forward is for lecturers in the field to discuss together what they see as the argumentational emphases within their subject, and particularly within the undergraduate or graduate courses they teach. What difference does it make at undergraduate or graduate levels? How does argument play a part in the core formulation of knowledge in the subject, and how are undergraduate students inducted into these discourses? What are the forms of expression? Could they be varied or extended so that thinking in the field is given better and fuller expression? How is assessment framed? Is it done so to bring the best out of students and to differentiate their performance? Is the assumption that 'a lot has to be learnt before any argumentation takes place' a tenable position? Or could it be that such a position is one that favours simplistic pedagogies and a reluctance to engage in dispute, controversy and argumentation?

Finally, how best can students' progress from their studies at pre-university level be exploited so that they find argumentation in their chosen discipline(s) easier and more engaging? It is universally the case that studies in the pre-university are broader and more varied in a disciplinary sense than at university. It is also the case that in the pre-university years, the differences between disciplines are being formed: territories are staked out, boundaries set and policed, discourses established. To what extent is the emergence of epistemological and pedagogic differences made explicit, and to what extent are these differences compared? It is through such discussion and exploration of such disciplinary differences that both lecturers and students can see the particular strengths and demands of their subjects and thus navigate these more readily in the first and second years of undergraduate study wherein rapid understanding of the rules of the particular game they are playing can be developed. In this way, students can make faster progress, avoid the misunderstanding about expectation that sometimes occurs with lecturers, and give themselves a greater chance of success.

The Practical Dimension

Activity 4.1

Referring back to Chapter 2, compose, in your academic team, a text such as Storey's *Writing History: A Guide for Students* (and if you are a historian, improve on it). Your handbook for students in your own institution could become, in due course, a title in a published series.

Activity 4.2

Undertake in-depth interviews with colleagues in your own department or faculty or in another department. You could transcribe these and use the results in an analysis of the differences in approach to argumentation or simply see them as part of a professional conversation for your own – and the interviewees' – enlightenment. Alternatively, you could set up discussions in focus groups between colleagues within one department, or from a number of departments.

5
The Balance Between Generic and Discipline-Specific Skills

In this chapter, a proposal is put forward for a balanced approach to generic and discipline-specific skills development in argumentation at the institutional level in higher education. The chapter discusses which elements can be addressed generically and which need discipline-specific attention and treatment. Guidance on such balance will make for much improved policies and practices with regard to students' study skills across the sector.

Chapter 3 set out some generic models in argumentation, suggesting that different models had different functions. Chapter 4 looked at discipline-specific issues, tying the nature and development of argumentation to epistemological concerns. Chapter 5 brings these two approaches together and recommends a balance between the two.

It also looks at where argumentation stands in relation to the literature on academic literacy or literacies.

Generic Stages in the Development of an Argument

Some aspects of argumentation are generic or at least can best be approached generically and applied to particular disciplines and/or circumstances. It is helpful to have such generic guidance as (a) such guidance is of a more general nature and more easily memorable than more specific guidance and (b) a common set of models provides a basis for comparison between different disciplinary practices, thus highlighting the particular needs of each.

We noticed in Chapter 3 that there were various identifiable stages in the making of an argument: the generation of the argument; its development; the definition of stance or position; structuring; expression; refinement; and a testing of the soundness of the argument put forward.

Generation of the Argument

In contemporary academic argument, it is not so much a case of seeking out the places (*topoi*) for argument as seeking out the points of dispute and, to use the metaphor supplied by the history lecturer quoted in the previous chapter, drilling down at those points. Many students write less-than-riveting assignments because they fail to identify the points of dispute. Their work is, therefore, blander than it could be; they take certain truths for granted and see the generation of knowledge in the subject as uncontested and non-controversial. With such an approach, they cannot get out of the trap of expository prose in which they recount and describe the 'way things are'.

How are the points of dispute identified? This is a matter of knowing the territory of the discipline, or at least of the topic. Once that territory is traversed via wide reading, reflection, discussion, and exploration of primary and secondary sources, the points of dispute tend to emerge. These are issues that secondary analysts (critics, commentators) seem not to be able to resolve or agree on. To give an example: in psychology and fields of child development, the question of nature or nurture often presents itself. This question also has application in a range of different sub-fields and other disciplines, manifesting itself in disputes about inherent factors as opposed to longitudinal ones. Such questions can be couched dramatically and oppositionally as in formulations such as 'Is it nature *or* nurture that has the greatest effect on *x*?' or by offering the possibility of a spectrum of interpretation: '*To what degree* is nature a factor in the development of *x*?'

Points of dispute are like knots in wood, or bruises, or blockages in transport systems. They are points at which there is some problem, some seizure in the general flow of things. These point need attention for a harmonic state to be reestablished. Once identified, diagnosis of the problem needs a high degree of energy and concentration. It requires thought, a weighing up of reasons for the problem, and consideration of possible solutions. Such consideration makes for a more critical approach. Criticality comes naturally when faced with such problems, because there is a weighing up of various viewpoints and a distancing of the arguer from the problem itself that comes from the consideration of a range of viewpoints.

Once the point of dispute is identified, the problem can be clarified. Clarification is an important part of this stage, because it helps the solving of a problem if the problem can be accurately defined and 'contained'. Again, such clarification can be oversimplified, and oversimplification of a problem can lead to superficial and unsatisfactory solutions.

The generation of the argument, then, is in many ways like the generation of a research question for a dissertation or thesis: both the argument and the question need to be relevant, interesting, and problematic (to sustain momentum); both need to be precise, or the search for precision to be part of the process of developing the argument; both need to be manageable; and both determine the nature of the argument that follows (see Andrews, 2003b).

Development of the Argument

The development of an argument can be best served by the model devised by Kaufer and Geisler (1991). The model presents a line of argument from A to

B, with 'faulty paths' leading the discussion away from the main line to find points of reference for it. The process is rather like orienting oneself in relation to a number of reference points along the way, navigating a straight course by taking reference from key points in the landscape. The key advantages of this model at this stage in the development of an argument are that it requires the identification of a clear main thesis (the journey from A to B); it provides the discipline of thought that can distinguish the main path from faulty paths; and it prevents straying from the topic by recognizing that interesting avenues open up as we argue but making sure that we only go down those avenues as far as will help us maintain focus on the main path of our argument. In a further refinement of the model, the suggestion is that our points of reference can be some way from the main line of argument to begin with but get close to the main line as the argument progresses. Thus, arguments that might seem oppositional at the start of the journey are much more in support of the main line of the argument toward the end of that journey.

Another advantage of the journey metaphor as represented in Kaufer and Geisler's model is that there is no limitation on the length of a journey. This is not a model that is concerned with the length of an argument, with how many stages there are in it, and so on. Rather, it is concerned with two main features: the goal of the argument and the means by which we navigate our way toward that goal.

The Definition of Stance or Position

Developing a stance or position can be one of the most daunting aspects of argumentation for students, often because they understandably declare that they cannot know what position to take on a particular topic. This anxiety or reluctance to commit is often the result of not knowing enough in a particular field or on a particular topic to be able to stake out a position. However, such reluctance can be overemphasized, especially when it is realized that the adopting of a stance or position need not be a trenchant one, nor one that is radically different from previous arguments on the topic.

Part of the critical development of thought and of its expression are the seeking out of gaps in the existing literature and exploiting those gaps. Sometimes the gaps can even be created, thus engineering rhetorical space in which to speak/write. The gaps – these are spaces where it appears that previous work has failed to fully address the problem – can range from gaping holes to slight cracks. It is more likely that there are going to be cracks in the field than huge holes, and these cracks will take a good deal of work to identify and to fill.

The point that is being made here is that a stance in relation to existing work need not require the carving out of a whole new position, with its attendant backing (values, assumptions, ideologies) and warrants (technical means of joining claims to evidence). It can just as well be a tangential stance that sees some space for discussion. Such subtlety requires finesse of its own, but it is more likely for an undergraduate or graduate student to be able to make such points and take such a position. If the student feels, as he or she is reading a secondary work on a topic, there is something missing or that the interpretation is flawed in some way, there is scope for the taking up of a position.

Once the position or stance is established, there is a strong basis for a thread running through the assignment that reinforces the position by justifying it and developing it. The position itself can be questioned (via a counter-position, for example), thus adding more strength and colour to the argument overall.

Structuring of the Argument

The classical rhetoricians thought more about structuring arguments (*dispositio*) than about any other aspect. Despite – or perhaps because of –this attention to structure, the advice from Aristotle, Quintilian, and Cicero is conflicting. One definition of Aristotle's suggests that an argument is made up of two parts: statement and proof. This formulation is similar to the Toulminian conception of claim and grounds (proposition and evidence). It is not so much a rhetorical structuration of argument as a declaration of the minimal elements that make up an argument. There are then a number of configurations, from three parts upward, that are suggested for the structuring of arguments. Rather than recite these various configurations, I describe the constituent parts of an argument in classical terms and then cite the principle articulated by Quintilian that appears the most useful for contemporary academic usage.

The key elements are an introduction, the facts of the case (*narratio*), the statement, the proof (in the form of evidence and/or logical development of the statement), the counter-argument and its refutation, and the conclusion (*peroratio*). The most complex core of the argument are the statement and proof; the rest are rhetorical elements that support/embed the core argument and its delivery. There is no set length for any of these elements but, as a guide, it is not advisable to spend too long on the introduction and the conclusion. If there is to be a lengthy exposition, it had best come in the core of the argument, followed by a somewhat shorter counter-argument/rebuttal and 'facts of the case'. Other elements could be added to strengthen the argument. For example, two elements suggested by Toulmin might be added to the classical model: warrant and backing. The warrant is a technical element that justifies the linking of the grounds to the claim; the backing is more of an ideological foundation or values-based set of assumptions that gives the whole argument a rationale. These may be important to win a key argument or make progress in a negotiation; they also slow down the delivery of the argument itself.

Quintilian's reminder is salutary, however: the art of argument is to use those elements, in whichever order (and whichever number of elements are needed) best suit the purpose in hand. This is an important reminder, because it moves deliberations about the structure of argument away from formulaic patterning to a fitness-for-purpose approach that is, however, not entirely contingent upon the circumstances of the situation; rather, the available elements are structured according to need. So, for example, an argument could start with a counter-argument (an approach that first-year students find difficult to comprehend) or with evidence or with the facts of the case. It can move the various parts around, drop some of them, repeat some, and so on. It can vary in length. Not all of these variations are for rhetorical effect; some of the structuring can be deliberately ideational.

Expression of the Argument

There is often debate about whether the personal pronoun 'I' can be used in an assignment or whether it is best to use the passive voice and avoid any personal reference altogether. My own view is that the use of the first person pronoun is acceptable in most cases, especially if a personal view is included or called for in the assignment. For example, to refer back to the section on stance and position: if there is a distinct position to be argued, it would seem evasive not to express that position with the personal pronoun. It is not received knowledge that is being presented in such a case but a personal viewpoint underpinned by logical, quasi-logical, and evidence-supported arguments. In a thesis or dissertation, to give another example, there is often a space for the use of the personal pronoun: for instance, when the researcher is declaring his or her own prejudices or background so as to make the discussion of the research more transparent.

Having said that the first person pronoun is acceptable in some circumstances, it ought to be said that clear and uncluttered expression of what is to be said is a helpful stylistic quality. Some students' writing is overlaid with adjectives that convey enthusiasm or some other feeling; it is often useful to go through the draft of such an essay and think hard about whether these adjectives are necessary.

Refinement of the Argument

Refinement of the argument is largely a rhetorical matter, though rhetorical and logical concerns go hand in hand. The rhetorical dimension is prompted by attention to the audience. If it is an oral presentation to a seminar or a public (or private) defence of a position, as in a *vive voce* examination, the refinement will take particular forms; if the work in hand is a written piece – from a position paper through a research paper to a fully fledged dissertation or thesis – it will require different kinds of refinement.

Let us take an oral presentation to a seminar first. These are usually short (10 to 20 minutes) and are followed by questions. Whichever media and modes are used for delivery – straight talking, handouts, overhead or data projection, Web-based, or any combination of these – a number of rhetorical devices can help comprehension. These include reciting the structure and main stages of the talk at the start, so that the audience knows how to pace itself and how to place one part of the delivery in relation to others; the use of narrative, either as illustrative anecdotes during the talk, or as an overarching structural principle; re-capping the main points at the end; and so on. It is fairly well-accepted knowledge that if you give students handouts, they will look at them and begin to read them while you are talking, therefore being distracted from the main focus of attention. However, second-language learners in higher education have often asked for handouts to be given at the start of a talk, to aid understanding. It terms of refinement of the argument, it must be remembered that an informal seminar with peers is different from a formal oral examination of a dissertation; nevertheless, lecturers set more store by oral contributions to class discussion that they sometimes reveal. It is worthwhile, as a student, to discuss with lecturers what nature and degree of interest the lecturer really has in oral presentations.

Defences of dissertations and theses in *viva voce* examinations can be tense affairs. The students are on the defensive, having submitted their argument in the form of the written thesis. Whether the occasion is a public defence, wherein the outcome is usually known but the student now has to present his or her work to public scrutiny, or the outcome of a closed-door *viva* really does contribute to the determination of the result (as it does in borderline cases), refinement of argumentational approach can help.

For example, it is wise to consider possible counter-arguments to the *thesis* (in the sense of argument) put forward in the dissertation or thesis. It is highly likely that the examiners will put counter-arguments. If these have not already been considered in the written document, being prepared for what they might be and having answers ready (perhaps in the form of counter-counter-arguments) is a sensible move. There might be arguments put by examiners that are reasonable, and the student might wish to accept some of these; but blanket acceptance of all the counter-arguments will weaken the student's position and lay him or her open to accusations of a weak main thesis and poor argumentational skills as a researcher. In the end, the student has to judge how firmly to mount a defense and to what degree to accept some of the points made by the examiners. This process is made easier if the original written argument in the thesis is sound and if counter-arguments have been addressed in the written form.

Testing the Soundness of Arguments

Testing the soundness of arguments was, according to Toulmin, the main function of his model of argumentation. In other words, his model, used by the speech communication community as a model for the generation of arguments (and even by some as a writing process model), was not designed for those uses. Indeed, in the preface to the new edition of *The Use of Argument* in 2003, he expressed surprise that his model had been taken up in these ways.

It remains a very good model for testing the soundness of what has been put forward as an argument. At a stage in the composition process wherein a first draft has been achieved or a fairly full plan has been made or where the skeleton of an argument has been sketched in preparation for a fuller exposition, then the Toulmin model can be applied.

The first question that can be asked is 'what is the main proposition in the argument?' If it is unclear or if it is too deeply buried or is implicit, it will be difficult for an audience to see it. Similarly, if there is more than one proposition or if a number of subsidiary propositions sit in relation to the main one, there will be sifting out to be done so that the relationship of the propositions (whether hierarchical and/or logical) can be determined. There is a similar problem with the formulation of research questions, which is addressed in Andrews (2003b). The position and prominence of the proposition is an interesting question, and cultures vary as to how explicit and how up-front such propositions can be. For example, although the expectation in the European-American tradition is that the proposition will be explicitly stated and will come early in the argument, it has been the case in Japanese traditions that it is indiscreet to state the proposition too explicitly: subtlety and even deferral of the proposition to the end of the argument (in extreme cases, the proposition is not stated at all but is left implicit) is more common.

The second question, once the proposition or claim has been identified, is 'what is the evidence in support of the claim?' Evidence can take many forms (see Andrews, 2008, for a discussion of what counts as evidence in education), from anecdote and personal account to statistical evidence; from observation to a material object; from empirically gathered data to testimony from other (authoritative) sources. What kinds of evidence are used, and what the relative weight of those different kinds of evidence are, need to be considered and possibly explicitly discussed. What is often overlooked in the presentation of evidence is that evidence can take many forms. In a court of law, a photograph (for example, of a crime being committed) or some DNA record retrieved from a piece of clothing might be crucial evidence; equally, the oral account of a prime witness may be just as weighty. In an academic essay in the humanities or arts or social sciences, it is unlikely that such kinds of evidence will carry as much weight. Oral anecdote is looked on as flimsy evidence for many of these disciplines, especially if it is self-generated. The search for a degree of objectivity means that other forms of evidence come to the fore and are considered more weighty. For example, in a social science report, statistical evidence derived from empirically gathered data and subjected to statistical tests such as significance is likely to be more highly valued than an individual oral report. Conversely, a small number of qualitatively analyzed expert interviews could count as heavily as statistical evidence – or they could complement it. The question of what counts as evidence in education, to take one particular discipline or field of enquiry, is explored more fully in Chapter 11.

The third question to be asked is that addressed by Toulmin's 'warrant' category: 'what is it that enables the proposition to be linked to the evidence, and the evidence to support the proposition?' Deliberation at this stage begins to become more difficult, because it is not always easy to define the relationship between a proposition and the evidence that purports to support it. What can be said here is that much depends on the answers to the second foregoing question. Certain kinds of evidence are more telling in some contexts, and in some disciplines, than in others. What counts in a court of law or an engineering lab may be very different from what counts in a psychology essay or in a presentation or some aspect of literature and the media.

Making the warrant explicit, however, can strengthen the argument because the means by which the connection is made between claims and evidence are made clear. They can thus be justified and challenged – and defended.

Such defence may not, however, be sufficient – or indeed possible – without further backing. Toulmin's technical term for the sets of values and assumptions that underpin the way warrants operate in particular fields is exactly that: *backing*. Such considerations need not usually be addressed in assignments for academic disciplines in higher education, because it is taken for granted within universities that assignments work within certain agreed assumptions. These are rarely made explicit, because everyone is in the same boat (or is assumed to be). However, as a fourth question to ask oneself when testing the soundness of arguments, the question 'What enables me to think that these warrants work in this particular case?' is a good one to ask. Backing operates at the level of common values, ideologies, and theories. To explore the theoretical justification for an approach in an essay or another assignment is a good move, because theoretical perspective and critique enable not only justification of a position but critique of it and alternative possibilities at a fundamental level. The best assignments work down to this level, establishing a firm basis for the rest of the argument.

Finally, as suggested earlier, a very useful way to test the soundness of an argument is to challenge it with counter-arguments. Does it stand up to intense scrutiny from other positions? Do other perspectives shed critical light on the position that has been taken? Do all the various connections that have been made – between claims and evidence, supported by warrants and backing – hold up in equal measure when tested by another perspective? The counter-arguments can come in various forms: a direct challenge to the proposition or claim; the provision of new evidence or a challenge to the nature of the evidence presented so far; a questioning of the connections made between claim and evidence in the form of an attack on the warrant; and a more fundamental challenge to the values, assumptions, *mores*, and ideologies that have underpinned the whole edifice of the argument in question. Needless to say, good, strong arguments need to be prepared to deal with such counter-arguments. In Toulmin's terms, the rebuttal is the answer to the counter-argument; if embedded in the argument itself, it provides stronger defence if the written assignment is subjected to a later oral critique or if the examiner or marker of the assignment comes with his or her own arguments and assumptions that will be used to challenge those of the student.

The Balance Between Generic and Discipline-Specific Skills

'Balance' is a nice idea in theory. How does it work in practice?

First, the need for a balance in theory must be discussed. There is a need for balance, because much of the guidance that is given to students at universities is too generic. Students are thought to have a deficit in argumentational terms when they arrive at university or in higher and further education. That deficit is a result of the massification of higher education and the opening of a gap in the discourse skills that are required between what is used up to the end (or just beyond) compulsory schooling on the one hand and the beginnings of higher or further education on the other. The solution, especially in the United States, has been for general courses in argumentation under the umbrella of rhetoric and composition classes often run centrally in a university by a writing centre and/or by an academic department with an interest in rhetoric and composition (varying from rhetoric departments to English departments). There has been no such solution in the United Kingdom, for example, where the tradition of rhetoric died in the mid-nineteenth century under pressure for literature-based courses. In the United Kingdom, although there has been a move from 8 per cent to nearly 50 per cent of 18-year-olds going on to attend university over the last generation – and therefore a similar process of massification – there is no generic provision. Indeed, the provision of academic writing skills has been closely associated with pre-sessional and in-sessional courses and coaching for students of English as a second or foreign language. Only in a handful of UK universities (York, Queen Mary, the Open University, the Institute of Education of the University of London and UCL, for example) are there centres or courses that concern themselves with academic writing for all students. In these universities, the 'writing centres' tend to be optional for students – more like clinics they could visit optionally if they have a problem rather than compulsory introductory courses that are seen as a foundation to further successful study.

As discussed earlier in the book, the UK approach has been to leave the business of writing argumentational prose to the departments and disciplines. In general, the disciplines have neglected the responsibility, seeing it as something the students themselves should address. The assumption is that students will learn such skills by osmosis or that they will come fully skilled for work at the university level.

Somewhere between the view and practice, at one end of the spectrum, that argumentation is a generic skill that can be taught to all students at the start of their university education and, at the other end of the spectrum, the view and practice that argumentation is so embedded in the discipline that (a) it is assumed by lecturers to be already there in students and (b) is so specialized as not to be subject to any generic input, is a balance. The balance is not a pivotal mid-point where there is stasis or inaction. Rather, it is a hybrid set of practices that provide generic *and* discipline-specific guidance. Such a balance is necessary because it enables teachers/lecturers *and* students to gain an understanding that is important common ground: that the discipline's epistemological identity is partly shaped and certainly expressed by the discourses that take place within it; some aspects of these discourses, in which argumentation plays a major part, are shared with other disciplines. By 'discourses' is meant the ways in which talk and writing (and other modes) convey and represent the exchange of knowledge within the discipline.

How does such a balance manifest itself in practice? A Venn diagram (Figure 5.1) will help demonstrate the balance that has been discussed so far in this chapter in a generic and theoretical way.

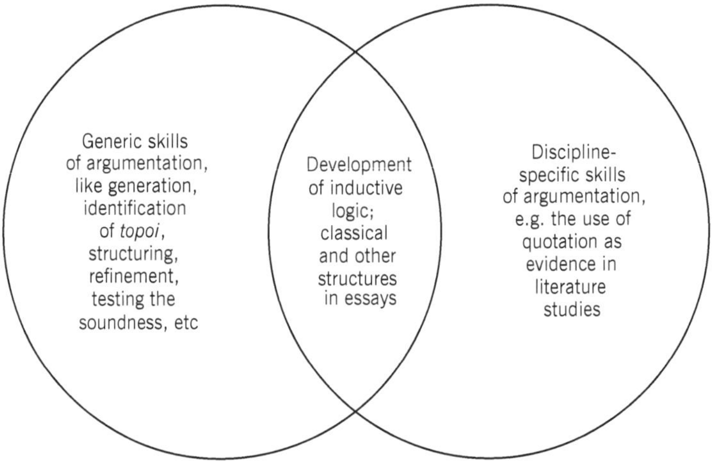

Figure 5.1 An example of balanced argumentational approaches in literature studies

In the foregoing case, students might benefit from a generic course that explores some of the generally accepted ways of approaching argument. However, such courses need to be balanced by input from the department on the discipline-specific concerns of those working in the particular field. In this case: how long can quotations be? Do they have to be indented and without quotation marks, or can they be represented in other ways? Which is better: the embedding of quotations within the fabric of the argument of an essay or an approach that clearly demarcates between the voice of the student and the voices of the writers he or she is quoting? Could an essay *start* with a quotation and, if so, should this be short, like an epigraph, or can it act as a starting point rather than a touchstone of the argument itself?

I have focused in the previous paragraph merely on the use of quotations in literature essays, but the fact that there are a number of (and more) questions that novice students will need to have addressed is indicative of the discipline-specific nature of argumentation. In such discipline-specific discussions, whether they take place in tutorial groups and/or via taught seminars and lectures, there is the possibility to mediate the guidance from the generic approaches to argumentation, as indicated in the space where the two circles overlap. Here, generic principles can be applied to the discipline in question. Take the case of inductive logic, for example. In some fields, inductive logic is seen as almost a contradiction in terms where logic is subjected to the whims of the particular and concrete. However, in literary study, which takes texts as its starting point, the thinking that goes on is largely inductive. It does not operate from propositions or claims but rather starts from the words on the page in front of the reader. Both through interpretation and appreciation, which are inductively logical analyses of the text and its nuances, through to more critically analytical approaches that bring theories or other frameworks to bear on the text, there is a to-ing and fro-ing between the inductive and deductive. Each level – that of the text and that of theories of text – is used to *interrogate* the other level. It is in such territory between the generic and the particular that much productive conversation can be had about how disciplines argue and what the arbiters of the discipline – teachers, lecturers – bear in mind as they teach and mark students' work within the discipline.

Argumentation and Academic Literacy/Literacies

Lillis and Scott (2008), in an article on defining academic literacies research, trace the reemergence of the field of academic literacy to the last 20 years. I suggest *re*-emergence, as the mid-part of the twentieth century saw a revival of interest in classical rhetoric as a guide to thinking and writing in the academy. They see academic literacies as drawing on 'disciplinary fields and sub-fields such as applied linguistics and sociolinguistics, anthropology, sociocultural theories of learning, new literacy studies and discourse studies' (p5) – all fields in which language and culture play an informing and underpinning role. The multi- and inter-disciplinary context for academic literacies is typical of the study of a nexus of practice: most academic literacy practice and research take place in language institutes, departments of rhetoric, language support units, English centres, and other units within universities and colleges that have the function of supporting the academic writing of students. In some higher education institutions, these centres are ostensibly for learners of English as a second or additional language, and the field English for Academic Purposes provides a focus for such activity. All too often, however, the assumption under which such centres exist is a deficit model in which the student is thought to lack something – usually competence in writing academic English. It is clear that problems in writing academic English are not confined to those for whom English is a second or additional language; they are also shared by many native speakers and writers of English.

The Lillis and Scott article addresses questions of definition: whether academic literac*y* or academic literac*ies* are the best way to frame the field. The spectrum that is drawn is from academic literacy at one end, with its assumption of a single autonomous competence in language use, and to academic literacies at the other, where the plurality of social contexts in which literacy is manifested and shaped is evident. The question for the present book is how argumentation fits into practices of academic literacy. (The singular form will be used for the rest of this chapter, not to signify an autonomous, single state to which students can aspire but as a simple way to refer to the spectrum as a whole.)

Let us first deal with the notion of a deficit model of academic literacy in higher education. Notions of deficit seem to be part of institutional – and some individuals' – thinking. In the case of institutions, some provision has to be made for those students who do not appear to have the requisite linguistic and compositional skills and capabilities for success in higher education. However, a deficit notion can easily turn into a prejudice. Some teachers and lecturers believe that 'overseas' or international students for whom English is not a first or native language 'cannot argue'; that they 'come from a culture in which argumentation is not encouraged'; and that they 'defer too much to the teacher, practising a passive and uncritical mode of learning'. My own experience of teaching at undergraduate, masters, and doctoral levels in higher education is that there is no such cultural deficit. Students from China (see Watkins and Biggs, 1996), Japan, Korea, and Taiwan working at the masters level in England or Malaysian students working in the United States seem to have no problem in arguing a case. There may well be a need for language support, but that is not surprising – and immersion in a 'Western' academic context for a year or more, with good supervisory, social, and institutional support, can make a great difference to the command of language. However, learning the academic rules of the game is the same for any student, regardless of background, and seems to be more a matter of the quality of the student than his or her linguistic profile.

It is also not surprising that it is student *writing* that receives a great deal of attention in higher education. Writing is the mode in which most assessment is couched; and the 'essay' is still the default in the humanities and in many of the arts and social sciences. A shift away from a narrow focus on text toward seeing composition in higher education as a matter of cogitation and communication has meant that academic literacy *practices* have come to the fore in the last 20 years. These include the acts and processes of writing; the need to make sense of what is discussed, read, and experienced; the social exchange of knowledge; and the power relations within which students essays find their place. In other words, there has been a shift to a more dynamic, more contextualized, more ethnographic way of seeing student writing.

In summary, we can say that academic literacy practices and research provide a location for the study of argumentation within the academy but that argumentation both is contained within its canopy and escapes from it. Argumentation is contained in the sense that it may well be that, institutionally, the location for academic literacy practices is the best place to practice and understand argument. However, in at least two senses, argumentation escapes from under this canopy: first, in the sense that a more diverse, ethnographic approach to argumentation (Prior, 2005) cannot be framed entirely under such a canopy, as it finds itself operating in a wide range of disciplinary contexts. Second, in that the forms in which argumentation takes shape may include the verbal, but may also include visual and other modes (see Chapter 6). We must also note that the canopy itself is different in different countries: in the United States, it takes the form of rhetoric and compositions classes in a range of different centres and units within the academy. In the United Kingdom, it has to date been located in units that were originally designed to serve the needs of second-language learners but which have expanded their remit to include academic literacy for all students, such as the Centre for Academic and Professional Literacies at the Institute of Education, London.

Interdisciplinarity

What happens to argumentation when there is more than one discipline at play in a course or programme? There is again a spectrum of practice to be considered here. Combined courses or programmes – for example, those in which undergraduate students study for a degree in music and education, or history and English – have to consider, at the curriculum planning stage right through to examination board levels, how their different epistemologies affect the student in terms of what is demanded and expected of the students. In the case of each discipline or field, the way in which propositions are connected to evidence, what counts as evidence, and what the main forms are in which argumentation is practiced are issues that need to be addressed. It can be a considerable strain on students to move from one disciplinary culture to another and to write successfully in both disciplines. However, at least there is the chance for the joint programme directors to discuss the issue and make explicit the expectations in each discipline.

The same problem occurs in programmes in which undergraduate students have a great deal of choice as to the modules or courses they take. So-called 'elective' modules are those in which a student in one department can take modules in another. He or she often enjoys the difference in approach, but it is rare in a compartmentalized, modular system such as this for the epistemological and/or discourse expectations to be made clear. Students are often surprised by their success (or lack of it) in a discipline different from that represented in their 'home' department; such success may be as much to do with happening upon the argumentational expectations of the new module as with its content.

Still more complex and potentially confusing for the student are semi-professional fields of academic enquiry, such as educational, management, or nursing studies, wherein a number of disciplines inform the field. The most interesting and academically sound studies in these fields acknowledge the complexity of the disciplinary background and work with one or more disciplines to shed light on problems that occur. Weaker conceptions of what it means to have a theoretical underpinning to such fields are those in which 'reflective practice' (cf. Schön, 1983, 1990) are the guiding principles. From such a perspective, the individual is the basis from which progress is measured and from whom critical perspective is gained. This is a foundation very different from a theoretical or epistemological one, in which the public history and patterning in a field of enquiry is taken as the basis from which progress is measured. Taking a reflective practitioner position means that the capacity for argumentation is reduced, because narration and personal reflection are the basis for enquiry. There is no reason why starting with a narrative, descriptive account cannot lead to a fully argued, heavily referenced piece of critical writing, but the temptation is to dwell on personal or interpersonal reflection rather than plumbing deeper to some disciplinary principles and lines of enquiry.

Finally, interdisciplinarity is particularly interesting if the two or more departments that have an interest in the student's progress make the rules of their own game explicit and then engineer a debate on the matter. Although most students do not want to go to levels of epistemological shaping of their discipline(s), an airing of such matters and boundaries can provide an extra critical perspective and can shed light on *why* knowledge takes the forms it does in a particular subject or discipline. Studies such as Bazerman's *Shaping Written Knowledge* (1988), on the emergence of the scientific article as a genre, can provide insights into why we frame knowledge in the way we do, how we express it and conduct debates within it, and consequently what we value in students' writing as they make their way in the discipline(s).

The Practical Dimension

Activity 5.1

The question of balance in the provision of guidance and support on argumentation in your discipline is a delicate one. Review the materials you provide for students: are they weighted toward the generic or the subject-specific? Is there more that you could provide for either side of the balance to improve students' understanding of the argumentational demands of the course? Furthermore, is the material you provide too concerned with surface matters of presentation and format? Are you helping the students to understand the epistemological shape of the field and the genres that operate within it?

Activity 5.2

Look at other departments' material with a view to seeing what you can learn from it with regard to study skills and, in particular, argumentation.

6
Information and Communication Technologies, Multimodality and Argumentation

A number of centres around the world are interested in the potential of information and communication technologies (henceforward ICT) to help teach and/or research argumentation. This chapter surveys the field. Using ICT to undertake argument, however, is not the same as multimodal approaches to argument. Much ICT work in argument is highly textual, but there is the possibility of a more multimodal approach, afforded by the use of images and sound on computer screens. Examples of such work by students are discussed.

An Example of an Undergraduate Dissertation

At various points in this book, focus is centred on student dissertations or 'long essays'. These are the summation of undergraduate student work for assessment, in which the best work is assumed to be done; they often come late in the degree course and often gain the greatest number of marks that are available on the course for any one assignment.

In a simple multimodal assignment that I discuss at the outset of this chapter, one student wrote her final-year dissertation on the range of marks made on paper by a 5-year-old boy, asking the question 'How do these marks demonstrate a development in written literacy?' This is in many ways an ideal first attempt at a dissertation: the topic is manageable in a few months' study. The case study approach allows an intense and small-scale focus. Issues of access are helped by concentrating on a subject – in this case, a 5-year-old boy – who was well known to the student and to whom she had access as a family member. Ethical issues were easily addressed and explored. I hope to show that the argumentation involved in the creation and production of such a dissertation is complex but one that can be enjoyed and developed by the student.

The topic is one that is attractive in itself. Intellectually, its attraction is great because of the possible and fairly well-researched connection between children's drawings and their literacy development. In the Introduction, the student makes a direct proposal: that there is a direct link between children's drawings and learning to write and that she will generate a theory to illustrate how this happens. The research questions follow from the initial hypothesis. They are (a) what is the range of marks made on paper by a 5-year-old boy and (b) how do these marks represent a development in written literacy?

Because this is a small *research* project, the argumentational structure of the dissertation is provided or, at least, a conventional, default template was provided. This is a template that can be followed, adapted, or ignored, but it is helpful to have it there for these purposes. The template is a structure that is broadly as follows:

- introduction
- context (or literature review)
- methodology
- results and analysis
- conclusions
- references
- appendices.

The template can be used with a short dissertation of 5,000 to 10,000 words, or it can be used with one 10 times that size. The Introduction consists of one page, is concise, and gives an idea of the work as a whole:

> This work is devoted to the topic of children's drawings. It is a study which aims to add to existing knowledge about children's drawings and how they show emergent literacy skills.
>
> My research takes the form of a case study, and the 'case' in question is a five year old boy. Over a period of time, I collected work which he had created on paper at home, which comprised written, drawn and painted creations.
>
> I am interested in tracing the development of marks made on paper. The data I have collected will be used to identify the characteristics of this process, and show how children develop their drawings in preparation for learning to write. I propose that there is a direct link between children's drawings and learning to write, and I will propose a theory of development to illustrate how this happens. My research question is as follows: 'What is the range of marks made on paper by a five year old boy? How do these marks demonstrate a development in written literacy?'
>
> The first part of the work will set the context for my study: I will discuss the foundations of the topic of children's drawings, and also explore related literature and explain the aims for my research in light of this. I will then explain the methodology of the study. I will describe and justify how I conducted the research, and critically analyse the methods I used. After this comes my results and analysis, which will show what the data revealed. Using others' writing on the topic for

> reference and comparison, I will develop my theory of how children's written capabilities develop from their drawings, according to the findings from my case.

In many ways, this is as near to a perfect introduction for a short dissertation as one would wish. It is not over-problematizing the issue; on the contrary, it makes clear and straightforward the problem to be addressed and how it will be addressed. It is an exercise in elegance and is significant and motivating for the researcher. It both sets out the propositions of the argument that will follow and persuades through its eloquence and clarity. It emphasizes, too, the importance of getting the scale right in undergraduate dissertations of this kind: take on too much and the apparatus falters; take on too little and the results appear irrelevant and insignificant. The methodology is identified at the start, and although case study can cover a range of methods and approaches, it is helpful to have the broad methodology labelled as such. What is also so refreshing about this writing is the motivation that shines through: it is both personal and academic, clear-thinking and inquisitive, formal and informal.

That personal tone is carried over into the chapter headed 'Context' – in effect, a modest literature review. The opening paragraph is disarmingly casual and enthusiastic:

> My interest in children's drawings stems from work I did one year ago. I find it fascinating to study the intricate depictions children make, and think it amazing that children are capable of learning how to represent a language using marks on paper. I am interested in how children's drawings show this in action – from the first geometric shapes to full words, crafted letters and understanding of syntax. It is this process which I aim to document in this study.

The prose is transparent. The penultimate sentence, for example, makes the last one crystal clear, though usually the appearance of two deictic references in close proximity would make for a lack of clarity.

The dissertation then moves into more conventional, more distant, academic mode:

> As Czerniewska (1992) states, the origins of all early writing systems lie in pictures: 'At some point in human development, pictures used for representing objects and events began to be used as symbols which could be combined to create messages' (p. 33). So is born the idea that drawings and writing are inextricably linked.

It might be seen as uncritical to make too close and absolute a connection between drawing and writing in the development of writing as a system (not all writing systems are pictographic), but the quotation supports the emerging thesis.

Although the present analysis of the student's work could go on in some detail about the many ways in which the dissertation develops, the focus here is on its argumentation. Having set out some of the theorists in the field, the student arranges these into two main groups (itself a critical act), pointing out differences between them and (within the limitations of a short undergraduate dissertation) differences between members of the same group. However, the key critical act is that she then states that in reading the various theorists in relation to the data she had collected, 'I found great theoretical gaps'. These theoretical gaps are not just rhetorical (though they would be useful in themselves). In the relatively new field of the connections between children's drawing and writing, they are *actual* theoretical gaps. In other words, the student could not find research and/or theoretical accounts, despite her extensive searching, that provided the explanatory power to make sense of the material she had collected. She concludes the chapter with 'I hope to produce work which fills part of the gap I propose exists in the literature'. Again, the modesty is not rhetorical, though the move fulfils a rhetorical function in helping the audience to set expectations that are not too high. The modesty is also genuine: the *hope* is to produce work that fills *part* of the gap that she *proposes*. It is clever writing, but it is also intellectually refreshing writing.

The dissertation then proceeds by identifying eight categories of mark making on the spectrum from drawing to writing: geometric marks, repetitive marking, 'busy' drawings, number- and letter-writing trials, representative drawings, explorations of colour, accurate number and letter writing, and 'other' marks (i.e., scribbles that did not fit into a group). Excluding the last category, the student then arranges these categories into a developmental sequence (Figure 6.1).

This multi-levelled sequence is geared chronologically to the time at which the marks were produced in the child's life. However, as there are horizontal and vertical dimensions to the model, there is scope for logical progression and multi-layered connectivity between the various categories of mark making. Taking examples at any one point would reveal a complexity about each of the creations by the child – and that is exactly what the student does. She selects nine examples of the child's work over the period of data collection and subjects each one to its own analysis. They become like mini-case studies and provide

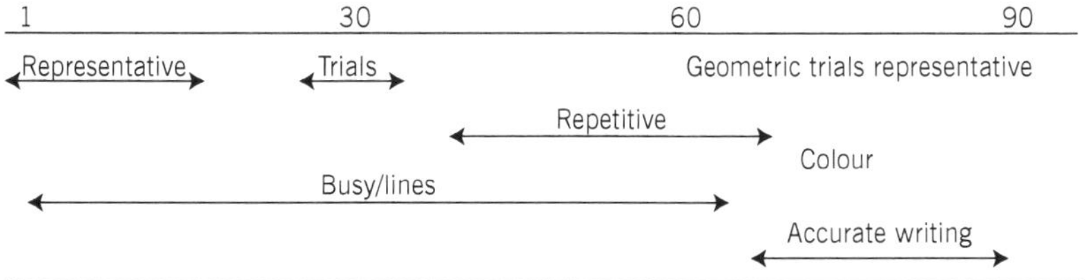

Figure 6.1 From an undergraduate dissertation (1)

Figure 6.2 From an undergraduate dissertation (2)

much of the bulk of the empirical part of the dissertation. Other artworks by the child are collected in an appendix and referred to as appropriate (Figure 6.2).

The student's commentary on this image is as follows:

> Fig 3 is an excellent example of children's work created with the use of geometric art gestalts. Philip has produced a symmetrical grid-like structure, in which he has filled every square with a rich display of colourful mandalas and combines (Kellogg, 1970). His mandalas take the form of repeated circular 'scribbles', which are undefined and seem hurried. I would hesitate, however, to define them as haphazard or careless…[he] has also created a number of combines in this piece, where he juxtaposes the circular mandala design with lines or zigzags. These geometric forms are common in children aged 2:6 [2 years 6 months], and if one saw fig. 3 away from the context of this study, one would assume that the piece was created by a child much younger than Philip. Later in this section, I will make an important point based on this observation, with regards to its implications for any proposed developmental stages theory.

The writing by the student is looking forward, knowing that she has other, more general points to make that will be supported by the evidence she is amassing. However, even from a relatively modest data set in an undergraduate research project, she is able to make observations through a combination of analytical limpidity, modesty, and intellectual curiosity that will have implications – as she rather immodestly states – for 'any proposed developmental stages theory'. In other words, she is aware that the work she is undertaking is core to cognitive and other forms of development and to literacy development.

Near the end (and to give only the lineaments of her study), she comes up with her argument:

> I argue that children's marks evolve with every single piece created. To miss even a few pieces of children's work would put one in danger of missing a whole new stage in his or her mark-making development… every production Philip made could have had hundreds of words of analysis dedicated to it.

One final point: the dissertation is about the relationship between word and image, but what questions are raised and answered by the multimodal nature of the dissertation itself? How does such simple multimodal composition have a bearing on the nature and development of the argument?

The assignment is principally verbal, with its rationale and structure laid out in words. The burden of the argument is carried in the words, but the illustrations do more than illustrate. It is true that the majority of the images are consigned to an appendix, providing further evidence or raw data if necessary to underpin the verbal argument. However, the core of the argument and of the dissertation is a sequence of nine images that have been selected by the student to represent the eight categories of her emerging model of development. Although she couches the model as one that moves from mark making to literacy, there is an understanding that emerges from the work that the picture is more complex that one suggested by such an uni-directional model. Instead, she posits a model that is multi-layered, that provides evidence of (and the possibility of) movement and interrelationship between word and image. The passage for the child becomes not so much one from primitive marks toward literacy but from a rich nexus of mark-making resources toward a yet richer one in which different modes are separated out and recombined to make meaning. The argument is elegantly made and is all the more persuasive because of the modesty of its scale and expression and the significant implications carried within it.

What Does Argumentation Look Like From a Modal Perspective?

What does argumentation look like from a modal and multimodal perspective? This question has been touched upon in Chapter 2 and is addressed again in Chapter 12. Here, consideration is given to some fundamental questions about the nature of argumentation in modes other than the verbal and what happens when modes are combined.

First, though, it is important to reflect on the nature of verbal argumentation. In both the oral and written versions of verbal language, the argument is (potentially) carried at two levels: at the level of the chronological account or narrative and at the abstracted level of generalities, ideas, propositions, and claims.

The connections at the narrative level are sequential and mostly happen in time (though time can be manipulated, as in flashbacks, forward projections, dream sequences, and so on). Sometimes, the forward drive of the narrative can *carry* the argument, as in a fable or parable. Sometimes, the narrative provides evidence to support an abstract argument, as in an anecdote used as an illustration or in the reconstruction of events in a court case.

The connections at the abstract level are logical or quasi-logical in that they might refer to logical sequences or take their cue from logic. They can be accounted for without reference to evidence and the argument summarized in a formula or single sentence: for example, 'It is argued that state support for a banking system in a period of financial crisis is the only way to shore up an economy'. This sort of statement looks very like those that are used in undergraduate essay titles, and the similarity is no coincidence. What is offered is a contentious statement that requires exploration, the provision of evidence to support and/or demolish the argument, and an opportunity to build a counter-argument or a supporting one. Such arguments at the abstract level require grounding in evidence to bring them to life.

Other characteristics of verbal argument are that it operates like beads on a necklace or, more hierarchically, like building blocks in a tower. The necklace analogy emphasizes the sequential nature of verbal argument, with one bead following another on the string but with them all being held together by the string (cf. the diagrams on argumentational structure discussed in Chapter 2). The building analogy draws attention to the fact that arguments often construct themselves around levels. At the foot of the building are data that become evidence when they are informed by the next levels up. The higher levels are categories and subcategories of argumentational propositions, built on the foundations of the lower levels.

Spoken and written verbal arguments have more in common than is often assumed. Elsewhere in the book, the differences between spoken and written argument are explored. These include the dialogic or multi-voiced nature of spoken argument as opposed to the largely univocal nature of written argument; the addition of body language in spoken exchanges; the relatively ephemeral nature of spoken argument as opposed to the written record; and so on. None of these differences is absolute.

What they have in common is more pertinent to this chapter. Apart from what is set out earlier, arguments can take place at sub-sentence level, as in syllogistic argument; they can take place in the form of sentences. Spoken arguments often operate at the level of the paragraph or extended utterance, which are then countered by another utterance; and they also work at the level of the whole text, in spoken and written genres. In other words, verbal arguments have the potential to be highly embedded, in that smaller argumentational moves can sit within larger argumentational structures. The smaller argumentational moves are not so much embellishment as part of the rich fabric of the verbal argument that is presented.

When we turn to the other major modes of communication – the visual, the aural and tactile – there is similar differentiation to be made between types of argument within each of these modes. However, for the purposes of the developing argument, let us concentrate for the moment on the differences between the verbal and the visual modes. Perhaps the key difference between the two modes is that the visual – let's start with a single still photograph – carries its referential suggestiveness within itself. It does not operate at two levels, as words do. There is no abstracted level at which the meaning is expressed. However, the *single* image *is* open to interpretation and thus to a number of possible *readings*. These readings are derived from the image and *suggested* by it.

Because the nature of the image is to suggest rather than to propose or declare, the abstract level of operation is less well defined than with words. The suggestions may form themselves in words, or they make take other less systemic form (a 'feeling', a 'sense', an 'impression'), but they do not tend to constitute an argument in the way that words can. Instead, we could say that the effect of an image within a broad rationalist paradigm that imputes meaning to signs is to *persuade* rather than argue. In other words, a single image itself does not constitute an argument, though it can persuade by virtue of its viscerality, its direct appeal to the senses and/or to feeling, its relative closeness to experience and the perceived world. It will, of course, be highly dependent on context. A photograph of a son or daughter lost in a war that took place 20 years ago will *move* the mother or father; it is persuasive in the sense that it changes the state of feeling or being of the viewer through what it *means* to that viewer. However, it doesn't *argue* in the sense of putting forward a set of propositions supported by evidence.

One could say that argumentation is possible in a single image if there is tension present and if that tension suggests two perspectives that are at odds with each other. In the following image of Jean Shrimpton, taken at the Melbourne races in 1965, there is tension between the foregounded Shrimpton, wearing the latest from London fashion scene at the time, and the backgrounded middle classes of Melbourne at the time, locked within a more conservative style. The rhetoric of this particular photograph is discussed in detail in Black and Muecke (1992), who provide a full analysis of a 'moment in fashion' (Figure 6.3). In argumentational terms, what can we say about it?

The tension present is a result of the contrast between the conservative status quo and the challenge of the new. What is more, the new is flaunting itself in front of the old, in a sense challenging it to recognize the new style. The success of that challenge is evident in the focused gaze of the old, albeit through dark glasses (themselves identified as a mark of the old look). The *argument* could be that (a) London was ahead of Melbourne in the fashion stakes in 1965,

Figure 6.3 Jean Shrimpton at the 1965 Melbourne Cup (courtesy of The Herald and Weekly Times Ltd, Victoria)

(b) in purely photographic terms, the foregrounding of Shrimpton and the backgrounding of the Melbourne set suggests a deliberate challenge, (c) there is more to the moment than a moment in fashion: what is implied is a cultural shift from age to youth, from constraint to liberation, from an age of formality to a more informal age, and so on. However, it must be noted that nowhere is the argument stated explicitly. Both the moment itself and the photographic record of it mark an iconic turning point that lends itself to *interpretation* and in which the arguments are *implied*. It is not even clear, in this case, that the effect is more one of persuasion, because it is not entirely clear who is persuaded and what he or she is persuaded of. The press reaction at the time, and the general response in Melbourne, was one of *resistance* to the Shrimpton look.

It would be possible to say that the photograph, because of its tensions, provides data that could be construed as evidence once one or a range of propositions is supplied. If persuasion is the larger functional category and argumentation is one of a number of operational means by which persuasion can take place, we can characterize persuasion as an effect of interaction between *people* and argument as a systemic, operational means to that end. The 'higher' category, persuasion, allows comparison between modes of operation; and argumentation, we could say, operates most comfortably in the verbal mode.

Figure 6.4 Visual argument from contiguity (courtesy of Mike Wells/Aspect Picture Library)

However, I am not entirely happy with the suggestion that the visual can persuade but cannot argue per se and so will pursue the investigation of how it argues further.

The tension that was identified within a single image can be made more obvious, and the argument made more explicit, if there is more than one image and if the differences between the images suggest contrast of a political kind. In the pair of images (Figure 6.4) , there is no need for words to make the comparison between the legs of the Pretty Polly advertisement and those of a starving Biafran man. It could be that these posters appeared alongside each other coincidentally in London, but whether they did or not, the analogy between them is stark and arresting. The fact that they are photographed together makes the tension between them more evident.

The next stage of visual representation would be the 'photo essay': the well-established genre in which a sequence of photographs carries the burden of an argument. In this genre, the narrative sequence is less important than the thematic unity of the series as a whole, though the Vygotsky-derived stages of concept formation, narrative development and argumentational structure (see Chapter 2) may be again useful in determining what stage of development a particular photo-essay has reached.

The fact that a photo-essay can argue a case is partly a result of the *number* of images, each one pinning down meaning via the context in which it is set (alongside other related images) and in which comparisons and contrasts are invited and with the narrative sequence coming into play, so

Figure 6.5 'Anyone for green tea?' (courtesy of Magimix)

that the principle *post hoc ergo propter hoc* is invoked. The range of possible interpretations is limited by the determining choice of the composer, who is providing more context, more definition, less of a floating image that can be interpreted at will.

So far, we have considered the verbal and the visual as separate modes and also looked at variations within the visual mode to gauge to what extent argumentation may be said to inhere and to what extent it may be said to be provided by the image(s) or suggested by them. What happens when the two modes are brought together? What kinds of argumentation, if any, are made possible?

The simplest place to start is with a relatively straightforward advertisement (Figure 6.5).

From the visual perspective, there are a number of features to note about this half-page advertisement: its black-and-white composition, in two distinct halves; its simple depiction of the product that is being advertised; the registered logo or graphic for the name 'Magimix' on the right hand side of the advertisement, balancing the photograph of the product on the left. All of these visual elements suggest simplicity and elegance of design: a minimal, functional and yet beautiful composition, so that the nature and intended (perhaps subliminal) effect of the advertisement reflects that of the product.

From the verbal perspective, the text is subtle. 'Anyone for *green* tea?' (my italics) suggests an audience that is a little more sophisticated than those who would simply not differentiate the kinds of tea they would drink. The website address on one side is balanced by the slogan 'Built better to last longer' on the other. The main textual presence is in the neatly boxed statement opposite the kettle:

> We've been designing products for over 30 years and we're constantly looking at ways to perfect them. Out latest creation is something special.

> The kettle's unique double wall jacket retains heat, so once you've boiled the kettle, any water left inside stays warm for longer. Which means, next time it's boiled you'll use less electricity, saving you money and helping save the environment. More tea anyone?

The verbal text appeals to potential buyers' senses of tradition ('for over 30 years') and continual improvement. The unique selling point is described ('the kettle's unique double wall jacket') and the fact that it might save you money *and* help the environment.

The aim is clearly persuasion: to persuade you to buy the product (and other Magimix products). How does the argument operate multimodally? First, I would suggest, by providing a design framework in which the eye can move from the catchy title ('Anyone for green tea?') to the image to the brand name, and range between these key points; then, by inviting the viewer to read the text that sits directly opposite and complementary to the image of the new kettle. There is work to do for the viewers, because they cannot see the inside of the kettle where the new feature is located, so they are invited to read about it. At the same time, the boxed nature of that verbal text is there to balance the simple visual image. A reader/viewer may take a different route through the reading of the advertisement, but the same principles of simplicity, elegance, comparison, balance, and minimalism apply. The argument resides in the whole advertisement and not just in the words or the image.

A more complex case of multimodalism is a composition by a masters-level photojournalism student for his final project, viewable at www.engladesh.com.

It is now commonplace for students on practice-based courses, at undergraduate or postgraduate level, to present a 'creative' or 'made' component in their final submissions. These are seen as the most important piece of work submitted for assessment and also as a final summation of the work on the course. They tend to be demanding of students' time, are highly wrought pieces of work, and often, as in the case of *Engladesh*, of high quality.

Engladesh is a documentary Web-based slideshow in sections, consisting of photographs, soundtrack with music and recordings from Bangladesh and London, voiceover narration by the composer, and graphics. It tells the story of 'Londonis' – Bangladeshi people of whatever generation who have moved to London. Crucially, it is the result of photographic and other research work in both Bangladesh and London, so there is a dialogic shuttling between the two places.

In multimodal terms, it uses the spoken, written, visual, and aural modes. There is always a visual presence, in the forms of photographs. Most of the time, these are accompanied by a soundtrack and, for much of the time, by a voiceover narration. The least used mode is the written word, but the title, section headings, credits, and some of the images contain words. Multimodal analysis would look at the affordances of each of these modes, plus the particular combination of the modes. My preoccupation in this chapter, however, is with the way in which *Engladesh* 'argues'.

Because the principal mode of communication is the visual, via photographic sequences, it is here that the argumentational analysis must begin. My analysis is necessarily interpretational, as there is no explicit argumentation.

The background title page has a photograph of silhouetted people, including children, under some telegraph wires. Against this background are foregounded three panels that contain images of the three 'stories' used to structure the work: stories loosely based on the characters of Habib, Wali, and Ayub.[1] Although the three panels are arrayed left to right along the foot of the title pages, and the Western reader/viewer is likely to read these from left to right, there is no compulsion to read them in that order. They could be viewed right to left or by starting in the middle. Immediately, then, we are in a position of being able to choose the route through the work; there is no determining argumentational line that takes us from A to B.

If we click on one of the panels, we are shown a sequence of images in a coherent narrative, accompanied by background music, contextual recordings from interviews and ambient sound, and voiceover. These individual stories are not much different from filmed (moving image) documentaries in their combination of modes and, like documentary films, they describe, depict, and argue a particular point of view (or a range of points of view). To take 'Ayub', for example, the sequence begins with two quotations in printed script: 'Bangladesh ranks 134 of 145 in the world corruption league table' and, seemingly connected on the *post hoc ergo propter hoc* principle, 'only because the vote was rigged'. These written statements set the tone and/or broadly define the theme of the sequence, which follows a returning Bangladeshi politician in his efforts to secure a political power base in his home country.

However, the stories in each section are not limited to a particular theme or to a particular character. Rather, they present a rich sequence of images depicting various aspects of Bangladeshi life. There are 59 images in the 'Ayub' sequence alone. It is these that are the core of the communicative experience: shot by the photographer and presented in sequence for the audience. The effect of having the images at the core of the artistic experience is to evoke and suggest arguments rather than to pin these down too closely.

If there is an argument for the work as a whole, it could be expressed as something such as 'We need to look more closely at Bangladeshi experience both in Bangladesh and in London, because the received assumptions on both sides – from Bangladesh and from London – must be re-examined'; or, to take a different angle, 'The dream that many Bangladeshis have, of a London-based paradise to which they aspire, is largely unfulfilled in practice'.

1 *Engladesh* has been updated since its first version, but this argument presented here still obtains.

Neither of these attempts at capturing the overall argument quite distils the effect of the whole artwork. The multimodal composition escapes neat abstract summary. Indeed, the interpretation of the argument is as much a matter for the viewer as for the composer.

Is 'argument' the right word to describe what is going on in the composition and reception of a work like *Engladesh*? In the eighteenth-century sense of the term, yes. The 'argument' for a chapter of *Gulliver's Travels*, for example, was the term for an abstract or summary of the narrative. In this sense, it laid out the skeleton of what was to be fleshed out in the full narrative of the chapter. In the case of *Engladesh*, the narrative in each of the three cases could be set out without ambiguity. This eighteenth-century view of an argument is not one to be discounted when thinking of argumentational power, in that the argument is carried in the bare bones of the narrative. However, it would not be fair to say that there is an overarching, abstract-able argument that could be stated in logical or quasi-logical terms in *Engladesh*. There could be a number of such arguments, depending on the viewpoints and sensibilities of the audience. The work does not pin down or state explicitly its argument, in this latter sense – nor does any work of art.

Deliberations about whether argumentation is the right term or concept to deal with multimodal creations is first a matter of considering alternatives. *Persuasion* is certainly taking place in all the foregoing works, most ostensibly in the advertisements. In *Engladesh* and in a single-image work, such as the photograph of Jean Shrimpton, persuasion is taking place in a general sense in that the photographer is using his or her art as a core communication tool to 'say something' to an audience. He or she wants the audience to be moved in some way, whether emotionally, politically, and/or intellectually. The desire for audience reaction is not paramount: the works could just as well satisfy the artistic drive of the composer and live in an archive without an audience, in which case the persuasion is self-directed, internal, enclosed. However, in being looked at by another, the work takes on a rhetorical meaning and function. Persuasion is, therefore, a term to describe a relationship between people, mediated by the semiotics of the photograph or photo-journalistic documentary. The *argument* in such works both sets up the persuasion and derives from it. Argument describes the lineaments of the work, sometimes embedded in narrative, sometimes explicitly stating its proposition(s) and providing evidence for them, sometimes operating somewhere between the two. In cases wherein multimodality is evident (i.e., in most cases), the foregrounding of one mode over another sets the level at which argumentation operates. If the burden of argumentation is carried in words, whether spoken or written, the potential for abstraction and logic is greater. If the burden is carried in music, ambient sound, or imagery, the affordances of those modes makes for a different kind of argument: one in which suggestion and interpretation are at the fore. It is a difference not so much of levels of abstraction as of the nature of the artwork. The framing of a piece – as in the documentary *Engladesh* – is artistic in that the work is highly framed. The audience is invited to enter the frame and then choose his or her route via a number of other frames and sub-frames (via 'Habib', for example, down to the individual images in that sequence). At each stage in the descent to particular images, one frame contextualizes and gives a particular kind of meaning to the next frame down; at the same time, each image in the sequence provides a resonance of its own that affects the reading of the work as a whole, permeating upward through the existing frames of the work. The same could be said for words, except that individual words are more concept-like in that they are already at a considerable stage of abstraction from the perceived world. It could be said that the verbal modes operate at a higher level of abstraction than images and that mathematical language (if it were used in these artworks) would be at a yet higher level of abstraction. The music that companies both words and images in *Engladesh*, because its constituent elements are rhythm, melody, harmony, and so on, seems to operate at a subliminal, emotional level – one that is not subject to abstraction.

In multimodal works, then, first it must be established what is the dominant or principal mode. The other modes can find their place in relation to the dominant one. Which is the dominant mode may be a matter for the composer or for the audience (or both) to decide. If there is no easily identifiable dominant mode, the *tensions* between two or more modes can be exploited by the composer and audience. The argument will lie somewhere on a scale from the inductive and suggestive at one end to the highly abstract and determined at the other.

Argumentation and Information and Communication Technologies in Higher Education

In a number of research studies over the past few years, Caroline Coffin, Ann Hewings, and others at the Open University in the United Kingdom have undertaken research on the relationship between argumentation on the one hand and ICT on the other, both at school level and in higher education. In the present book, the concentration is on higher education, though some of the studies based in schools and the pre-tertiary sector (e.g., Coffin, 2004, 2007; Coffin, North, & Martin, 2009; and Martin, Coffin, & North, 2007) are worth reading for the light they shed on practices in higher education.

For example, Painter, Coffin, and Hewings (2003), basing their study on three online tutorial groups as part of a distance MA in Applied Linguistics, found that whereas it is usually assumed that students have more freedom and more chance to interact with one another in online (synchronous and asynchronous) environments, it was the tutor's presence in managing the discussions that was often the key factor in the perceptions of the quality of interaction. The authors claim that the jury is out on the question of whether tutor presence is always effective. Their focus is primarily on the degree of argumentation that was evident in the students' work, both in online interaction and in written assignments that followed.

One overall perception was the striking absence of argumentation in online discussions. Instead, there was an emphasis on consensual discussion and an absence of conflict, heat, or even tension. Such consensuality was seen by the researchers as a need to provide a social glue to make the asynchronous discussions work and also perhaps as a result of the fact that most of the students were teachers and so would have been aware of the importance of online etiquette. In a sense, then, the discussion served to validate one another's views rather than challenge them or subject them to any kind of critique (a pattern seen also in school-based small-group discussion, wherein social cohesion of the group is seen to be more important than disinterested pursuit of ideas). However, the intervention of the tutor was one way in which argumentation could be kick-started, with challenges coming from him or her to the seemingly cosy consensuality. Questions like 'Why is this the case?' and 'Can you connect the previous statement you made to another's point of view?' generate causal or pre-causal links in the discussion, moving it gently toward argumentation. Indeed, the research found that the greater the degree of tutor intervention of this kind, the more likely chance was there to be argumentation and critical reflection.

Coffin, Painter, and Hewings (2005) 'aims to extend the research conducted to date' on computer-mediated communication and argumentation 'by drawing on notions of genre and generic staging developed within systemic functional linguistics (SFL) to focus on the character of argumentation within two electronic conference discussions located in a postgraduate module in applied linguistics' (p42). In particular, the study focused on the issue of how argumentation was structured 'and whether contextual variations such as tutor role and the design of the discussion task influenced the way in which different points of view were put forward and negotiated' (ibid.). The authors' review of research to date on the relationship between computer-mediated communication and argumentation comes to no clear conclusions other than the suggestion made earlier that it is more likely that argumentation thrives in face-to-face undergraduate and postgraduate discussions than in synchronous or asynchronous online discussions, because of the drive toward consensuality:

> It appears then that studies conducted to date are largely inconclusive as to whether CMC environments promote effective argumentation. One likely explanation for this is that it is not necessarily the medium (CMC) per se that promotes argumentation but rather the type of pedagogic activity engaged in within that medium. Another possible explanation for the disparity in the findings lies in the variation in

> the methods used for analysing argumentation, not all of which may be well adapted to illuminate the arguing process within a CMC environment. It is for this reason that we propose in this paper an alternative method of analysis.
>
> (p. 43)

Before discussing this alternative method of analysis, it is worth saying that consensuality need not be a condition in which argumentation is absent. Discussion can move toward consensus via argumentation, in which the moves made by the participants are more supportive, less challenging than would be the case in arguments that get their metaphorical modelling from conflict or debate (see Costello and Mitchell, 1995).

The authors refer to the same study as in Painter et al. (2003) discussed earlier but give a more through account of the methodology and in particular to the data analytical approaches:

> [W]e...applied a generic analysis to the data we had collected, considering each posting in terms of its overall purpose (or purposes), its structure and its linguistic characteristics. Where previously described genres or stages of argument were recognized, they were identified as such, and where the data required the recognition of additional elements, these were labelled according to their function.
>
> (p. 44)

This coding approach using applied linguistics techniques to examine the contributions made by participants on the online discussions revealed more in the data than the previous publication. Different kinds of argumentation – from claim and counter-claim to the positing and testing of hypotheses; from stating a proposition to confirming it and then expanding it (elucidation); and what the authors called 'reasoned observation', in which the speaker/writer argues with him- or herself – all appear in the transcripts. The important move forward that this paper provides is that it shows that while, on first appearance, a discussion carried out online between students may seem devoid of argument (and is usually given more argumentational shape and purpose by tutor intervention), there is a foundation of argumentational potential in such discussions. This may manifest itself informally, given the nature of small group discussion (whether computer-mediated or not) and thus be harder to analyze and perceive, but it is certainly there in the characteristics of the dialogue. Although the authors do not claim to be able to gauge whether the quality of argumentation is any better in computer-mediated or face-to-face contexts (such judgments would need criteria to be worked out in advance), they do suggest that there is enough promise in the mediation of argumentational talk and writing through computers (especially when tutors are engaged) to warrant further research.

In a later study based on the same population (masters students on a course in applied linguistics), Coffin and Hewings (2005) focus particularly on 'engagement'. Drawing the concept from systematic functional linguistics, they define engagement as 'the systems of semantic options available to speakers and writers for negotiating and adjusting the arguability of propositions and proposals' (p. 6). The advantage of such a concept is that it allows the researcher to see how students make initial engagements with argument: how they enter, find spaces for, and engage with argumentation during the course of academic discussion and writing. Six subcategories of engagement are posited and used to analyze the data from the students: endorsement, distancing, non-endorsement, proclaiming (expect), proclaiming (pronounce), and probabilizing. To explicate some of these categories: distancing involves a moving away from the claims or proposition made by another interlocutor and is seen as a discreet way *not* to agree with someone without actually saying so. Proclaiming (expect) with expectation is a category in which a proposition is put forward as a 'given', or as 'common sense' that would seem to require no questioning. Proclaiming (pronounce) conversely signifies an intervention in an argument wherein the position is clearly stated and is usually in counterpoint to what has just been stated, or builds upon it. Finally, probabilizing is a tentative mode of intervention whereby an idea is put forward as contingent and as one of a possible range of viewpoints.

These categories are useful in charting the ways in which students can engage in argumentation with their peers. Although the findings of the research projects undertaken by Coffin and her colleagues in the first part of the 2000s suggest that the quality of argumentation is enhanced when tutors manage and direct it, the seeds of online peer argumentation are evident and can be encouraged. What these studies show us is that there is potential for argumentation and that raising students' awareness of how argumentation operates can be helpful. They can use it to (a) engage more deeply and critically with dialogue in the classroom or in computer-mediated communication, (b) challenge one another's assumptions and positions without losing peer group solidarity, and (c) build bridges towards their written assignments, wherein they might use online discussion as evidence of arguments that have been put forward and learn the range of techniques themselves that might be transferred from speech to writing. In particular, the concern that many students have that argumentation is too critical, too 'negative', can be allayed by the introduction of tentative and provisional ways in which argument might be engaged. These more subtle forms of argumentation can stand as pedagogic ends in themselves, or they can be seen as stages on the way to more-explicit, more-challenging, and more-critical forms of argumentation. If the communities of argumentation are established early on so that the process is accepted and encouraged without there being personal or group fallout, the chances of developing higher orders of argumentational thinking are established. Indeed, based on the same data set, Hewings and Coffin (2007) investigate the transition from multi-party computer conferences to single-authored written assignments in more depth, looking particularly at the use of the pronouns 'I' and 'we' in academic writing by students.

Although the foregoing studies are all based on masters-level study, there is no reason why they might not also apply to undergraduate interaction via computer, as indeed they do to peer-group and teacher-led on- and off-line discussion in the pre- or post-university sector.

A fundamental distinction that needs to be made in the comparison of computer-mediated argumentation on the one hand and written argumentation on the other is the seemingly simple – but actually complex – distinction between informal oral genres and formal written genres in academic discourse. 'Dialogue' as it appears in computer-mediated exchanges usually appears in written form. The written dialogue, however, is informal and is characterized by the patterns that are evident in spoken interaction, with some key exceptions. In written online (synchronous and/or asynchronous) exchanges, there is more time for reflection, for the shaping of a response (this could, for example, be drafted and honed offline and then inserted into an online discussion) and for a relatively more formal pace at which dialogic exchange takes place. There is always the possibility for other voices to come online and to engage in the dialogue or, indeed, for some voices to cease to be part of a group exchange. There is also the possibility for interlocutors to refer back to what was 'said' (written) earlier in the exchange and thus to build on, or synthesize, or counter the direction of an argument.

This multi-voiced procedure – whether it is or is not further mediated by a tutor – is different from even relatively informal written assignments. The principal difference is that the written assignment is almost always the product of a single voice – that of the writer. He or she may, again, synthesize other voices into one voice, make quotations, refer to existing published or other works and, in a range of other ways, *incorporate* a wider range of voices into his or her work, but the fundamental fact remains that the single-voiced author is in control. He or she can therefore *marshal* the argument more fully than in a truly dialogic situation (speech or online conversation), putting more emphasis on structure, on the developing of a line or lines of argument and, perhaps crucially, building conceptual hierarchies into the argument via planning and the execution of such plans. In short then, an online argument is more likely to be accretive, associative, and lightly argumentational (in that it is important to preserve the cohesion of the group) than a written argument, which can be more hierarchical, relatively more logical in its exposition, and – if necessary – accentuate difference.

A new set of studies was initiated by Hewings, Coffin, and North at the Open University in the extensive report for the Higher Education Academy, *Supporting undergraduate students' acquisition of academic argumentation strategies through computer conferencing* (Hewings et al., 2007), undertaken at roughly the same time as the studies by Andrews et al. (2006b) and Torgerson et al. (2006), also for the Higher Education Academy, that provide some of the data for the present book.

The Open University study focused on one of its undergraduate distance-based courses, 'Perspectives on complementary and alternative medicine'. Using categories and approaches honed in the studies discussed earlier, the researchers found that online conferencing on this course was often marked by fewer explicit logical links than one would expect in written and/or formal argumentation and by a complexity of strands of argumentation, not all of which reached a conclusion. Preliminary analysis of written assignments deriving from the courses and from the computer conferencing suggested that the informal, inconclusive nature of argumentation in conferencing did not affect the more formal nature of the written assignments in that there was no clear bridge that could be described between the two forms of engagement. One of the conclusions of the report is that course designers and tutors – one could add students, too – might take advantage of the hybrid nature of computer conferencing in its position somewhere between speech and writing. They could, for example, exploit the informal, tentative, co-construction of knowledge, the reflective processes, and the more gentle challenges that come with the conferencing territory, building on these to posit more explicit and assertive propositions that in turn could be challenged and developed.

Conclusion

This chapter has tried, first, to separate multimodality from the impact of new ICT, though accepting that there is a degree of overlap between them brought about principally through the affordances of computer interfaces. It has then examined instances of work in various modes and of multimodal work to see where, and how, argumentation operates. It has teased out the relationship between argument and persuasion, seeing the first as operational and embedded in the work and the latter as a relationship between people. Finally, it has looked at a number of studies that examine the effect or impact of ICT on argumentation; and how argumentation interacts with such new technologies. We return to the question of multimodal argumentation in Chapter 12, wherein new directions for the study of argument in higher education are charted.

The Practical Dimension

Activity 6.1

Examine the regulations and guidance in your own department about the undergraduate or masters dissertation. To what extent do they give scope for multimodal argumentation? Does the guidance assume a writing-only approach? Is argumentation explicitly addressed and, if so, how? Do the regulations and guidance need to accommodate multimodality?

Activity 6.2

Look at the website www.engladesh.com – the work of a masters student in photojournalism who, at a university in London, gained a distinction – indeed a comment of 'beyond outstanding'. What attributes does the work have, and which of these pertain to argumentation?

7
Further Evidence from Research

This chapter refers initially to research previously completed by the author as part of a project for the Evidence for Policy and Practice Information and Coordination Centre. The work was collaborative, undertaken with Carole Torgerson, Graham Low, Nick McGuinn, and Alison Robinson, who are duly acknowledged (see p. iv). The project consisted of a systematic research review of argumentation at school level; the synthesized research is presented here to show where students who come into higher education might have come from in terms of argumentation; and what lessons could be learned from a close look at school practice. The bulk of the chapter looks at the implications of the report for higher education.

Argumentation at School Level: Lessons for Higher Education

What can research into argumentation at school level tell us about what comes before argumentation in higher education, and what can we learn from successful practices that might be adapted or carried over to higher education?

With colleagues at the University of York, I undertook a systematic research review in 2005 to 2006 to answer the research question 'What is the evidence for successful practice in teaching and learning with regard to non-fiction writing (specifically argumentational writing) for 7- to 14-year-olds?' using methodology designed by the Evidence for Policy and Practice Information and Coordinating Centre. The review was undertaken in collaboration with the UK government's Department for Education and Skills (Andrews et al., 2006a). A distilled, more critical version appeared as Andrews et al. (2009) in an article for the *Cambridge Journal of Education*.

In essence, results from the systematic review showed that certain conditions are either assumed or have to be in place to create a climate for successful practice. These were not specific to argumentational writing but included a writing process model in which students are encouraged to plan, draft, edit, and revise their writing (the kind of model proposed by Graves, 1983); self-motivation; some degree of cognitive reasoning training in addition to the natural cognitive development that takes place with maturation; peer collaboration, thus modelling a dialogue that might become internal and constitute 'thought'; and explicit and very clear explanations for students of the argumentational processes to be learned. These general conditions are important to mention, because, all too often, the background conditions for pedagogic change are *not* mentioned in research or in the implications of research for practice.

In addition to the general conditions, specific strategies were identified that have contributed to successful practice in teaching and learning with regard to argumentational writing for 7- to 14-year-olds. These included 'heuristics' (i.e. scaffolding of structures and devices that aid the composition of argumentational writing – in particular, planning that is extensive, elaborated, and hierarchical and can make for more effective argumentational drafting and completion of essays); the use of oral argument, counter-argument, and rebuttal to inform written argument; the identification of explicit goals (including audiences) for writing; teacher modelling of argumentational writing; and what some research reports call 'procedural facilitation' (i.e. coaching).

This is not the place for an extensive account of the research review that led to these results and, in any case, the results pertain to the 7- to 14-year age range. However, the implications of this study for this book need to be drawn out, in particular with regard to the transitions that students make (and have to make) as they move from primary/elementary education to secondary/high school; from high school to university/college; and from undergraduate courses to (post)graduate courses. My basic thesis here is that much remains the same from stage to stage but that the demands of argumentation increase and that new strategies and techniques have to be learned to meet the demands.

Implications for Higher Education

The 7- to 14-year-old literature review has a number of implications for practice in higher education. First, it should be noted that the conclusions of the review fall into two sections: the conditions that are assumed or have to be in place for the successful practice of argumentation and the heuristics or specific strategies that can be used to enhance argumentation.

Second, not all these indicators of good practice are operational in school education. Higher education cannot assume that students come to universities and colleges equipped with an understanding of the conditions necessary for argumentation and competence in the skills necessary for enhancing it. Far from it. However, knowing something of what students do bring from their previous experience is essential to educators in higher education. There are relatively few studies in the transition from school to college/university. Mitchell's work (e.g., 1992, 1994a, b; Mitchell and Andrews, 1994a, b) deriving from projects funded by the Leverhulme Trust in the 1990s in England is one exception.

Third, there are lessons to be learned from both the conditions that have to be in place and from the specific heuristics that might be employed.

Implications: The Conditions that Have to Be in Place

Of the five conditions just mentioned , we can perhaps take self-motivation for granted in higher education. That may be a dangerous assumption, because there are many students who enter higher education without such self-motivation. A learner who is not self-motivated is likely to be passive in learning style and approach. Such passivity is unlikely to lead to argumentation in speech or writing, because argumentation depends, to an extent, on taking a stand, the active marshalling of ideas from different sources, critical engagement, and a certain degree of abstraction. The unmotivated learner is also likely to produce merely expositional and/or descriptive work and so will not attain the higher grades that are awarded for argumentational skill in a subject. We must, however, distinguish between extrinsic and intrinsic self-motivation. The very term *self-motivation* suggests an intrinsic drive; however, in some cultures, self-motivation can derive as much from extrinsic (e.g. the desire to seek a particular grade, responding to parental encouragement and/or pressure) as from intrinsic motivation.

Of the other four conditions, each one has a particular bearing on and application in higher education.

The presence of a writing process model in which students are encouraged to plan, draft, edit, and revise their writing is helpful to argumentation. As is seen later in this chapter, hierarchical planning is an essential stage in forming a strong argument. It helps provide structure, direction, and relevance to the question in hand. Students in higher education will use a range of different planning techniques, according to purpose, but it is rare to see instruction or guidance in planning at college and university levels.

Drafting is a more common practice, especially since the advent of word-processing. Higher education institutions differ in relation to the attention lecturers and professors will give to student drafts. Some rule it out completely, expecting the student to submit an essay or other assignment with no input from the lecturer at all. Others offer to read one draft of a student's work, concentrating on matters of content, structure, and orientation. Yet others are more solicitous in also proofreading students' work prior to submission, especially if the students are working in a second language.

My view is that intervention by the lecturer during the process of composition is far more effective than providing feedback after the event. If a student's draft of an argument is wanting in any respect, changes can be suggested or questions asked about them, on the draft itself or in discussion with the student. Students are more likely to learn through intervention by the lecturer at this stage, as they have to consider the questions or suggestions and decide what to do about them. Experience suggests that once the assignment is formally submitted and assessed, it is the grade rather than any formative feedback that is the principal interest. Adoption of the writing process model does imply that students will edit and revise. Editing and revision at a deep level are, however, often missing if students decide merely to tinker with the composition. They might need support from writing centres in the processes of planning, drafting, editing, and revising their work to enable argumentation to have a firm basis in thinking and rethinking.

The close connection between composing and thinking leads us on to the second condition that the research review deemed to be necessary to successful in argumentation: some degree of cognitive reasoning training in addition to the natural cognitive development that takes place with maturation. Such cognitive reasoning training sometimes goes under the name of 'critical thinking' and, in its generic sense, it can take the form of de-contextualized heuristics in thinking. The critical thinking movement has its origins in philosophy for children (see Lipman, 1976) and a well-developed literature. Essentially it distinguishes itself from thinking via the addition of a reasoned, contestable, meta-aware dimension about how problems are conceived and addressed. Like many formulations with the prefix *critical* ('critical literacy' being another), critical thinking suggests a politicized, self-aware, reflexive activity. It is not discussed in detail in this book because it operates at a more abstract and generic level than argumentation, and it is not so closely bound to modes of expression and communication. Nevertheless, it is helpful to note that the literature review sees it as essential condition for successful argumentation.

The third condition is peer collaboration, thus modelling a dialogue that (it is hoped) will become internal and constitute 'thought'. This Vygotskian formulation is a particularly interesting one, as 'peer collaboration' can take various forms. What it refers to in the research literature is discussion between peers, either in pairs or small groups or in whole-group seminars chaired by the lecturer. Such dialogue, usually in speech, can indeed provide important ground for the development of thought and its subsequent expression in writing and in other forms. However, the translation from a lively, engaging, interactive and challenging discussion does not always translate so readily. The processes of transformation from the various voices of a face-to-face or online discussion are complex, but essentially they involve the distillation of a number of voices into one voice (that of the writer/composer) and reflection on which of the voices in an oral exchange gains precedence in the later, written version. Furthermore, whether the exchange of views in a peer dialogue constitutes 'thought', in due course, depends on the quality of the exchange.

The last condition, explicit and clear explanations for students of the processes to be learned, presents the lecturer with a challenge that is at the heart of this book. Can the learning processes in a particular subject or discipline be sufficiently articulated to make them helpful to students?

Consideration of this condition requires lecturers to first work out what the processes of learning – and more specifically of argumentation – actually are. Debate about these processes involves epistemological reflection, pedagogical issues, and consideration of the needs of the learners themselves. All too often, these processes are tacit or implicit. They are avoided or skirted or dealt with summarily and briefly in handbooks or in introductions to the discipline. To improve awareness on the part of students of the rules of the game in any particular subject/discipline, it is recommended that lecturers not only dig down as far as the epistemological level at the start of academic courses but return to epistemological and pedagogical issues throughout the course of study. The needs of individual learners can be addressed in tutorials and personal correspondence with students, and the time devoted to such engagement is highly appreciated by students. We look at the guidance given by some departments about the ground rules in their disciplines elsewhere in the book.

Implications: Specific Activities

Heuristics

The first practical recommendation from research since 1990 is for the use of 'heuristics' (i.e., devices that aid the development of argumentation, such as scaffolding, planning, and sequencing). These heuristics require a good deal of thought; indeed, it is at the planning stage of the composition of an argument that deep structural thought probably best takes place. Such thought is refined and developed later in the actual writing of sentences and paragraphs, but the early stage of planning the work in hand is crucial.

Plans can take various forms, so what is proposed here is a typical sequence of development. This sequence can be varied according to need.

Given any topic, an initial stage is *brainstorming*. This is where the topic is noted at the centre of a page (or at the top) and the brain is allowed to associate any idea or lead that seems relevant to the question or topic in hand. Such relatively open (but at the same time controlled and focused) brainstorming can reveal unexpected possibilities. Links between the various ideas may occur as the brainstorming takes place, or they could be made after it has taken place. The result will be a loose web of associations around a central topic.

The next stage is arranging the clusters of ideas, sources, and the like into a *pattern*. This is a crucial stage, because the patterning, although it needs to be formed into a sequence for the purposes of writing, need not fall into a sequence at this particular stage. Because the stages from brainstorming to sequencing are often short-circuited, the final sequence of the argument is often less impressive than it could be. An intuitive sequential structure, for example, that follows associative links rather than logical or quasi-logical ones

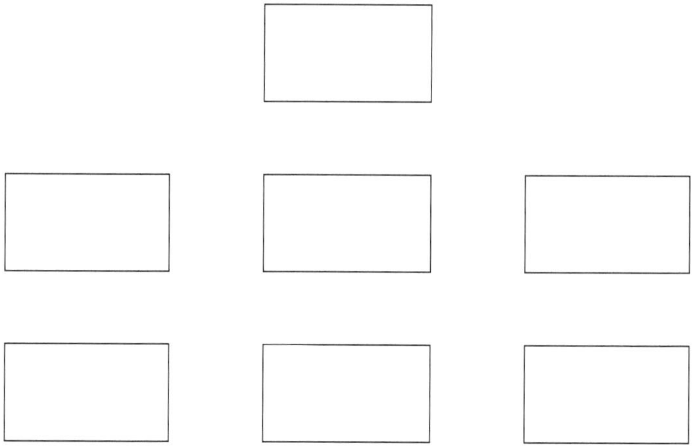

Figure 7.1 Hierarchical pattern

will make for a weaker argument – especially if the reader/audience cannot follow the intuitive path of the speaker/writer/composer.

One way to arrange the initial pattern is *hierarchically*. The following pattern (Figure 7.1) provides an example:

This pattern of seven clusters of ideas and/or data has a vertical dimension and a horizontal one. Indeed, the horizontal one is yet to be fully operational at this stage. We tend to think, metaphorically, of the proposition or claim or idea or thesis being at the top of such a diagram, because of its abstract, generalized nature. Equally, we think of grounds or data or evidence or sources as being at the foot of such a diagram, because they 'support' the claim. (Try reversing the hierarchy; it is possible to see claims supporting the interpretation of data.) What the three levels of phenomena indicate in the foregoing diagram is that there are often intermediary claims or intermediary kinds of data that bridge the gap between claims and data. These are not 'warrants', as such, in the Toulminian sense but are simply levels of generalization. More than one intermediary level can be built into a plan but, for the purposes of illustration, we will work with a three-tier plan for the moment. Figure 7.2 shows an example of how such a plan could work.

The clustering at intermediary level in this proto-plan is based on kinds of data, but the results gathered from the various types of data may suggest different points of view and thus become less methodological than substantial. For example, the data from documentary sources may suggest that there *is* a clear indication of an English literary heritage, even though the notions of such a heritage might be several and/or confused. The data from encounters with people and their opinions may suggest that there is no sense of an English literary heritage. Data gathered from observation may suggest the situation is somewhere between these two extremes. In other words, clustering of

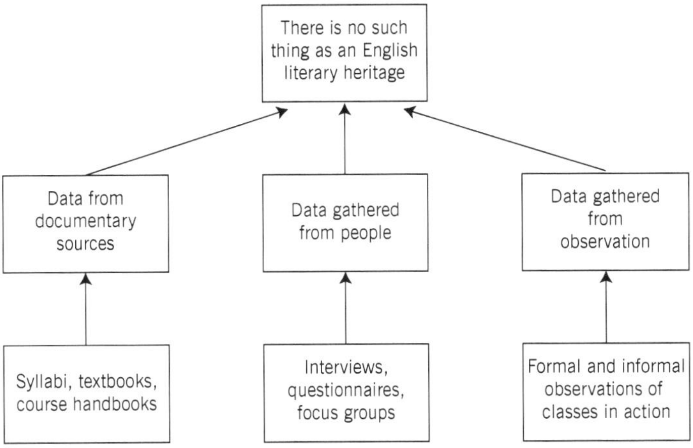

Figure 7.2 Example of hierarchical plan

a methodological kind might suggest clustering that provides substantial elements in an argument; and also provides matters of dispute, tension, and difference that can provide the basis of critical discussion.

Furthermore, such conceptual patterning can offer the writer or composer an obvious way in which to structure and paragraph the composition. Each of the foregoing boxes offers the possibility of at least one paragraph (building blocks in the construction of an argument).

When it comes to *sequencing*, there is more freedom than some of the classical rhetoricians allow. In the previous example, the sequence could be as in Figure 7.3.

It could be said that this skeletal argument is in nine parts: an introduction; three pairs of sections on different kinds of data (different approaches to addressing the question); a chapter on synthesizing the data sets; and a conclusion. There is no reason that the structure could not consist of seven sections, or five, by losing one or two of the pairs of sections – or an even number by dropping the synthesizing section and incorporating it in the conclusion. Somewhat hidden in the horizontal or sequential pattern of the final plan is the hierarchy (a more vertical structure) that was the result of the work of the second stage of the process. However, the presence of such a vertical patterning strengthens the structure and, therefore, the nature (and quality) of the argument as a whole.

The vertical structure gives organizational structure and clarity. It allows for a transparent and simple arrangement that benefits both the composer and the audience. It also does more than that: it provides more space for criticality. Being critical, as we have seen elsewhere in the book, is one of the essential criteria for successful argumentational writing at the higher education level. The vertical spaces between the various elements are where connections of

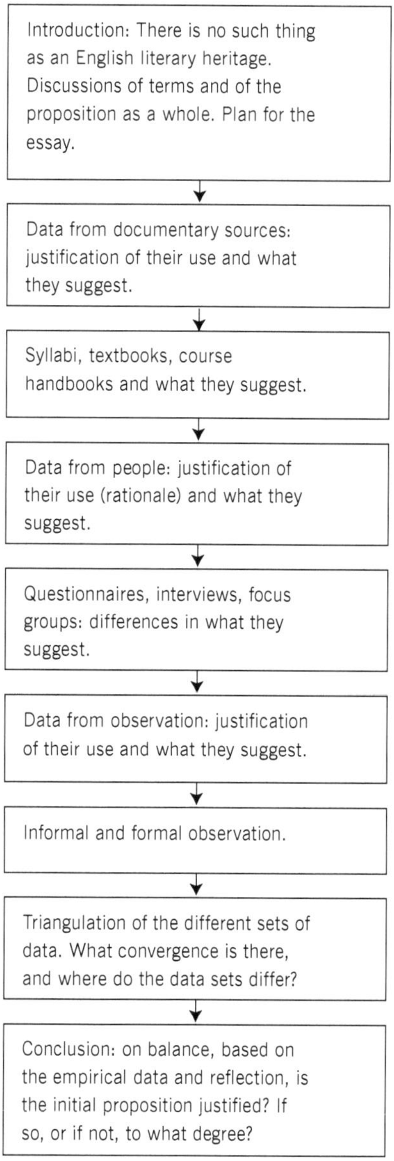

Figure 7.3 Sequencing

category are made. In the foregoing example, it is assumed that data from documentary sources are going to be relevant in debating the question of the English literary heritage. However, that assumption (or 'warrant', to use Toulmin's term) can be challenged. Facing such a challenge is grist to the critical mill, in which nothing is taken for granted and the sceptical spirit is at play. Setting up such spaces, through the very design of the argument at

Figure 7.4 3 + 1 sequencing

Figure 7.5 1 + 3 sequencing

a macro-level, thus opens up more spaces for criticality and more chance of success in the composition.

Toulmin's model, in which a warrant is required to justify the link between a proposition or claim on the one hand and data or grounds on the other, can, therefore, be applied in a limited sense to connections between parts of an argument. By asking the question 'What enables us to make the connection between a claim at a particular level of abstraction and the evidence supporting that claim?' we bring in a dimension to the business of writing essays and academic assignments that increases the quality of argument.

The three-level hierarchical plan, as previously outlined, is just one of the patterns that can be used to map out the structure of an argument – or part of an argument. Consider the following, all of which suggest different configurations of argument (Figure 7.4) and all of which can be used to work out what is the best pattern for the particular (part of an) argument in hand.

In this pattern, one cluster of ideas or data is separated from the others, to suggest difference and possibly contrast. This pattern can be useful for suggesting that either the majority cluster is the position to take and the outrider is an aberration or, conversely, that the distinctiveness of the outrider is a position worth considering seriously in opposition to that of the majority. This particular pattern can easily be reversed (Figure 7.5), when it comes to sequential structuring, for rhetorical purposes.

When two different positions are set up in contrast to each other, elements of hierarchical patterning can be used to make comparisons between how the hierarchies work. In this case, not only are the proposition and evidence weighed against each other but the interconnecting warrants and backing can be compared, too. This basic pattern is particularly useful if there are two seemingly exclusive sets of arguments that need to be compared (Figure 7.6).

There are other patterns that can be generated; and those here may be developed further, combined, and adapted to particular purposes.

Yoshimi (2004) focuses on whole arguments in discourse rather than on systems or principles of argumentation. His model provides a useful alternative method of tracking the shape and derivation of arguments,

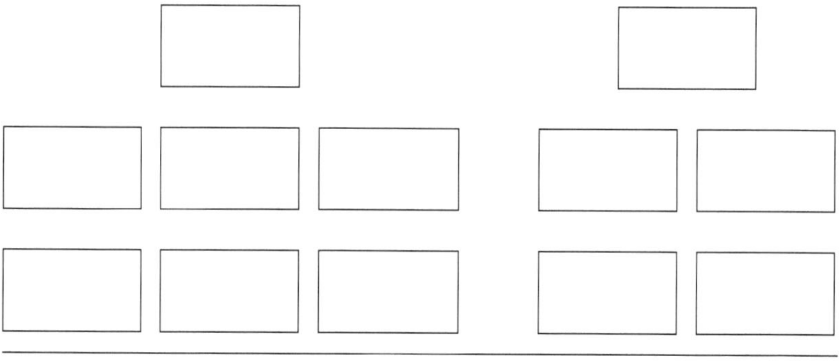

Figure 7.6 Combination of hierarchical and sequential structures

whether in speech, writing, or other modes. What is interesting and useful about Yoshimi's 'rooted digraph trees' model is that it graphically displays the blocks or boxes via which an argument can be constructed, but it also gives freedom to the composer/writer to vary the length of strands of sub-arguments; to include any number of strands; and to see what the particular basis is for any of the strands.

There is an organic feel about the structure. There is none of the hierarchical structuring that has been mentioned earlier in this chapter in the research on 7- to 14-year-olds' writing. Nor is there any highly developed sense of different functions of aspects of an argument, as in Toulmin's work. Rather, what we are offered (more like the work of Kaufer and Geisler) is a compositional tool. Such a tool may be very useful in the stage between brainstorming the ideas for a piece of argumentational composition on the one hand and mapping out the sub-strands or the elements of the argument on the other. To date in the book, there has been no mention of sub-strands. Yoshimi's work provides the possibility of seeing argument as being composed of a series of strands, not necessarily logically connected. If the diagrams were turned 90 degrees, with the claim or proposition at the top, we would see that the sub-strands appear like tentacles or roots, providing sustenance and support for the main proposition.

The other advantage of Yoshimi's model is that logical and quasi-logical connections between boxes on any particular strand can be critiqued by simply reading *against* the direction of the sub-arguments. Any one of the articulations can be questioned and critiqued (Figures 7.7 to 7.9).

The Use of Oral Argument, Counter-Argument and Rebuttal

The use of techniques from oral argument to inform written argument is underplayed, though it is not without difficulties. The principal means of assessment in higher education is via written assignment or examination. Oral assessment still only plays a minor part, on the whole.

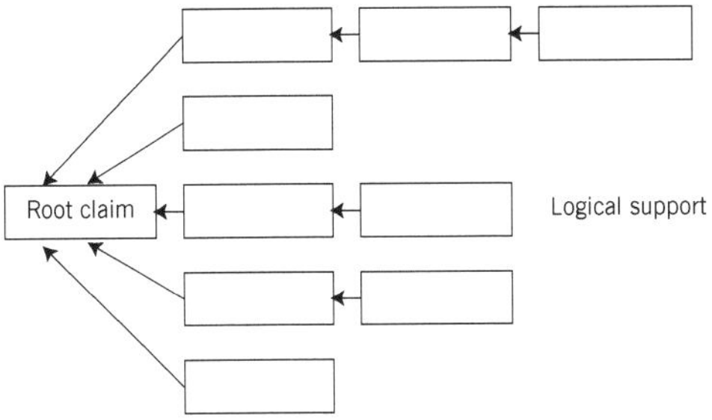

Figure 7.7 Structure of debate, represented by 'rooted digraph trees' (1) (Yoshimi 2004, reprinted with permission)

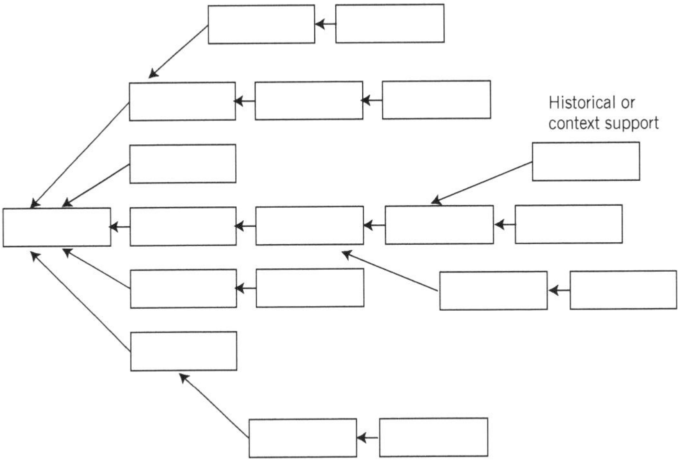

Figure 7.8 Structure of debate, represented by 'rooted digraph trees' (2) (Yoshimi 2004, reprinted with permission)

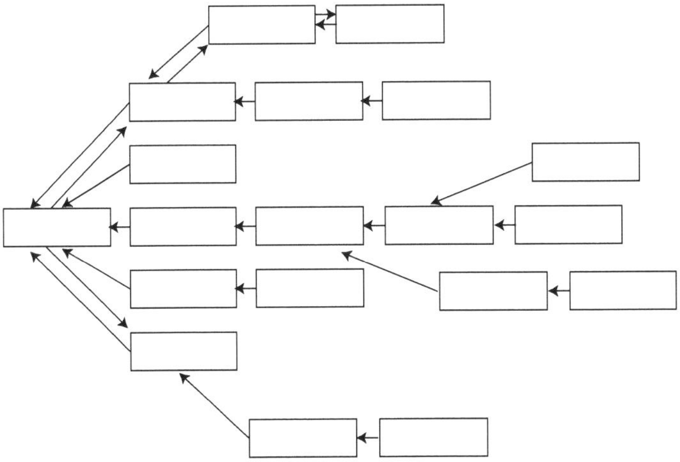

Figure 7.9 Structure of debate, represented by 'rooted digraph trees' – how to represent counter-argument/debate (Yoshimi 2004, reprinted with permission)

It is not always the case that a good oral argument – say in a seminar or discussion – translates neatly into a good written argument. Indeed, it is often the case that those who are good at arguing orally are not so good at putting the argument in writing and vice-versa. Nevertheless, rehearsal of an argument in speech before committing it to paper can raise some of the issues that need to be addressed in writing. Furthermore, the largely dialogic mode of speech can translate into dialogic forms of writing. Such forms of writing might remain below the surface in a largely monologic piece of writing, or they might rise to the surface where the writing is more obviously dialogic. One of the advantages of oral rehearsal of an argument is that the nature of dialogic exchange can provide counterarguments or rebuttals to a particular proposition that is being formulated.

As mentioned in Chapter 4, the article by Larson et al. (2004), 'Disfluencies in comprehending argumentative texts', is an account of a study of 79 native English-speaking introductory-level psychology students at Northern Illinois University. The study found that the students were

> not proficient comprehenders of natural, written arguments. They identified only about one-third of the main claims and reasons, they selected reasons that could not possibly support their stated claim, and they often identified a stated counter-claim as the main claim.
>
> (p. 220)

The results showed that the students were aided by a brief tutorial that explained the process of argument comprehension 'as long as they were not given the task of reading to rebut' (ibid.) Students did not always know that an argument can begin with a counter-argument.

This is an interesting set of findings. First, there is the problem of identifying the claim or proposition that is the keystone of the argument. If that cannot be readily identified (and, admittedly, it isn't always clear in writing what the main claim is), it is very hard to proceed with understanding the nature or flow of the argument presented. Second, the students 'selected reasons that could not possibly support their stated claim': in other words, the connections between claims and evidence were not clear to the readers, so they made inappropriate connections, Third, 'they often identified a stated counter-claim as the main claim'. Put together with the reluctance to rebut, the fact that students did not always know that an argument can begin with a counter-argument and the confusion between claims and counter-claims make the whole process of reading (and by implication, composing) argument very difficult.

Some training in reading against the grain of a supposed argument would help alleviate the problem and produce sounder and rhetorically more polished arguments. If we go back to the Yoshimi model (Figures 7.7 to 7.9), we can run the arrows in the opposite direction to the flow of the argument at any point to test the validity of the connection being made. This process of reading against the grain has much in common with Toulmin's notion of 'rebuttal' in which the connection between the claims and the grounds is challenged. It could also be the case that rebuttals could enter the Toulmin model at any point: there could be challenges to the very conception of the claim; challenges to the nature and validity of the evidence itself; and a direct challenge to the backing (set of values, *mores*, disciplinary *habitus*, and conventions) and to the way the warrant works. Those who are used to debating orally will know the techniques of attacking your opponents at the weakest places in their arguments. Conversely, in terms of defence, debaters need to know their weak points so that they can acknowledge them, strengthen them, or shore up an argument against a challenge.

Explicit Goals, Teacher Modelling and Coaching

The last three practical ideas identified from the systematic review for helping to improve the quality of argumentational composition can be grouped together, as they are concerned with the way the teacher or lecturer relates to the students. Of the three, we can take the use of explicit goals and coaching as part of the general pedagogic repertoire. They are important, and though they enhance argumentational competence, they also apply to other forms of learning. Rather, this section concentrates on teacher modelling.

The modelling of argumentational writing by teachers is rare. Despite the writing process movement in schools and higher education, teachers and lecturers spend little time taking students through the processes of their own writing in a particular genre or meta-genre. The advantages of such modelling are considerable: students see a teacher grappling with a problem that they have set; they see how the teacher solves particular compositional problems; they see a sequential process in action; they are going to be interested to see what solutions the teaches comes up with and how his or her argument develops; and, not least, they are going to be interested personally in the substance of the argument the teacher puts forward.

Disadvantages include showing only one way in which an argument can develop (this can be avoided by offering and exploring alternatives during the modelling process) and a tendency toward the primitive pedagogy of *progymnasmata*, wherein a rule is set out, and a genre is modelled through a typical example and then is imitated by the students. The danger in both these tendencies is that the student becomes a passive recipient of 'teaching' that has little bearing on their practice.

In general, though, there is space for more modelling of the *processes* of composing argument so that students can use the tools and approaches for their own ends and as liberating structures in the construction of their own personal knowledge.

Transitions in Education: How Does Argument Change?

Much of this chapter has been concerned with the implications of research into school-level argumentational writing. The concentration has been on commonalities between approaches to argument at the various stages of education, from teaching for 7-year-olds up to university level education. Before turning to the characteristics of argumentation at the various stages, it is worth reinforcing the point that many of the approaches to teaching and learning argumentational writing and composition *are* generic and common to the different stages.

However, arguing is not the same for 7- to 11-year-olds as it is for 11- to 14-year-olds. Again, it is different for 14- to 16-year-olds, for 16- to 18-year-olds, and for undergraduates and postgraduates (further differentiated as masters level and doctoral level students). What are the characteristics of argumentation at each stage and how do students build on one stage as they grapple with the next one?

7 to 11 Years

Approaches to argumentation at this stage are divided between those who follow a largely Piagetian or neo-Piagetian line on the one hand and those who follow a Vygotskian line on the other. Essentially, the first camp sees argumentation developing slowly and in a proto-argument stage, from 'concrete operations' (cf. William Carlos Williams's maxim of 'all ideas in things') toward – but not reaching – the 'formal operations' stage. Argument from this point of view is hardly possible but proceeds as best it can without the ability to move from one abstract concept to another. The thinking processes are largely inductive. The second camp sees argumentation as part of everyday discourse, the structure of which is embodied via 'inner speech' to thought. The movement is from the outside to the inside, as it were, using dialogic structures to inform the shape of argumentational thinking. Vygotskian approaches to argumentation, though not stated as such, would be neither deductive nor inductive: the relationship between things and ideas is there in the theory of concept formation but, in terms of everyday discourse and the way it shapes thought, the main process is one of an interaction between society and the individual. Society is seen to shape the individual mind more than the individual's shaping society. There is plenty of scope for argumentation in this phase, as indicated in Andrews and Costello (1992) and Andrews, Costello, and Clarke (1993).

11 to 14 Years

Though the specific stages laid out here do not necessarily correspond with the way educational provision is organized in different countries, it is possible to say that around the age of 11, pupils do tend to move to middle or high schools in the expectation that a different cognitive stage has been reached; that 'subjects' begin to come to the fore, thus carving up the curriculum epistemologically; and that classrooms may begin to look different, reflecting different approaches to pedagogy. Piagetians would say this is the stage at which logical operations begin to have an impact on the way thinking takes place. The implications for argumentation would be that no longer would research 'swim around' a topic but that logical abstract connections might be made between ideas. Along with this movement to abstraction, the emergence of particular written and multimodal genres, such as the critical book review, the multimodal advertisement, and the comparative essay, differentiates the field of composition. There is thus a two-way movement that makes for interesting tensions and challenging learning experiences: toward abstraction at higher levels of thought and simultaneously (and more laterally) toward increasing differentiation between genres.

14 to 16 Years

In the English educational context at least, and in other countries where there are public examinations at 16 or 17 years of age, the external pressures of assessment begin to test students' bodies of knowledge. The increasing definition between subjects reflects an increasing influence of epistemological shaping on the curriculum. It is at this stage that the formal ways of setting out scientific experiments, or the ways in which evidence and propositions are related in the study of literature, begin to be marked out. It can still be said, at this stage, that the genres that are promulgated, expected, and assessed are *school genres*; that is to say, they are forms of argumentation that are required by the school and the public examination system as it tries to differentiate between students. This is also the stage at which is becomes clearer which subjects encourage and develop argumentation and which see it as an aspect of a higher level of thinking that has not yet been reached. It is too crude to say that the more bulk that is expected of students, the less they are likely to be asked to argue, but there may be a connection between the development of argumentation and thinking on the one hand and the proliferation of material on the other that does not value thinking as much as accumulation of knowledge.

Criteria for the marking of essays and other works by teachers and examination boards will reflect the degree to which argument is valued. If part of the purpose of a public examination system is to differentiate, it may well be that the ability to argue is one of the most telling ways in which such differentiation is demarcated.

16 to 18 Years

This appears to be the phase of critical importance for development. Whether a student is going on to higher education after this phase or developing skills for use in the world of work (or both), there is added emphasis in 16- to 18-year-olds' curricula on argumentation. In England, A-level examinations continue to have a strong hold on this phase of education and are one of the most specialized systems in the world. Some students take as few as two or three subjects (most now take four in the first of two years) of their own choice. Although they are not called disciplines as such, the beginnings of disciplinary convention come into play. Teachers are keen to get the highest standards in work from students, and the essay establishes itself in the humanities and social sciences as the defining genre. The predominance of the essay is such that, at times, it seems to over-dominate. Students are set several essays a week, each of which takes a good deal of research, structuring, and execution. The default nature of the essay means that it becomes a genre with which one must gain fluency; it is used as a catch-all for the development and production of knowledge. Such centrality to the business of learning and assessment in this phase can mean a great deal of pressure for students.

The genre largely remains unspoken and unquestioned, however. Marking by teachers tends to be on the subject, not on the way in which knowledge about the subject is expressed or articulated.

In educational systems where there is more breadth, there is more chance of variation in the text-types that are used. A student taking a typical baccalaureate in Europe would cover science, philosophy, literature and the arts, and mathematics. Such a breadth of learning does not necessarily require a breadth of genres in which to write, but it is generally the case that such a breadth exists. The epistemological pressure from below tends to produce a range of genres: reports, short prose answers, letters, reflective logs, and the conventional essay.

Undergraduate Education

Much of this book is about argumentation in undergraduate education, so all that needs repeating here is that the entry into disciplinary practices is perhaps the key shift at this level. Where that entry is deferred, as in the United States wherein the first two years of an undergraduate education are often more broad-based, the compensating preparatory work of rhetoric and composition classes is undertaken. However, movement into the disciplines does require an understanding of the discourses that operate in different fields and an ability to move across fields (or, at least, step outside them so that it is clear what the nature of the discourses are).

In this section, the focus is on the transition from school to university. First-year students bring with them to university a knowledge of a way of working. Like riding a bike, it does not seem to be a body of knowledge or even a set of skills; it has been absorbed into the individuals' mental systems during the process of education. Many students will carry this set of skills right through their university years, never developing it further. Even the most highly equipped students, in terms of study skills and a predilection for learning, may take weeks or even months to get used to what is expected at university level, if it is not made explicit at the start of the course and again a few months later when the students are used to the conventions of the course, their lecturers, and the university. The crucial questions are what counts as knowledge in a particular discipline? What is the position a student should take in relation to a body of knowledge: deferential, critical, or a mixture of both? More pragmatically, what styles of composition gain most marks?

It can be a difficult transition if the student does less well at university than he or she did at school. Yet it is almost inevitable that the student *will* do less well, as is discussed elsewhere in the book, because of the notion of starting with a *tabula rasa*. There is no scope for 'improvement' in grade terms if a student starts at the top: from that position, there is nowhere to go but down, and such a trajectory does not feel right or is not in the best interests of the student. So a combination of factors – the new discourses of increasingly specialized disciplines, a pressure to move from a low start to a better grade, and increasing independence of the learner – all conspire to make for a less intense experience than the previous phase but nevertheless a fairly steady ascent up the discoursal mountain.

Postgraduate Education

Under 'postgraduate' or 'graduate' education, I include masters-level and doctoral studies. There is less difference between the two than between under- and postgraduate, especially as at doctoral level there has been a proliferation of types of doctorate in the twentieth century, many of them incorporating more teaching and more coursework than implied by the conventional PhD degree.

What appears to distinguish postgraduate education is increasing specialization. Such specialization will require its own forms of discourse, its own conventions, its own forms of expression and articulation. In terms of argumentation, there is more emphasis on argument itself, with the lineaments of argumentation being required to be shown. A potential irony and tension here is that, as students are expected to show increasing originality and even a contribution to public knowledge, the forms in which they are asked to do are increasingly conservative. Only where there are enlightened practices in higher education and where the lecturers or gatekeepers of knowledge have thought about the possibilities of *how* new knowledge might be expressed does new rhetorical space open up for students. However, the exploitation of new rhetorical space is a risk, and one that must be taken carefully with research supervisees or others who wish to push the boundaries. Such students must be encouraged to push boundaries but must be guided by lecturers to ensure that the students do not suffer for their cause by a loss of grades.

It is at this level, and beyond, that new forms of doctorate, discussed later in the book, are important.

The Practical Dimension

Activity 7.1

Attempts at simple structuring and restructuring were suggested at the end of Chapter 3. In this chapter, they are taken further. Build on these experiments in structuring to create your own patterns for argumentation in your own disciplines or subjects. You can use a set of picture postcards, as in the example suggested in Chapter 3, or work this time with abstract propositions and evidence. Try building arguments like those depicted by Yoshimi, or design some new structures.

Activity 7.2

The systematic research review is a genre with particular techniques associated with it and is undertaken by small teams. You might wish to undertake a current research review with colleagues in your own team on a topic you are teaching or a research bid or article you are writing together. See Torgerson's *Systematic Reviews* (2003) for a short but comprehensive and authoritative guide on the approach.

8
Students' Views on Argumentation

Undergraduate students have their own views on argumentation and its place in their discipline and in higher education more widely. This chapter reports on an empirical study in which first-year education studies undergraduates interviewed other undergraduates in a range of disciplines. There is remarkable commitment to understanding the function of argument but also a strong sense among students that argument is not addressed – or made explicit by – lecturers. It is a hidden 'rule of the game' that students need to know more about. Furthermore, the reemerging issue of 'student voice' in further and higher education is one that needs to be borne in mind in negotiating how, where, and why argumentation takes place.

Students Interviewing Other Students

Four months after they had started an interdisciplinary programme in educational studies, I asked a class of undergraduates to interview one another – or someone else they knew – on what argumentation meant in their subjects, if it meant anything, and how it was manifested and taught. We had explored some of the basics of argument and also reflected upon the different demands of the last years of schooling and the first of university education. The interesting thing about this group as far as argumentation was concerned was that they were taking the course in educational studies as a subsidiary subject in a combined degree. Their principal disciplines included geography, psychology, chemistry, literature, medicine, mathematics, archaeology, politics, physics, environmental science, sociology, biology, writing and performance, social policy, and history of art. Students were asked to reflect on the recordings of their interviews with one another and then to write a summary of one page or so on the interview.

In geography, for example, argumentation was seen as central to the course.

> However, even with this being the case, it appears that at the beginning of the course no sessions were set aside to help students learn how to write a good essay…in fact the student's knowledge on how to make a good argument had carried on from the student's previous knowledge on the matter.

It is not clear how that 'previous knowledge' had been acquired – whether it was imbibed as part of the pre-university courses for 16- to 18-year-olds or whether there was explicit instruction on 'how to make a good argument'. This geography student saw two ways in which argumentation could be learned at university level: from discussions with peers, in which a range of different ways of presenting ideas would be experienced, and from written and oral feedback on assignments.

Written and oral feedback were also mentioned by a psychology student. She had read psychology journals before starting the degree course to see how best to write in the field, and such reading had also given her experience in reading and comprehending research in psychology. She acknowledged the importance of argument in her studies and in the presentations and assignments that she was required to produce. On the nature of evidence, she said that it was just as important to find evidence to counter your own hypothesis or position as it was to support it and that counter-evidence often led to better hypotheses, better arguments.

A chemistry student saw argument differently. First, he saw it as a series of (often, empirical) facts used to prove a point and, second, as a technique via which to undermine an opponent's argument. Acknowledging that the subject is more fact- and logic-based than humanities or arts subjects, this student felt that argument is used in chemistry to prove theories and processes 'to be exact, instead of arguing an interpretation of certain events or a certain critical hypothesis'. Because much of the work is based on theories that are unproven, the work of the student is to find evidence for or against the theories to improve them. 'Evidence', in this case, might be in the form of mathematical or symbolic means in the interests of succinctness and clarity. This student also felt that argument was enjoyable because it was useful in revealing 'weak arguments and incorrect reasoning in his own and others' work', thus providing a form of learning in the subject. There is a more in-depth study of this chemistry student's work further on.

Learning from others was also the tenor of a student from history of art, who found that not only in academic groups but in galleries and museums the justification of a position by a presenter was a very useful and illuminating practice for her to observe and that such skills were needed by her to make presentations within her own course. She believed that the way the classes were structured, with frequent presentations by students, encouraged her to learn from others and to develop her own argumentational skills but that she could improve faster through a slightly more formalized expression of argument, as in debates. Interestingly, she also felt that whereas argumentation was not quite so central to history of art as to history, the interpretive character of history of art 'can be easily developed into an argument which needs developing in several ways'.

Other views from a range of other disciplines were that, in archaeology, for example, it is important to learn to argue 'because so many things are open to interpretation and there is never one answer' and that although it did not appear to be part of formal teaching, it was a vital part of the discipline. In physics, the structure of argumentation usually took the form of making a statement and then proving it was true using scientific evidence to ensure the reader or audience can also believe it to be true; that evidence was largely through 'mathematical and symbolic means, figures proving that experiments conducted were 'good science''. A student from environmental science expressed the view that unlike a subject such as history, wherein the argument is based on events that have occurred and are compared and contrasted with the input of personal perspective (no doubt informed by belief and value systems), science subjects seemed to be based on observable factors. According to this student, the argument in science subjects seemed to be concerned with justifying methods and explaining why certain statistical tests were better than others for particular purposes. Another student from environmental science, however, expressed the view that argument is mainly utilized in the discipline to put forward new theories or claims and that 'primary, secondary or tertiary evidence is often used to compare current trends with previous hypotheses in order to counteract the detriments of preceding theories with the advantages of the new'.

Whereas much of the rest of the book is concerned with in-depth analysis of argumentation in education, history, electronics, and biology, here we concentrate on argumentation in a medical course, in mathematics, in psychology, in politics, in literature study, in nursing, and finally in chemistry.

Case Study 1: Argumentation in a Medical Course[1]

In this case, the summary of the interview on argument is presented in full, both to give a flavour of the way the students approached argumentation, interviewing and summary in general, but also to provide insight into a particular case: that of an undergraduate medical course.

> The medical course…is based on training for a future career as a doctor. In this way, whilst undergraduates are not expected to research cures themselves by conducting experiments, they are constantly asked to make judgements on various illnesses, and back up their diagnosis with logical reasons.
>
> A doctor has to deal with life and death situations, and so it is imperative that they are properly trained to make quick decisions as to which route to take. There may be a variety of possible courses, and they need to be able to have these skills to justify to other doctors who may not agree, giving informed reasons to back up their proposed theory.

1 Case study authors are thanked in the acknowledgements section.

> You can 'prove nothing in science', but there is a generally accepted method of action that accompanies a particular sequence of symptoms that they call a 'protocol'. It is the identifying and differentiating between very similar symptoms that proves difficult, as there may be a vastly different set of diagnoses from similar symptoms.
>
> The course…values the training of how to reach these judgements very highly, and much of the course involves class discussions (problem based learning), practical experience ('clinical placements' and 'clinical skills'), and essays. In these a student must write on a particular chosen subject, demonstrating different theories from a field of enquiry and discussing arguments fairly and with justifications…
>
> At times they have to write essays like 'Are pharmaceutical companies our friends or enemies?' Although this would involve an in-depth study to see if they would benefit (or otherwise), it is also a student's particular morals and beliefs that count in these circumstances. They would defend their decision with evidence and 'logical' statements, and show a clear pattern to their reason.
>
> Many of the arguments made in medicine are from 'ruling out' other possibilities and seeing what you are left with. The extreme variety of diseases that there are, mean that there is always going to be arguing involved.

There is much to discuss here in terms of argumentation. The first point to note is that undergraduate medical education is no longer just a matter of clinical training but has moved to a paradigm in which making judgments, communicating them to patients, and taking appropriate action are at the heart of the training. Second, the making of judgments and decisions often has to take place quickly, in a pressured situation. Such pressure makes it all the more important that judgments are made on the basis of sound evidence and appropriate hypotheses; if such judgments become intuitive for experienced doctors, they are nevertheless based on high-speed reasoning. Third, it appears that in medical education, as in other fields, arguments are rehearsed and demonstrated to fellow students and lecturers in essay form (and in presentations, most probably, though these are not mentioned). Whereas the essays are more obviously addressing controversial topics, such as 'Are pharmaceutical companies our friends or enemies?', the machinery of argument is brought to the surface, and the argument takes on the form of formal debate or a written version of debate (the 'for-and-against' model). There is an analogy here with practice in biology, for example, where issues about the environment (climate change, pollution, biodiversity, etc.) are raised to ask students to marshal scientific evidence in support of a position. Questions of ethics are raised in such debates, providing another dimension for argumentation in undergraduate science and medical education. It is interesting, too, that the foregoing case study makes the point that 'it is also a student's particular morals and beliefs that count in these circumstances'. The classical rhetoricians knew this, and the moral dimension of argumentation is present in Toulmin's model in the 'backing' that underpins the warrants that connect claims to grounds.

Case Study 2: Argumentation in Mathematics

One of the early definitions of argument, now largely obsolete, is from mathematics and astronomy: 'the angle, arc, or other mathematical quantity, from which another required quantity can be deduced, or on which its calculation depends'. The spatial, navigational aspect of the calculations of angles and arcs is not unrelated to the movement and progress of argument in the Hegelian model of thesis, antithesis, and synthesis, but it is another early (Aristotelian) definition of argument as 'proof' that seems to be at the heart of contemporary mathematics, at least at undergraduate level. Argumentation was seen as important by the undergraduate interviewed in the multi-disciplinary class, because of its attempt to prove or disprove a mathematical statement. According to this student, to argue is to attempt to prove, and looking at how other arguments have been proved and studying the methodology ('showing the working' in school parlance) helps to improve argumentational skills in the discipline. For mathematicians, such proof is not a matter of opinion or belief (although none of the students interviewed wished to go down to deep epistemological or culturally informed levels to ask why such proofs worked) but a matter of accuracy: 'Mathematically, arguments are very clear, because in order for something to be true mathematically, it must be 100% true'. Calculation in mathematics is seen to be arguing toward a solution, so that '3+4' is an argument the solution of which is '7'. In other words, what appears on either side of an = sign must balance, and such a process of balancing on either side constitutes an argument.

The emphasis on mathematics appears to be more on proof than on disproof, perhaps because there is the operation of two different languages at play: verbal language, largely for discussing and justifying; and mathematical languages (numbers, algebra, etc.) that are the core abstract languages of the discipline. If proof and disproof take place in one 'code', there is more room for slippery logic because the code itself is being used to prove the point. When another code is used, it is less likely that one can be used to prove or disprove the other, as a degree of outside perspective is added. The student interviewed suggested that he used argumentation 'to prove existing theories' as at introductory undergraduate level, the skills needed to create new theories were not taught. To quote from the student summary of the interview with the mathematics student:

> 'Proving your own theory requires rigorous mathematical proof', and so students are asked to present proofs for existing theory 'from already existing known facts or by showing that the opposite is not possible' as a way of testing knowledge learnt. This is sometimes done through oral presentations, which may have a peer of lecturer response. Although there may be an opportunity for a question and answer session following a student presentation, this would simply be to ask about something that maybe wasn't understood.

In other words, discussion between students at the early stages of a mathematics undergraduate course is largely expositional and clarificatory.

Case Study 3: Argumentation in Psychology

In the following account of argumentation in psychology, the interviewee, a first-year student, suggests that the benefits of argumentational thinking and expression go beyond those learned and applied in the discipline itself. The account begins with the interviewer recording the problems with making argument applicable to undergraduate psychology:

> Having chosen someone to interview in the department of psychology, I found it was hard to make the questions applicable. I found that… psychology relies more on the research and understandings of others, rather than on being able to make one's own contributions. The information is gathered from secondary and tertiary sources such as journals. Similarly, students are expected to take readings from reports of different experiments [and] are expected to critique and discuss the implications; they are not asked for their own opinion…
>
> The work that is required of the students is in the form of essays, which must demonstrate knowledge and research taken from the report readings. In the essays students are also expected to discuss and not necessarily side with a particular argument, all of which must be heavily supported with evidence. Practical reports are often used in the students' evidence and they follow a logical format: an introduction, the method/procedure, the results and then how the results can be applied to previous works. The examiners also expect a clear understanding of the topic being discussed and a logical structure to support the arguments and ideas being put forth. Similarly, there needs to be an up-to-date and relevant spread of research; the examiners are looking for an accurate selection process and of course all knowledge must be referenced. The idea of writing essays is to get students to compare and contrast the different arguments being put forth by different researchers,

particularly working on the students' analytical skills and not so much their own argument.

As an extra-curricular activity my interviewee is on the netball team and as a result, when discussing tactics she has to adopt a diplomatic and sensitive approach towards others, whilst getting her own argument and opinion across for the good of the team. She is able to listen to others' perspectives and views and try to associate with them and understand them, which makes it easier to put forth her own views as she is respected. As a result, she feels argumentation is vitally important, in and out of the classroom.

What is different about the practices in psychology for an undergraduate student? It has been discussed elsewhere in this book that the terms argument and argumentation are not always easily or appropriately applicable in some disciplines. In this case, the interviewer has had initial problems identifying what aspects of academic practice might come under the umbrella term of 'argument', but she does find that despite the fact that the term is not much used, the actual practices include much that is argumentational. We have seen, for example, that the gathering of secondary and tertiary sources (as in history) involves a second stage that is pre-argumentational: the weighing up of one source against another. Again, as in history, primary sources can be used to interrogate secondary ones and secondary to interrogate tertiary, and so on. Such interrogation and movement between levels of source open up the space for critical commentary, for the identification of gaps and mismatches, and for the gradual development of personal rhetorical and intellectual spaces for argumentation. In the case of psychology, primary sources may include documentary evidence as in history but may also be the results of experimentation, observation, and other empirical methods: such sources may be found in others' work and, if possible, reinterpreted, but may also be generated by the students themselves.

The default genre of the essay appears again in psychology, as in humanities and social science disciplines. Interestingly, the structure of the psychology essay follows the 'logical format' of that of scientific articles, except that the undergraduate essay appears not to have a literature review. Foregrounding the method/procedure section, as is suggested in the interview account, would suggest that what students learn is – as has been expressed elsewhere with regard to science and mathematics – that methodologies and methods are central to the activity of these subjects at undergraduate level. In short, how conclusions are arrived at is more important that what they are. New propositions and claims are rarely put forward; instead, the student is apprenticed to the discipline by learning how it operates, not by interpretation of the generation of new public knowledge. As the interview states, 'the idea of writing the essays is to get the students to compare and contrast the different arguments being put forth by different researchers [including recent research], particularly working on the students' analytical skills and not so much on their own argument'.

Case Study 4: Argumentation in Politics

On a spectrum of the degree to which argumentation plays a foregrounded and central part in disciplines, sociology, and politics might be the most obvious candidates. Both share an interest and preoccupation with social and political theory and its connection with events and social phenomena; both operate largely in the verbal code; and politics, in particular, is a discipline in which belief, conviction, and opinion play a large part. The interview with the politics undergraduate is illuminating in a number of ways, not least with regard to how the discipline operates:

> When I interviewed the politics student, he said that argumentation was incredibly important in politics, and said that if a student could not argue well, that student would not do well on this course.
>
> The student told me that he had learnt to make good academic arguments, mainly through seminars, as opposed to written work. [In such seminars] the students would have to argue their point well, in order to try to convince the others in the group that their opinion was the best…
>
> He has done very little written work for the course so far [the interview took place in the middle of the first year] as the course is mainly based on having discussions and debates. However, for the few essays that they have been asked to do, they are asked a question, and have to argue their opinion on this question. Written feedback from the tutor is received for these essays. This feedback comments on how well the student has answered this question, but mainly on how well the student has argued his point on the topic. In politics, there are no right or wrong answers; everybody has a different opinion. This is why argumentation is so important for this course.

Politics is unusual in its emphasis on the oral; the discipline seems to take its cue from the conduct of politics in public life, wherein exchanges in government at local, regional, national, and international levels as part of a democratic process are conducted largely in speech, with briefings and recording in writing. It is evident that where there is a democratic approach to a discipline and where there is not a body of authoritative knowledge that has to be learnt via the transmission mode of teaching, argumentation flourishes; where there are texts and other phenomena to be interpreted, argumentation flourishes in a different way; and where the disciplines are more based on the public accretion of knowledge, the scope for argumentation becomes limited to 'proof' of existing theories. The latter is simply a different kind of argument:

one that concentrates on method rather than on the substance and processes of what is being argued.

Case Study 5: Argumentation in Literature Studies, Writing and Performance

Unlike the cases in the sciences, wherein there is considerable emphasis on method, evidence, a deductive approach to argumentation, and the testing of hypotheses, the study of literature starts from a different position. Whether the subject is called 'English literature' or is the study of literatures in other languages or in translation (or both), the material is given in the form of literary texts. These texts are, in a sense, the 'evidence' from which investigation begins. The process, then, is a forensic one in which interpretation, inductive argumentation, and critical commentary are the means by which the 'discipline' operates. Whether 'discipline' is the right term for a field that has notoriously ill-defined boundaries and in which a wide range of theories are brought to bear on literary analysis is questionable. However, whether the study of literature is termed a discipline, subject, or field of enquiry, there are argumentational processes that operate and that students need to learn.

If aspects of more productive ('creative') activity are included, such as writing and performance, different kinds of argumentation are also brought into play. In the following account, the range of argumentational activity is described and discussed:

> In this particular course there are several ways in which the students learn to make good academic arguments. It seems that the main form is via oral feedback; much of this is during tutorials where one-on-one work takes place and an essay is read together with advice being given to secure a more tightly structured argument. This particular student also said that feedback is written on the back of essays for reinforcement and handouts are given out with advice on structure. During tutorials, essays are swapped and the students mark each others', discussing ideas with their tutor. In classes, examples of bad essays are shown and the reasons given; this degree course even goes as far as offering courses on structure in their essays, which are optional.
>
> In this course, essays are the only form of written work the students have to do. The interviewee said that logic isn't required to write essays, but they must have a clear structure for their argument, which relies on primary evidence from the text being studied, and secondary evidence from their own individual research.
>
> Arguments were asked to be made in essays, in oral and visual presentations where parts of a film were shown, and also as spontaneous participation in group discussions. When asked about the effect her

> classes had on reading and making arguments [the student] said that due to the number of people in classes, many different viewpoints had to be taken into account. This makes a difference in written work, as in previous years at school ideas were set.
>
> An experience that the interviewee thought as important in learning how to make a good argument happened during a tutorial the [previous] term. She said that her tutor pointed out to her, in discussing an essay, that if a particular point in an argument had to be split up and put in a different part of the essay, she must state this – otherwise it suggests confusion.
>
> As ways of improving her learning in making arguments, the student felt that she must read as much as possible to see how others arrange their arguments and ideas. She also recommended allowing as much time as possible in between planning and writing essays, so thoughts can settle.
>
> Finally, as this student does a lot of acting and performances as extra-curricular activities, she says that [argument] helps her to get into the perspective of the character and improve her analytic skills.

There is a great deal to discuss in this account of a first-year's work in the study of literature. First, we see again that, as in history, 'feedback' whether in oral or written form, is a key way in which the argumentational abilities of students are improved. Lecturers, tutors, and professors spend a considerable amount of intellectual energy in providing such feedback, and it is seen as important and highly valued by the students, especially if it comes via one-to-one sessions ('tutorials'). Second, there is a degree of peer critique in that students look at one another's essays. There is no doubt mutual support in these sessions but also a spirit of positive criticism that can be very effective. Third, unlike the Renaissance rhetorical approach of using *progymnasmata* or exemplary models to teach written forms, these students look at bad examples of essays in their field, learning from them how not to argue. Such an approach can teach as much as a good model and also be more amusing.

Fourth, the idea in literature study that 'logic isn't required to write essays' needs explication. Elsewhere in this book, I have argued for 'logical or quasi-logical' argumentation. Strictly speaking, logical argumentation is a sub-field of argument studies that draws on classical logic and the study of fallacies and syllogisms and/or mathematics. It is formulaic, tightly controlled, and informed by philosophical analytical principles. It has no real place in the study of literature, which operates at a different level of generality. Whereas mathematical logic and logic per se operate abstractly or, in the latter case, at the level of short propositions ('Dermot is a penguin. All penguins like cold weather. Therefore Dermot likes cold weather', to give a banal example), literary texts, on the whole, do not. They provide rich, textured language that is consciously crafted and often conscious of itself, and they provide the grounds for inductive arguments arising from, and consistent with, the text itself. In terms of syllogistic logic, then, literary essays are not the appropriate medium and vice versa. Instead, these essays employ a quasi-logical approach in which the structure of the essay as a whole draws on logical patterning. To give a very simple example: the conventional 'compare and contrast' essay that is common for pre-university students of literature and the lineaments of which are also present in the critical fabric of the undergraduate essays in the discipline operates via a tried and tested structure. The content and thematic nature of the works are first discussed, followed by consideration of the position or stance of the writer and the 'writerly voice'; then there is attention to language, rhythm, and other stylistic features. Finally, a judgment may be made about the quality or respective merits of the work(s) being studied. Though this structure is not set in stone and may be varied according to the preferences of the writers or the demands of the tutors, there is a quasi-logical nature to the descent from broader issues (theme, position) toward detail (linguistic and stylistic features) and a quasi-logical momentum to the sequencing of the paragraphs or sections. The design of the structure can often be flagged in an introduction, so that the reader/examiner is clear as to the direction being taken. In essence, then, logic is manifested in the humanities essays in terms of discourse structure: the sum of the rhetorical choices made by the writer.

The notion that 'at school ideas were set' is not new and has been researched previously by Mitchell (1994a) and Mitchell and Andrews (1994b). The somewhat disturbing result of that 1990s research was that students had given the impression that in English literature study at sixth-form level (16 to 18) in England, 'we all end up thinking the same'. This result may have been the effect of a particularly directive teacher and a group of relatively passive students at the time, but there does appear to be a systemic stage of induction into the study of literature that is more about appreciation than critique. Such consensus making is, perhaps, a necessary step toward a more differentiated, individual purchase on literature for students: one they are encouraged to develop on undergraduate courses in literature and certainly at masters level and beyond. The undergraduate student quoted in the preceding interview appears to enjoy the number of people in the classroom and the 'many different viewpoints [that] had to be taken into account'. If these viewpoints move beyond opinion into well-argued, textually based, and even theoretically based modes, the study of literature can be a vibrant and highly argumentational practice. The great advantage of the subject in this latter respect is that, except where the text itself is in dispute (usually the focus of study at more advanced levels), the text is stable and provides the evidence on which the arguments can be built.

A final point pertains not to the study of literature but to writing and performance – the more productive side of textual study. It is interesting to note that the student in question does 'a lot of acting and performances as extra curricular activities' (these can also be done as part of a degree programme itself) and that argumentational training allows her to get inside the character and 'improve her analytical skills'. Thus, choices made by an actor in the interpretation and delivery of a part are a result of weighing up the possibilities that are inherent in the text/script. Such a 'weighing up' is both a critical and argumentational task in the service of a seemingly physical, linguistic, and emotional presentation is a matter of *arte est celare artem* – the art is to hide the art.

Case Study 6: Argumentation and Discussion in a Vocational Course

So far, the case studies have been in academic subjects and disciplines, but what happens when the degree is in a vocational field – in this case, as part of a nursing or management degree? The interviewee here focuses on talking about learning the conventional methods used in the assessment of workplace risks and hazards and about learning the relevant health and safety legislation and case law that operate 'in order to be able to act as a competent advisor to management in the workplace'.

> In classes, where the majority of work focuses around meeting the minimum health and safety requirements of the law, the term 'discussion' is preferred to that of 'argument'. The reason for this is that the suitability of a solution is more open to exploration than direct challenge. In Health and Safety, advice is given with direct reference to legislation and case law and so, as long as this advice takes account of all relevant legislation, there is no real question of right or wrong, only one perhaps of quality [and interpretation].
>
> Legislation itself could be argued about, but this is beyond the scope of a Health and Safety practitioner. Disputes of the law are more for the consideration of lawyers. It was also pointed out that, as students, 'discussion' seemed a more appropriate term as the class were all learning and did not have the breadth or depth of knowledge or experience to be confident of a 'right' answer.
>
> One area where this student felt the term 'argument' would be more appropriate was when a case was to be made to management to go beyond the minimum health and safety requirements of the law (either with a written report or through verbal [oral] negotiations). In order to improve working conditions within an organization, management would need to be persuaded that the benefits of these improvements would outweigh the costs. Moral arguments could be made but arguments to implement better working practices were more likely to be successful where they were supported by numerical and statistical evidence that long-term savings could be made for the organization.

> Things that this student considered important in making an effective argument were making sure that your arguments support your position, using appropriate forms of evidence to support your claims, foreseeing possible objections and recognizing your own limitations. Where there is opportunity for two-way argument, active listening is considered an important skill ('you should listen rather than wait to speak'). You should be open-minded and always accept the possibility that you may be wrong.

The point about 'discussion' as opposed to 'argument' is one that is often raised by students and by lecturers, principally those who are concerned to preserve a strong degree of cohesion in the group in which they are operating and who see 'argument' as a divisive, sometimes aggressive, activity. On occasions, the preference for discussion over argument is based on an unconscious or conscious predilection for harmony. In this case, the preference for discussion is that learning about health and safety matters is seen as 'more open to exploration than direct challenge'. Such topics and such contexts encourage complicity rather than critique, though there is an opportunity for argumentation in the interpretation of law and guidance. As the student points out, lawyers may wish to debate points of dispute in the law itself.

However, the related point that '"discussion" seemed a more appropriate term as the class were all learning and did not have the breadth or depth of knowledge or experience to be confident of a "right" answer' requires some unpacking. Clearly the notion that, as the class is in the process of learning about health and safety, they are not yet in a position to argue about it, is one that is reflected also in biology and other subjects wherein it is felt that one cannot argue until one has gained command of a certain level of proficiency or competence in the subject matter. Both 'breadth' and 'depth' are required, from this point of view, so that critical perspective can be gained and argumentation can begin to flourish. However, the question about the need for 'confidence of a "right" answer' is worrying. Pedagogically, students may be able to reach better answers to problems by attempting to devise hypotheses and test them with argumentational procedures; by questioning received wisdom with new evidence and/or new propositions; and by applying existing conventions and laws in real contexts, thus interpreting the received wisdom for themselves. Such processes are needed to keep the intellectual dimension of learning alive, to engage students in learning about matters such as health and safety where there is ostensibly less room for argument, and to further the field itself.

Indeed, the student herself indicates that when called upon to go beyond the legislation, argument might be a more appropriate way to proceed. If management (those responsible for seeing that the law is properly applied) need to be 'persuaded' that working conditions might be improved by the further development of the legislation or its interpretation, a case could be made that would entail argumentation. It is interesting (and entirely sensible and pragmatic) that management would be more likely to be persuaded if the argument were not only morally driven but backed up by 'numerical and statistical evidence that long-term savings could be made for the organization'.

Finally, this particular student sees that the factors that are important in making an effective argument include not only the features that we have previously encountered in the book ('making sure that your arguments support your position', 'using appropriate forms of evidence to support your claims') but moves that involve thinking outside the box and imagining oppositions to the argument being put forward. These include 'foreseeing possible objections' (Toulmin's category of refutation in the face of a challenge to the connection of grounds and claims) and 'recognizing your own limitations'. This latter aspect of argumentation is one that (post)graduates are well aware of as they begin to add to public knowledge through their masters or doctoral dissertations but that undergraduate students, more used to entertaining the ideas in a field than having to apply them to the wider world of knowledge and/or practice, are not often asked to consider. Nevertheless, being aware of the limitations of an argument is not only a necessary conceptual and intellectual act of modesty; in rhetorical terms; it can strengthen the position of the rhetor or speaker/writer in that he or she is shown to be aware that his or her argument is relative, limited by the democratic processes in society, and thus subject to objection and critique and inevitably partial. The best that can be hoped for is to create the strongest possible argument in a particular context and hope that the ideological current helps it to carry the day. To quote the student whose final statement might serve as an appropriate epigraph for this book as a whole, and, wider still, for argument itself, 'you should be open-minded and always accept the possibility that you may be wrong'.

Case Study 7: A More In-Depth Look at Argumentation in Chemistry

Previously, it was noted that there were several key points that a chemistry student wanted to make to his interviewer about argument. A fuller account of the interview is given here, as it reveals much about the way argumentation operates for this student in his chosen subject:

> Carlton [a pseudonym] is a second-year Chemistry student, halfway through a four-year course. He mainly studies with around 120 other chemists in large group lectures, taken by one lecturer, or in tutorial groups which consist of around four other students and a tutor.
>
> Carlton defined 'argument' in two different ways on two separate occasions during the interview. Firstly, he identified it as a series of facts used to prove a point – his work is often based on empirical facts, which he then must use to explain his processes during experiments

or tutorial work. He also said that when arguing in this way, he tries to pre-empt what an opposing chemist would say, in order to undermine his argument, so that he may in turn invalidate their argument.

Carlton acknowledges that his subject is perhaps more fact- and logic-based than for example, History or English, but explains that argument is just used differently in Chemistry – it is used to prove theories and processes to be exact, instead of arguing an interpretation of certain events or a certain critical hypothesis. Carlton practises this technique by producing work based on a question (or questions) set by his lecturer or tutor – there are often a number of different ways of completing one question, so, whilst doing the work, Carlton must also argue why his way of completing the question is the best method – this may even sometimes trigger a debate with his lecturer or tutor, in which each will seek to prove the other's method wrong.

Much of Carlton's work must be based on theories which scientists are, at this stage, unable to prove, therefore Carlton must be persuasive in his work, and argue as to why his work is correct in the light of these unproven [and sometimes unprovable] theories...

Carlton has also given over four presentations to his tutorial group in his time at university, during which he has argued his opinion on a particular method of practical analysis, and on the effectiveness of certain chemical processes, against his tutor and other members of his tutor group. Carlton finds these debates intimidating, yet stimulating, since it means that he must be more resourceful in his argument, and draw on many different areas of his knowledge in order to prove his theory or make his point.

Carlton prefers mathematical or symbolic means; he thinks that these are more succinct and clearer to the reader or audience. He thinks that the more long-winded approach taken by some of his peers can be confusing and can lead to their arguments being lost amongst flowery sentences and pretentious, meandering arguments in which they often contradict themselves, and lose sight of the point they were originally trying to make.

Finally, Carlton says that he enjoys arguing. He believes that it is useful in discovering weak arguments and incorrect reasoning in his own, and others' work. He says that he finds that he learns through argument and listening to others arguing their points. He tells me that, in his opinion, arguing within his subject is a useful way to improve your knowledge of the area under discussion, and these benefits can be carried over into other areas of study within Chemistry.

This account is, in many ways, the most detailed and insightful so far into the nature and operation of argument in a discipline or university subject. In addition to the points made at the beginning of this chapter, there is much to say about the way argumentation is employed in chemistry.

The first use of the term is in accord with the Aristotelian notion of argument as evidence: in Carlton's words, 'a series of facts used to prove a point'. There is nothing in the interview to explore further what the 'series' may be or how it is constructed in chemistry, but it is clear that these are 'facts' that are the result of previous or new empirical work. There is also no discussion of what the nature of a 'fact' in chemistry is. 'Facts' in this discipline, and others, are theories that have been proven and are then taken by the community with an interest in the field to be 'given'. They acquire factual status in time, through consensual acceptance and use/habit. They are not open to challenge, as they are agreed to be 'the case'. Such 'facts' are, however, open to challenge, ultimately, as was the belief that the earth was flat and has edges. In fact (though we must hold back from wordplay and self-definition), 'facts' themselves are taken in chemistry to be part of the argumentational repertoire – in a way that would not be the case in a more interpretive subject such as literature or philosophy. If we wished to unravel what is assumed by the phase 'a series of facts used to prove a point' in chemistry, we could so do with an elaboration: 'a [logical or quasi-logical] series of [generally accepted common truths, which were once hypotheses, and are now known as] facts used to prove a point [which, in turn, is a proposition or claim that posits some new position, new knowledge]'. It can be seen, then, that the progress of knowledge in chemistry is a matter of the positing of new hypotheses, some of which become reified as 'facts' that, for a time, provide support for claims/propositions and a stable relationship between theories and facts. The driving force here is new ideas…and thus a new theory of the nature of knowledge and learning, to be taken up and discussed in the final chapter of this book.

The second use of the term argument for this student is in relation to trying 'to pre-empt what an opposing chemist would say' in order to undermine his [sic] argument. It is clear from what follows in the interview summary that the undermining of an opposing chemist's argument is not purely for rhetorical purposes. Rather, it is to get a better handle on the truth of the position being argued and on a good explanation for the 'facts' or evidence/data being presented. That such debate could take place both in large lecture format and in the smaller, more intimate forum of the group tutorial (or somewhere between these two in terms of formality and scale) is testament to the robust culture of argumentation in science, and in chemistry in particular, as expressed by this student. Such contesting of the best theories to explain the data could make for engaging teaching and learning. It is seen as part of the 'method' of science and assumes that one element of the equation is stable (the data), which then becomes different kinds of evidence according to different perspectives, viewpoints, or hypotheses. Whichever of these explanatory heuristic tools has the best explanation for the data becomes its theory – and then the data becomes evidence (and ultimately, fact). The process is well articulated by the student earlier. It is fascinating to read the description of a process in learning chemistry (and in pushing forward knowledge in chemistry) that is 'intimidating, yet stimulating' because of the risk-taking involved. The searching out of new hypotheses to explain the data and the contestation of these hypotheses in the course of a tutorial or lecture seem at the heart of learning. In the process of such debate, persuasiveness is important, though it cannot be mere rhetorical persuasiveness (as in Aristotle's notion of argument as the art of persuasion). It must be grounded in good data, discovered by sound methodology.

One of the striking things about this summary of work in undergraduate chemistry is that Carlton claims that some of his study is based on theories that are unproven or un-provable. The floating (ungrounded) nature of some theory in chemistry creates a different situation in which argumentation might flourish. Whereas with grounded claims the connection or warrant holding these two elements together is contestable (though often, it can be imagined, without reference to competing backing for the warrants), in the case of floating theory, it can convince only in terms of its elegance, persuasiveness, and seeming consistency and comprehensiveness. How can such theory be contested? Probably only by competing theory that is more elegant, more persuasive, more seemingly coherent and comprehensive. Such theory will appeal to higher reason and to intuition (perhaps the same thing?), just as Einstein's theory of relativity was unproven for some time…until a form of proof could be discovered, validated, and undertaken.

There is much else in this account of one student's views on argumentation in his subject. To focus on one more aspect: it is reported that Carlton prefers mathematical or symbolic means of argument, as these are more succinct and precise than – the implication is –verbal arguments. The characterization of these other means of arguing as 'meandering' is interesting. It is true that verbal language, as opposed to mathematical language, is a looser, fuzzier medium for argument. Words have shades of meaning, often (but not always) pinned down by the immediate linguistic and circumstantial context. It is possible to chart the course of an argument sentence by sentence, but it is the larger structure of argument that is charted by words, on the whole. I have argued elsewhere in this book that the formalistic, artificial creation of statements (usually very short sentences) in syllogistic argument is itself a fallacious approach to the examination and testing of arguments in the world. As we reach higher levels of verbal language units – the sentence, the paragraph, the text as a whole, series of texts, and so on – the possibility for making and understanding logical and quasi-logical links between statements become greater. Although there is more room for interpretation, there is also more room for argument itself. Such arguments will not 'meander' if they are well structured both horizontally, in terms of their logic, and vertically in terms of the hierarchies of concept that they address.

The Practical Dimension

Activity 8.1

There are a number of simple teaching and research activities that can tell you more about the way students see argumentation. With any year of your undergraduate cohort or with postgraduate students, have them interview one another about argumentation and submit a transcript and/or summary work as an assignment, as in the work quoted in this chapter. You could develop this approach into a pilot, small-scale, or even larger-scale research project within your institution. Use any documentation that is issued in handbooks or as guidance to inform students about the place argumentation plays in the assessment of their work.

Activity 8.2

Arrange a meeting, possibly through your staff development unit, with colleagues from other disciplines, subjects, or departments. Compare notes on what argument means to you, as lecturers or teachers in that field, and how you might develop it. In particular, you might look at the feedback that is provided for students and the feedback that they provide for you on the matter.

9
Students' Essays and Reports in a Range of Disciplines

There is a strong tradition in some undergraduate and even graduate programs of what can be called 'critical reflective writing'. At its best, this kind of writing is personal, committed, critical, scholarly, and reflective. Such writing manifests all of the qualities that would be expected of writing at higher education levels and is likely to attain high grades for the student. At its worst, however, the critical and scholarly dimensions seem to be absent. The writing is personal and reflective and perhaps not even committed ('committed' suggests commitment to a cause or position, which would need to be articulated and preferably argued). It tends to the descriptive, toward narrative rather than argument, its principal *raison d'être* appearing to be authenticity, sincerity, and personal expressiveness. Such writing is often found in 'journals', which are indeed more like diaries, personal autobiographical accounts, and chronicles than they are like academic assignments.

I am exaggerating the difference between journals and academic essays to make the point that just as the academic essay can go too far in one direction and become arid, the personal reflective journal can, if allowed, become indulgent and over-personal. Though believing strongly in the presence of the *voices* (not the single 'voice' of post-Romantic educational discourse) of the individual learner in academic writing, I believe also in the presentation and discussion of *ideas*. The entertaining of ideas and concepts requires clarity, and such clarity is aided by criticality on the one hand and comparison with existing ideas (sources, existing works, literature in the field – all aspects of scholarship) on the other.

Academic reflective journals, at their best, can therefore be used both as preliminaries to more formal academic writing and as an academic form in themselves. If the latter, the expectation would be that such writing is deeply reflective (Schön, 1983), drawing on reading, and motivated by a sceptical spirit rather than one of deference and obedience.

Two Examples

Two examples of third-year (the final year on most undergraduate courses based in England and Wales) essays follow: one from music (opera and music theatre) and one for a literature course (Shakespeare on film). In each case, here is the opening paragraph of the essay.

Literature Essay Opening

> Ostensibly the role of women in Shakespeare's writing seems a negligible one – they can be seen purely as wives, sisters, daughters, mistresses or servants of the male protagonists, functioning only as subservient confidants or messengers. Yet Shakespeare allows them to subtly influence their male counterparts, as Lady Macbeth most famously infects Macbeth with her corrupt ambition, awarding the females a significant status within the plays, kept secret by their outwardly deferential nature. In performance – on stage and on screen – the director and the actresses play a considerable part in unearthing that secret influence through moulding the portrayal of women in Shakespeare... In film these feminine narratives are constructed technically, by the way the director 'photographs women, in close-up, in mid- or long-shot, in tracking shots; by turns intensifying concentration on a face, an eye, a foot or impassively observing, or drawing back, marooning women in compositions that register isolations and them as objects'.

This essay opens promisingly with a single word, 'ostensibly'. Right from the start, the distinction is made between what appears to be the ostensible case and what actually *is* the case. The opening up of such a gap gives the student both a rhetorical and an argumentational space to exploit. She can exploit such a space subtly by making a small and transitional point or, as appears to be the case in the essay, she can make the distinction a major thematic and structural element of the essay as a whole. The brilliance of the adverb 'ostensibly' as the tuning note, as it were, of the essay is that it requires completion; it is as though we are entering the discussion in the middle or as though we are off balance to begin with – a state that needs addressing by the essay itself. Though it would not be in anyone's interests for every essay to begin with such syncopation, the advantages here over more staid beginnings like 'This essay will discuss...' or ' In Shakespeare's day...' are clear.

At this point, it should be revealed what the actual essay title is. It appears that this title is of the kind given to the student, not created by her: 'I believe that Shakespeare was a feminist, and all the plays I direct analyse the roles of women from that ideological point of view' (Michael Bogdanov). Discuss this view of the presentation of women in one or more Shakespeare films.' The student does not address questions of film until line seven but uses her first seven lines to set part of the foundation for how she will build toward answering the essay question. That foundation consists of the view that Shakespeare's women are more powerful than they might (ostensibly) seem.

From line seven onward in the rest of the opening paragraph, the essay moves swiftly into a sharp focus on the question in hand, approaching it from an interesting technical point of view in film: 'in film these feminine narratives are constructed technically'. The author then bolsters her new point of view with a quotation, appropriately referenced (from Rutter, 2007, p. 246). The rest of the essay discusses the opening thesis in a number of plays, as required by the question.

As a first paragraph of a summative essay (i.e., an important 5,000-word essay in terms of the overall grading of the degree), this is promising in that it is fluent, accurately written, and readable; it also has opened up argumentational and rhetorical space in which to give the student room to manoeuvre and to provide a critical dimension. Conversely, its setting out of the terms of the argument – and how it will address the essay question – is muddied by the pivotal phrase 'unearthing that secret influence'. The opening lines of the essay suggest nothing secret about women's roles in Shakespeare ('covert' or 'subliminal' might have been better terms), and the verb 'unearthing' suggests an archaeological dig for meaning and influence. As a 'segue' between the broader theme of women's powerful roles (despite their seeming marginality) and the more specific topic of the narrative construction of feminine roles in film, it is a little weak. Such weakness makes the development of an argument difficult for the student in the rest of the essay, because there is no clear connection made between women in Shakespeare and women on film – which is what the essay question requires. At best, then, the essay is likely to be a blend of critical points and discursive writing: it received a very good mark but not among the highest that were possible for this assignment.

Let us turn to a different essay by the same student. This one is from a course on music and is the result of an extended series of workshops and a production of an avant-garde opera, *Staatstheater*. Unlike a conventional academic essay, this takes the form of a reflective, academically infused journal.

Music Essay Opening

> Our production of Mauricio Kagel's *Staatstheater* (1971) was created over a period of four months and became a devised collage of isolated images and actions, many of which were inspired by or lifted directly from Kagel's score for the piece, and many of which were created by the company during our improvisations and rehearsals. The nature of Kagel's score allowed us to be flexible; while we carefully followed his compulsory directions, for example that the piece should begin with *Répertoire* (the section focusing on poised presentations of

> props), we also developed strands of the piece which were unique to our own ensemble's strengths and ideas. The process was governed by a combination of score as a blueprint, the director's vision for the production, and our collective skills and contributions. Loré Lixenberg, our director, took on the role (as in much devised theatre) of the 'conceptualist', and led our initial improvisation, gradually moulding each idea that showed potential to become one of the building bricks of the final production.

As in the first essay, the writer dives in at the deep end. That, in itself, is an impressive quality: it suggests that not a word will be wasted, that the student is intent on getting straight to the heart of the question; it is also arresting for the reader. In the second sentence, we are focusing on 'the nature of Kagel's score' (though its nature is not elaborated upon until later in the essay). The second sentence itself is complex and counterpointed: first, an interesting opener ('The nature of Kagel's score allowed us to be flexible') followed by a contrasting set of clauses ('...while we carefully followed his compulsory directions, for example that the piece should begin with *Répertoire* (the section focusing on poised presentations of props), we also developed strands of the piece which were unique to our own ensembles strengths and ideas'). The writing is cogent, fluent, focused, and treads a fine line between reportage, as required by the journal approach, and the more abstract, impersonal, referenced nature of the academic essay.

The title in this case is 'Explore the process of 'devising' music theatre as a member of a performing ensemble, weighing up how much of this collective rehearsal process has influenced the final production and how much has been determined by Kagel's original score'. It is a gift of a title, because there are several points at which it invites critical exploration and distinctions – what we have earlier referred to as the opening up of critical space. First, in the inverted commas around the term 'devising', suggesting that the term may be accepted in some quarters but controversial in others. Second, in the invitation to 'weigh up' the collective rehearsal process against the determination of Kagel's original score. There is also the chance of some in-depth scholarship, suggested by the term *original* – that may refer to the score per se as opposed to the performance, but it may also suggest that Kagel's original score is not the only score and that some exploration of different versions may be in order. The student exploits the potential for creative ambiguity in her next concise but powerfully clear and suggestive sentence: 'The process was governed by a combination of score as a blueprint, the director's vision for the production, and our collective skills and contributions.' The added dimension in that sentence is reference to the director's vision – not an element asked for in the essay question but nevertheless one that the student feels is important to interpretation via the collective rehearsal process.

This added dimension is developed in the fourth and last sentence of the opening paragraph: 'Loré Lixenberg, our director, took on the role (as in much devised theatre) of the 'conceptualist', and led our initial improvisation, gradually moulding each idea that showed potential to become one of the building bricks of the final production.' The opening paragraph thus ends, as did the opening of the first paragraph in the literature essay, on a contrapuntal note: there is creative imbalance, some degree of turbulence, and most definitely the promise of more to come. The reader is persuaded, at the end of this crucial opening to the essay, that not only will the student answer the question but that she will go further and add new insights to the problem posed. Indeed, the essay was rated in the highest category by its markers.

The quality of this journal/essay is clear in its final paragraph, where it returns to address the question directly and concisely:

> Ultimately, our production of Mauricio Kagel's *Staatstheater* was inspired by his score, containing some elements specifically derived from his instructive blueprints, but [it] predominantly relied on the skills, resources, contributions, and techniques discovered during our devising process. The fundamental structural make-up of the piece, determined at the very end of the process once we had all the elements of the production in place, was vital to its success as a performance, a significance which reflects Brecht's philosophy, that 'the superobjective in Brecht is superstructure' (Mitter 1992, 53). Stoppard notes that 'if you don't work in theatre you would be surprised by the obsessive concentration on the adjusting of timing, duration, volume, intensity, colour and speed of a hundred or two hundred production cues' (Stoppard in Silvers 2001, 5) – it was our obsessive concentration on the structural detail that communicated Kagel's intention of reabsorbed, recontextualized opera. Kagel himself was a pioneer in devising music and sound pieces in a workshop environment here. We followed his example to create a uniquely personal production, true to our own talents and yet representative of the crumbling, subverted '*Staatshteater*' which Kagel sought to portray.

The question is answered with the help of the intervening evidence between the introduction and conclusion; but what is impressive here is that the conclusion becomes more than a conclusion. It draws in further references – to Brecht and Stoppard – to point the argument forward to other questions, other levels. The mere awareness of those levels provides further perspective on the question in hand. However, what really takes the journal/essay to a new height is the last phrase: 'the crumbling, subverted 'Staatshteater' which Kagel sought to portray'. We are made aware of a new dimension that is largely unexplored in the current essay but which reflects back on it, providing yet more critical nuance. The resonating nature of that final phrase has a similar effect to the 'ostensibly' of the first essay: it points beyond the essay itself and gives the reader the impression of an ongoing dialogue within an engaged and critical mind.

The End of the Essay?

There is no doubt that the essay is a noble and well-established genre in higher education, at least in the United Kingdom, Canada, and Australia. In undergraduate composition classes in the United States, there has been a move to break away from the essay form to more specific text-types such as the 'position paper' and the 'research paper'. The context for teaching essay writing skills is also very different in higher education from that in Australia or the United Kingdom. According to Hill (1995, p. 171),

> in universities in the United States, all entering students are required to take a course designed to enhance their writing skills. In this course, they are exposed to kinds of writing tasks that they will likely encounter during their university education, and they are given practice in the types of general cognitive skills – analysis, argument, interpretation – that will be expected of them. While the instructors who teach these courses are not usually trained extensively in logic and argument analysis, part of their job is to teach students some general principles of effective argumentation and to evaluate the argumentative essays that their students write.

Womack (1993) calls it the 'default genre' for the assessment of understanding, not only in higher education but at the upper levels of school and college education too. In earlier work (e.g., Andrews 1995, pp. 9–18) I've explored the etymological origin of the term *essay*, coming as it does into English from the French *essai* meaning an 'attempt'. The term's derivation from words meaning 'first drafts' or 'attempts' is not reflected in the current use of the term to describe finished assignments submitted for assessment or examination. Although students might be generally assumed to be attempting an analysis of a certain section of knowledge to demonstrate their emerging understanding of it, it is usually assumed in higher education that once the essay is submitted, the die is cast. The essay (the definition recorded in the *Oxford English Dictionary* is the one generally applicable in schooling and higher education: 'a composition of moderate length on any particular subject, originally implying want of finish, but now said of a composition more or less elaborate in style, though limited in range') represents the state of a student's understanding and is assessed accordingly. The submission and the response (assuming a response of high quality) have a formative function, but their principal function is to gain a mark or grade on the way to a degree. In this respect, the essay is more like 'an offering to a great personage' – one of the definitions of 'essay' in the *Oxford English Dictionary*.

A Very Short History of the Essay

Although the modern essay is assumed to start with Montaigne and Bacon, the derivation of the Renaissance essay is from the rhetorical speeches of classical Greece (and before) through sermons, *progymnasmata* (in effect, form and style exercises in the grammar schools of the early Renaissance), occasional pieces, and other short expository forms. As Gross (1991) points out in *The Oxford Book of Essays*, the form 'can shade into the character sketch, the travel sketch, the memoir, the *jeu d'esprit*' (p. xix) but its distinguishing marks after Montaigne are 'intimacy and informality' (ibid). This casual – or seemingly casual – style allows for the expression of discursive thoughts, not necessarily logically structured. However, the forms of the essay employed in school and higher education have departed significantly from those expected in literary magazines or as features in newspapers. Though the latter are characterized by an intelligent informality, the former are bound by assessment demands, school/university genre conventions and 'structure'. And yet, even within the convention of the school/university essay, there is a spectrum ranging from the explicit, abstract, and logically structured at one end to the more personal, idiosyncratic, and expressive –'a loose sally of the mind', to quote Dr. Johnson – at the other. It is this spectrum that makes sets of criteria for the assessment of essays so difficult to compose and apply and, more important, for students to interpret.

Despite Corbett's (1965) seminal work for college students on what classical rhetoric can offer to shape academic writing, the essay has been a matter of concern in the last 20 years in school and higher education. Freedman and Pringle (e.g., 1980) set the tone with their analyses of the problems faced by school and university students in composing essays, whereas in the United Kingdom, debate focused largely on secondary-level school writing (Wilkinson et al., 1981; Medway, 1986; Assessment of Performance Unit, 1998). Swales's exploration of genres in academic writing (1990) moved the debate into the field of social discourses and, in the 1990s, there was increasing concentration on the topic at secondary (e.g., Andrews, 1989, 1995; Sheeran & Barnes, 1991) and tertiary/higher education levels (e.g., Andrews & Mitchell, 2001; Cockcroft & Cockcroft, 1992; Creme & Lea, 2003; Heilker, 1996; Mitchell, 1994, 1997; Mitchell & Riddle, 2000; Newkirk, 1989; Womack, 1993).

There has been criticism of the essay genre and form itself from feminist perspectives, largely centered on critiques of the 'impersonal' academic convention of not using a genuine persona in writing, for adopting 'we' as a falsely collective voice, and for suppressing emotion 'even though the issues addressed have a passionate resonance in the conduct of human affairs' (anonymous reviewer). Some feminists (and anthropologists, social scientists, and others) have championed narrative accounts as being closer to a true voice of authority in academic discourse. Litosseliti (2002, abstract) argues that construction of 'women's language' as 'irrational and emotional affects the organization and content of arguments, specifically by producing an additional conversational burden for the women participating in the arguments'. Lamb (1991) and Meyer (1993) argue against argumentative conventions in the academy. In the edited collection by Berrill, *Perspectives on Written Argument*, Lamb (1996) suggests that argument – the mode that validates the essay – is seen from a feminist perspective 'in pejorative terms, as an expression of patriarchy' (p. 258) and sees the challenge as creating a rhetorical space that is not marginalized and yet avoids the pitfalls of the patriarchal mode; the creation of such a space will retain and celebrate the personal voice (e.g., avoiding bland and authoritative use of 'we', so common in the traditional essay) but at the same time recognize that the audience is academic. The approach is rhetorical, arguing that 'who can write, and why, using what forms, are always questions to ask' (p. 262) in composing for the academy. From another perspective, Giltrow (2000), as has been noted in Chapter 1, suggests that 'argument' is too abstract a concept to be useful in composition practice in universities because of its ideological associations with academic convention and patriarchy. The feminist drive, on the whole, has been to move the underlying metaphors for the exploration of argument and the essay toward metaphors of construction, dance, and journey and away from metaphors of war (Berrill, 1996); away from argument as persuasion, with its dependence on logic for making validity claims, and toward argument (and the essay) as exploratory tools in the pursuit of knowledge; and away from argument as adversarial to more consensual conceptions (Costello & Mitchell, 1995).

Concern about the essay, therefore, is expressed on a number of counts: the poor performance of secondary school-age children in argument as opposed to narrative forms; the stultifying nature of the academic essay form and its effect on the expression of argument; the structural weakness in argumentation at conceptual and 'arrangement' levels; the inadequate nature of evidence provided to support claims; the conflation between 'assignment' and 'essay' in students' minds; the lack of explicit criteria and/or guidance from tutors on the writing of the essay; the lack of personal conviction or 'voice' in the writing; and unacknowledged assumptions about the patriarchal nature of the essay as a genre.

Why is the Essay So Central to Assessment in Higher Education?

There are a number of reasons that can be put forward for the centrality of the essay in higher education. First, it is a genre and text-type in which *explicitness* is a key characteristic. In an essay, you spell out connections, whether the essay is expository or argumentative. There is little or no suggestiveness or nuancing in the essay: everything is 'above board'. Second, the essay sits firmly within *the rationalist and humanist paradigm*; it is supported by a belief that discourse in words is important and that the presentation and exchange of ideas is fundamental to human civilized discourse. Third, it is a genre that lends itself to persuasive discourse, again in an explicit way: ideas are paraded, supported by evidence, linked into meaningful sequences, and commented upon in order to *persuade* the reader of the strength of the writer's position. These related qualities make the essay eminently *assessable*: that is probably the main reason why the essay has such a hold on assessment practices and conventions in the academy. Any academic will confirm that, despite the presence of other forms of submission in the academy, the essay allows tutors/supervisors/lecturers not only to gauge the student's understanding but to differentiate between students and thus arrive at a marking list. The essay, then, is the genre par excellence for assessment in the academy.

If you take a conspiracy view of affairs, you might say that the centrality of the essay in the academy is a subtly insidious form of gate-keeping in that the 'ground-rules' (Sheeran & Barnes, 1991) for success are not always spelled out. Despite the presence of handouts on 'what makes a good essay' – which vary from obsession with surface form, such as attention to referencing systems, proof-reading, and the like to vague advice on 'structuring your ideas' – it is often not clear what tutors mean by an 'essay' and what students understand by it. When there is a mismatch between tutors' and students' expectations, trouble can ensue. This trouble is compounded by tutors who write elliptical or shorthand comments in the margins of essays, such as '*non-sequitur*' or '?', or simply concentrate on the surface features at the expense of any real attention being devoted to the structuring and expression of ideas in the essay.

In ideal circumstances, conversely, tutors set out the ground rules, respond to student outlines or drafts, and write full and explicit responses to work once it is submitted. An example of the ground rules is given here:

> A typical assignment is characterized by strengths in relation to some of the assessment criteria, and weaknesses in relation to others. Therefore, in reaching a decision about the grade to be awarded, the balance between strengths and weaknesses is assessed.
>
> Work of PASS standard will typically demonstrate the majority of the following characteristics where applicable:
>
> - a satisfactory understanding of the main points and issues in the assignment
> - a clear and logical structure
> - a well-sustained sequence of ideas

- development of a well-substantiated argument, claim, or theory
- evidence of critical engagement with substantial and relevant literature
- sound analysis of the main points and issues, with reference to literature where appropriate
- the relating of conclusions to arguments made and evidence presented
- critical reflection on own experience, where appropriate
- expertise in key aspects of the specialist field
- little or no irrelevant material
- no errors of fact that detract significantly from the content of the assignment
- no unsubstantiated value judgements and in addition, for a research-based assignment involving the collection of empirical data:
- evidence of critical engagement with methodological literature
- satisfactory presentation and analysis of the data gathered.

Some analysis of the language of such guidelines or ground rules is necessary. First, it should be pointed out that the diction is cautious: 'work of PASS standard will *typically* demonstrate the *majority* of the following characteristics *where applicable*' (my italics). Like the term 'normally' in much assessment discourse in education contexts, there is always room for variation when it comes to the presentation of actual texts for assessment. One could argue that the criteria are couched so cautiously as to be useless; a student could argue, for example, that none of the criteria was *applicable* to his or her work because that work sang to a different tune, or that the *majority* of criteria were inapplicable. Perhaps, also, the majority of criteria that were applicable could be the ones that were least important (there is no hierarchy of value). Second, when it comes to particular criteria, what is 'satisfactory' or 'well-sustained' to one person may be unsatisfactory or unsustained to another; relevance is relative; and 'where appropriate' is a slippery phrase, apparently revealing what counts as appropriate but actually leaving to the marker's judgment the definition of propriety. Despite the ambiguous nature of the diction, 'work of REFERRAL [i.e., close to fail] standard will typically demonstrate failure to meet several of the pass criteria or one of them in a more significant way'.

The interesting thing about this set of ground rules is that despite the fact they are relatively explicit, international students on an MA programme still did not feel that they made sufficiently explicit the requirements of the assignment. There was no guidance, for example, on the structure or subheadings of the expected assignment and therefore no guide to the essential shape of the genre or text-type expected. It is possible, in a wish to be liberal enough to allow a range of text-types, that the course had unwittingly forced the students into a guessing game of what form and format it was expecting. They, therefore, would feel safer reverting to what they took to be the structure of the conventional essay: introduction, development, conclusion (itself a distillation of classical rhetorical structures).

Alternatives to the Essay

So much for the conventional essay. What about alternative forms and text-types? Perhaps because of the Yeatsian maxim that 'ancient salt is best packing', students seem reluctant to abandon the essay as their preferred form for submitting coursework. Another reason for their timidity might be that they would rather the devil you know than the devil you don't know. I want to examine some examples of students' work that do not follow conventional format to look at the possibilities and problems therein. I will discuss four examples: essays written in metaphorical mode, Socratic dialogue, autobiographical writing and an unconventional thesis – a thesis that eschews the conventions by combining narrative, autobiography, poetry, and figurative writing in its 'argument'.

A visiting Italian student recently submitted an essay on language diversity and multilingualism that was not only clearly articulated, well structured, well argued, scholarly in its range and depth of referencing, and so on – all the general criteria expected of an undergraduate essay to meet in the humanities – but written with imagination, commitment, and verve. It used the device of a gardening metaphor to give it an extra dimension. Its title, 'On the art of gardening', was played out in sections entitled 'All around the garden', on identity, passports, and ethnic capital; 'Say it with a flower' on individual and collective experience of bi- and multilingualism; 'Say it with more flowers' on the debate on assimilation, multiculturalism and 'what's in between'; 'Uprooting obsolete gardening practices' on the anachronistic nature of monolingualism; and finally, in appendices listed as 'Small flowers'. Here are the opening words of the Introduction (it should have been titled 'Come into the garden'):

> 'Language diversity makes the language more difficult to tend' (Garcia, in Baker, 1998). Gardeners need to protect rarer flowers, control those that spread quickly and naturally, increase those in danger of extinction, and maybe add more flowers to make the garden more attractive to the outside environment. In fact, the garden of the 21st century – and all that is around it – is no longer static and fixed...

And so the essay progresses through its argument to its first-class rating. Essays of lesser quality tend to either fall short on some of the criteria listed here or they misconstrue the nature of the essay and the nature of the contract with the marker of the essay – the gatekeeper of standards and of the text-types approved by the academy.

The Socratic dialogue, by definition, takes dialogic form. That is to say, the argument proceeds explicitly, as in the conventional essay, with the entertainment of abstract propositions, the provision of evidence to support them, and other devices. In a sense, the Socratic dialogue is more explicit than the essay in that the two or more voices (e.g., references, an implied counter-locutor) that are usually distilled into a single authorial voice in the essay are here revealed for what they are: at least two voices. A typical example of the beginning of a Socratic dialogue in translation is this:

Socrates: I dare say, Lysis, that your father and mother love you very much?
Lysis: Certainly, Socrates.
Socrates: Then they would wish you to be as happy as possible?
Lysis: Yes.
Socrates: Is a person happy when he is a slave and cannot do what he likes?
Lysis: I should think not.

The potential weakness of Lysis's position is already exposed by Socrates, who goes on to argue that a young person can never do entirely as he likes and, therefore, cannot be happy. In Socratic dialogue, the dice are weighted toward Socrates: he uses the interlocutors to reveal the inadequacy of their position or reasoning, demonstrating the truth of an argument through exposure to underlying principles. The pedagogical approach is similar to that of a teacher who, through questioning, uses students' responses to demonstrate a case rather than following and answering student questions.

When the Socratic dialogue is used as a form of response by undergraduate students, the relationship between the questioner and answerer is not so much one of an authority figure and an apprentice as between two voices in an internal dialogue. In the following extract from a 4,000-word 'essay', a student has presented a series of photographs and is exploring the theoretical aspects of framing:

> *What are you trying to say by showing these photographs?*
>
> I was trying to convey the idea of the power of framing. By framing images we are shaping what is shown and sometimes creating a false impression of an event. Through this kind of framing we can learn that we must not believe our first impressions. We must learn not to stereotype…A frame gives something a focus and so can manipulate an image to disfigure the truth. By framing something we are forcing our selection onto others.

The device of question-and-answer gives the student the opportunity to be self-critical, to reveal his or her underlying assumptions – and, by revealing the ideology underlying the propositions that are put forward, opens up the possibility of criticism. The oft-repeated demand on undergraduate and postgraduate students, viz that work must be 'critical', is made more accessible by a simple device such as question-and-answer format.

Examples of reflective critical autobiographical work in students' assignments are rarer than we might imagine (such is the emphasis on the disinterested voice) but, nevertheless, a combination of a personal positioning and an authoritative critical exploration of an idea is possible. In the worlds of journalism and *belles lettres* (cf. *The New Yorker*, *The Guardian*, *The London Review of Books*), personal essays of this kind are common; they sit in the tradition going back to Montaigne, Bacon, and Addison and *The Spectator*. In a first-year undergraduate essay on the spectator's role in drama/theatre, a particular student begins by reflecting on being a spectator at a major soccer match in a crowd of more than 67,000 people:

> I pictured the game without these onlookers, a ball being kicked around, players doing what they do best but for what purpose? I tried to imagine a goal being scored without the roar of appreciation and joy that filled the stadium immediately afterwards, and how the players would feel having just missed a goal without the clapping which followed to say that it was a good effort and it doesn't mean it's all over. It was a difficult vision to conjure up in my mind, one that felt wrong and pointless...

The essay continues by comparing the role of the audience in literature, art, and theatre:

> An audience member of a theatre production has similar responsibilities to that of a viewer of a painting, in that they have the choice of whether or not to be fully indulged [sic] in the performance or stand back and simply watch so as to constructively criticize. Their obligation to artists, however, differs greatly in that their participation in some cases is essential to the success of the play.

Throughout the essay, the student weaves her own experience as a drama/education student and as an actor, with a critical appraisal of the role of the audience in different contexts. She cites other works on the topic so that, in the same way as for a dialogue, she is able to bring in other voices – as in the conventional essay.

My third examples relate to the doctoral thesis – a text-type that is bound by tight convention and might be termed a very long essay. I wish to draw attention to two types of writing for the PhD/DPhil, however, that break the convention and thus tell us something different about writing a large-scale argument at doctoral level. First, a number of years ago, I co-examined a PhD thesis that did not look like a thesis. Although it was bound in the conventional way, it consisted of sections of narrative, poetry, blank pages, highly figurative writing – and sections of conventional argumentative/discursive prose. This experimental *Tristram Shandy*–like work left out many of the explicit links and structures of the conventional thesis (e.g., signposting) in favour of gaps and silences for the reader to fill. Reading the thesis was, therefore, a hard but enjoyable task: as a reader, I had to make my own connections between the various sections and respond to implications and explications in the work. The other external examiner and I were clear that the candidate should be awarded the PhD: the work fulfilled all the criteria for the award, though we did ask for a brief *vade mecum* at the start to advise the reader of his or her role. Our request for a brief note to the reader at the start to alert him or her to the challenge ahead was perhaps a gesture toward explicitness and the conventional form of the essay/thesis. Reading the work made us think all the more clearly about the top-down and ideas-based nature of the essay and of its hold on conventional practice at doctoral and lower levels of performance in the academy.

My second example of unconventionality in writing at doctoral level is the case of a current student who, in her early drafts of a literature review on discourses of schooling in an Asian country, is writing with personal commitment and verve: one might say, from anger:

> Discourses in…high schools nowadays still very much accord to the management style of old capitalism and the ethos of dictator politics. Mass control and authoritarian teaching are adopted [from the start]. Schools are very much mass-production factories, small business companies which constitute the mainstream economic power in [the country], or concentration camps with bottom-line workers (students) who do [not] understand what they are doing and middle managers (teachers) to pass messages from the top (the principal) and supervise them in their work (making sure students attend and are awake in every class, wear correct uniforms and do the jobs asked even when they are already dog-tired). The goal of this factory is mass production (scores in the examination) and the profit for this factory exceeds that for the students.

At this stage in the writing, the prose is not supported by references to existing research; rather, it is driven by intense personal commitment. Later, the student refers to authorities in the field of social critique and discourse analysis to underpin her argument. However, the intense personal writing is framed by references to *The New Work Order* (Gee, Hull, & Lankshear, 1997) and followed by close reference to works about the ideologies concerned and about the social and political context in the country in question. Such writing cannot be considered arid; on the contrary, the political positioning and commitment are a welcome quality, framed as it is within the checks and balances of academic discourse. Our role as supervisors of this research is to help the student maintain the energy, critical edge, and passion of her research while at the same time ensuring that she does what is necessary to fulfil her lesser aim: the achievement of a successful thesis and the award of a PhD. We wish more students wrote with such commitment.

The Personal Voice

I showed an earlier draft of this chapter to undergraduate students in an 'Argumentation in Education' module, offering them the chance to comment on its argument and also to see whether the experience of other students chimed with their own. One student wrote

> I have found during my short time at [the University] that one's own personal style can be an asset or a handicap depending on the assessor. For example, you enjoyed your student's metaphor of global languages and a garden. I have tried metaphors and anecdotes (admittedly some too puerile) on some lecturers and have had them dismissed as not academic enough. Consequently I have become more impersonal in my writing.

Whereas 16-year-old students at the General Certificate of Secondary Education level have been encouraged since 1986 to combine personal response with a more 'impersonal' understanding of a subject, sixth forms and higher education seem wedded to the notion that the essay should be written with an impersonal voice. It is as if there is a hierarchy of the personal/impersonal in the grading of essays: for the bottom grades, it is acceptable to express opinion in a personal way (but usually unsupported by evidence or reference to the works of others); in the middle grades, convention dictates that the personal voice is erased and the impersonal, detached voice is favoured; perhaps only in the highest grades is the personal allowed back in, as long as it is supported or forms part of a work that is heavily referenced and evidenced.

The student just quoted, however, has retreated to the impersonal because of a perceived inconsistency between tutors: some welcome divergence from the norm, others don't. Those who don't like it feel that 'metaphors and anecdotes', for example, are inappropriate in the academic genre of the essay, perhaps because they move the work away from the rationalist, explicit, distanced voice they are looking for. The challenge for departments in higher education is to debate such variation and work out in a common policy and practice so that students are neither disadvantaged nor confused and so that students can find the appropriate form of expression for what they want to say in assignments. In such debates, it is likely that lecturers and teachers will get behind the surface forms and their associations and begin to concentrate on the arrangement and expression of ideas. The key move forward pedagogically will be to recognize that, on the one hand, finding the right channels for expression, growth, and learning in written assignments is a rhetorical issue that needs attention but that, conversely, lecturers need to broaden their sense of what is possible in higher education assignments and be clear about the extent and nature of that variation.

Conclusion

Is the essay dead? No. The essay, both in its literary/journalistic form and in its shape as the default genre of assessment in schools and in further and higher education, is alive and well. Part of its longevity is a result of its flexibility, its ability to adapt to different functions. Although it reflects the rationalist paradigm, underpinned by argumentation and in turn by logic, dialectic, and rhetoric, it gives students the space to inject personal perspectives, to alter the sequence and play with the tone of the genre. Abreactions or alternatives to the essay – like the Socratic dialogue, the autobiographical critical reflection, the book review, the diatribe/tract – can be seen as true alternatives to the default genre, or they can be seen as alternative versions of or routes toward the essay, keeping it alive by offering access to its essentially multi-voiced nature, drawing attention its explicit, rationalist nature, or offering a different angle for the writer/reader. Refreshing a genre like this, or indeed challenging more vigorously its dominance as the default genre of the academy, is what keeps the most important qualities alive: clear thinking, exchange of views, reasoned commitment, and lively expression.

The Practical Dimension

Activity 9.1

The default genre for assessment in the humanities, social sciences, and some of the arts is the essay, often running to about 5,000 words in length. Consider what alternative forms of writing and composition are possible and how they might be incorporated into the range of forms in which work can be submitted. Criteria for assessment may be no different for these alternative forms than for the essay, but you will need to make sure they are fit for purpose.

Activity 9.2

Revisit the criteria for the assessment of argumentation in undergraduate and/or postgraduate assignments in your discipline or department. Do they mention argumentation? Are there ways in which the criteria could be made more detailed or more explicit, so that students can be guided as to the kinds of argumentation that are expected? What do students think of the criteria?

10
The Significance of Feedback from Lecturers

In this chapter, the views of lecturers are considered, based primarily on feedback to writing assignments by students. The principal focus of this chapter is on how professors and lecturers negotiate and establish the parameters of argumentation in their disciplines through feedback; how they encourage and 'police' these parameters; and how alternative forms of argumentation can be accepted into academic practice.

Feedback at Undergraduate Level

One of the most highly prized aspects of an undergraduate or postgraduate university education is feedback, partly because it is usually individualized and (hopefully) formative and detailed. Feedback comes in oral and written forms, sometimes in small groups, sometimes in large groups, but more often than not in individualized written feedback to assignments. It is sometimes a controversial topic. Students are keen to receive feedback on the work they submit, both in terms of a summative grade and in terms of formative diagnostic feedback on how they can improve. The latter kind of feedback needs to come at a point in the term/semester or the course when it can be used; in other words, it needs to be delivered at critical points in the student's development so that it has maximum effect. If it is delivered after the event, it is likely to have minimal or no effect.

Two kinds of feedback are presented here, both from a first-year course as part of a three-year history degree: first, written feedback on a coursework assignment; second, comments on performance in an examination essay and on the course as a whole.

The feedback on the coursework essay indicates that it is for the course 'Historical Perspectives'. The student's title is 'Gender and Society: an Analytical Comparison of *Dislodging the Centre/Complicating the Dialectic* by Laura Tabili and *Labour History and the Gender Turn* by L. L. Frader'. The essay cover sheet that students are required to attach to their submitted work contains spaces for an assessment of English and presentation (in this case, 'very good' throughout with one exception – checking for typing errors) and for structure and argument. The sub-sections of this category are overall structure, clarity of argument, relevance to question, use of evidence, and clarity of conclusion. Sadly, none of these are completed in the example.

The comments, however, are extensive:

> This is a very good essay which discusses gender and society in the texts by Tabili and Frader. You have clearly really thought about their different approaches – how they compare and differ, their advantages and disadvantages and how you feel about their approaches. It would have been useful to have been told a little more about each article – what period are they attempting to cover and where? You consistently compare both writers throughout the essay – a good approach which encourages strong analysis. Your essay is written well and is neatly presented – thank you. There are a handful of errors to correct. As the overall theme which you needed to reflect upon was society (of which gender is just one part) it would have been beneficial for you to make the link more clearly.

The feedback gives an overall impression (reflected also in the mark of 64/100 – that represents just below the mid-point of a 2.1 degree class in the United Kingdom, which means 'very good' – the top class of marks (known as a 1st) would be in the 70s and above). It appears that the student has the broad conceptual, thematic, and methodological/procedural structures in place: comparison, similarities and differences, advantages and disadvantages. This structural opposition at the heart of much argumentational writing is a pattern that derives from Kant and Hegel and manifests itself in the 'for and against' model of high school essay writing. Furthermore, the student 'consistently compare[s] both writers throughout the essay'. Such a technique gives the student writer the possibility of making comparisons sentence by sentence and paragraph by paragraph and in broader structures throughout the essay, thus enabling a richer argumentational texture in the writing. There seem to be two major criticisms: that we needed to know more about each article and that a stronger, more critical link between society and gender would have been helpful. Perhaps it is these qualities that would have raised the overall score into the 'first' category?

The two criticisms are at the same time easy and difficult to address. At one level, unpacking the relationship between gender and society is a major task and could not be easily undertaken in a history essay, let alone in a sociology one. The best that could be done would be a concise, highly referenced paragraph revealing that there is a complex relationship between the two concepts and highlighting some of the points of dispute of tensions within it (and going on to exploit those tensions). At a lower, less analytically conceptual level, providing more detail about the two articles that are compared is ostensibly straightforward. However, the essay should not be packed with descriptive detail or exposition, and a student would have to tread carefully to make sure that his or her commentary on the two texts was critical, sceptical, and relevant to the analysis in hand.

Finally, what is disappointing about the feedback is the general, procedural nature of it. Much of it could apply to any essay (the generic qualities we discussed in Chapter 3), though in this particular case there is little if any attention to argumentation. Some of the attention is devoted to the accuracy and presentation, and annotations on the essay itself are all about that aspect. It is as if the lecturer has a template in his or her mind, and the essay – as student offering – is measured against that template. The template itself may take the form of a set of criteria that, by their very nature, are going to be generic.

A second piece of written feedback is worth comparing, for this one comes in response to an examination essay. These essays are 'end of term' (end-of-semester) summative essays and count directly toward the overall degree class. In this particular case, the essay is written (by a different student) for the module 'Modern period – general' under the specific title 'Why did Europe remain at peace between 1945 and 1991?'. Unlike the feedback to the previously discussed essay, this one does have an indication from the lecturer as to the structural and argumentational qualities. In terms of overall structure and clarity of argument, it is rated as 'Satisfactory', and in terms of relevance to the question, use of evidence, and clarity of the conclusion, it is rated as 'Satisfactory to Good'.

The feedback reads:

> This exam essay shows an engagement with the question, but struggles to provide a nuanced answer. The student touches upon the right areas, but could have made more of it [sic]. She could have challenged the question more, e.g. was Europe at peace during the period concerned, and is the absence of war the only benchmark of the existence of peace? The student mentions Soviet interventions and almost notes dictatorships; an exploration of these aspects could have led to a more analytical answer. The introduction contains a strong factual error, suggesting, with other signs, a lack of proofreading. Some claims are also questionable (see. e.g. p1 on détente; or pp2-3 and p5 on the death of ideology – which would need better explanation). At times, the student gets slightly distracted. Overall, the argument could have been clearer, with a better structure that links each point to the question. This is nonetheless a good attempt.

In many ways, this is better feedback, as it concentrates on the substance of the argument in the student's essay. In a more general comment on the student's performance on the course as a whole, there are indications that the student in question needs to 'resist the temptation to include too much', with an acknowledgement that such a move forward will be hard work. It is a move that concerns concentration on the question in hand rather than a comprehensive account of the topic in question. From the third sentence in the preceding feedback, the lecturer homes in on the actual substance of the question: 'Was Europe at peace during the period concerned, and is the absence of war the only benchmark of the existence of peace?'. Such a challenge appears to suggest that students should question the terms of the question that is posed or that they have posed themselves. Such a high degree of criticality is prized as long as the exercise does not become one of increasing etherization of the topic; if the criticality is brought to bear on the question in hand, and if it reveals new perspectives on the question, it will be highly rated by the lecturer. In other words, the question set for the essay is not taken at face value but used proactively (almost aggressively, certainly sceptically) to shed further light on the topic.

Such a 'reading' of the question set – or a self-critical account of a title that is generated by the student him- or herself – seems essential, not only in history essays but in other disciplines, too. This is especially the case wherein the discipline is focused on words and in which the assignments take the form of verbal essays: English, modern foreign languages, classics, politics, sociology, and so on. That these disciplines cover the arts, humanities, and social sciences is interesting. In some art subjects, for example music and fine art, *writing* a response may not be such a prized form of expression for the student. However, in history of art, musicology, and other disciplines that are *about* another mode of expression, then words tend to come to the fore.

In short, the feedback to this particular essay is rich and works at a number of different levels. It is about the substance of ideas and historical knowledge exhibited by the student; about structure and rhetorical matters; and about surface features ('a lack of proofreading'). Such feedback repays close reading by the student if he or she is to improve as a response to it. It provides no easy formulae for improvement but rather encourages the student to raise the level of critical attention in a number of ways.

Feedback at Postgraduate Level

I look in this section at various kinds of feedback at the doctoral level. I am jumping from undergraduate feedback in the previous section to doctoral on the assumption that readers can work out the gradations in between. Feedback is also best provided against explicit criteria that the student is aware of and is working to.

Typically, postgraduate feedback will be more extensive than at undergraduate level because of the smaller number of students that lecturers engage with and because the students are working more individually and at a higher academic level. Feedback is highly prized and, indeed, essential to student progress. The examples I discuss here are my own, and I have anonymized the students to protect their identities. These examples are presented not as exemplars but for the attention (or not) that they give to argumentation, which I draw out in my discussion of each piece of feedback.

Feedback is fairly formal at the doctoral level in these cases in that it addresses the 'candidate', but it is always made available to the candidate so that he or she can benefit from it and improve his or her own revisions of the submitted thesis or future work.

Here is a first example of a preliminary report, used to inform discussion in a *viva voce* examination and made available to the student:

> This thesis explores what primary children *do* in their writing in English. It focuses on three genres or text-types – diary, letter and story – and via the work of six principal participants, aged between 8 and 10 in [a particular country's] primary system, analyses textual and syntactic aspects of the work. The thesis proceeds from an introduction, which sets out the research questions and the broad context for the research, through chapters on the local context, on the theoretical framework for the study, and on methodology to a series of chapters which analyse the texts in detail. There follow a brief chapter which considers the potential for the study of texts and signs in mixed-code use, and then a concluding chapter which examines implications of the study for practice and future research.
>
> The candidate is at pains to point out what the thesis is not trying to do. It is not intended as a study of second language use (even though the participants are native speakers using English as their second language); nor is it a study of the processes of writing and composition. Rather, its principal function is to describe the textual and syntactic features of children's writing at a particular stage in their development. Accordingly, the research questions are framed to ask 'what do children do in their writing with regard to syntactical and textual aspects?' and 'what would a method of analysis look like?' to achieve clarity with regard to the first question. Secondary questions look at developmental and cross-genre issues.
>
> The principal (substantial) research question is well framed, though it might be repeated in full throughout the thesis rather than in its shorthand version, 'what do children *do* in their writing?'. Nevertheless, the focus is clear and consistent throughout. There is no doubt that the question is answered. The second main question is less satisfactorily answered in that there is not much originality nor discussion of methodological issues. Given the main research question, however, there isn't much scope for such discussion as the candidate uses tried and tested methods from previous researchers in the field. The subsidiary questions are answered in the course of the thesis, but without much evidence to substantiate the claims made (in that, for instance, it is hard

> to make generalizations about development with such a small sample). Strategically, then, the candidate might have done better to focus on the main question and left the others to be answered *passim*.
>
> In general, I find the analysis competent and admirably detailed; the structure excellent; the reinforcement of the structure in clear introduction and summaries very good indeed; the bibliography well produced and comprehensive; and the presentation first-class. Despite my reservations about some aspects of the work – which can be summarized as a lack of critical perspective, a taxonomic urgency that seems to miss larger points about the writing and the fact that the thesis just touches on mixed-code writing – my initial impression is that the thesis should pass.
>
> I look forward to further exploration in the *viva*.

The first paragraph rehearses the broad argument that the student has put forward. It tries to understand that argument and to use it as a basis for the comments that follow. It is important for responses to do this so that that there is a common foundation upon which further discussion can build; and it is particularly important, in argumentational terms, that the examiner (or teacher, lecturer, responder) is sensitive to the paradigm in which the student is working. If, for example, an examiner has a preference for research methodologies that provide the basis for quantitative analysis of data, it is going to be difficult for a student who has worked in a paradigm that assumes qualitative data are best suited to answering a particular research question. The examiner needs to be aware of the ideological framing of the research project and to gauge whether there is a 'fit' between the kind of question that is asked and the methodology and methods used to answer it.

Part of the response to the thesis is couched in the second paragraph, which acknowledges what the student is *not* trying to do. Such an awareness of selection and limitations for the research project is helpful to state, as a student, in the body of the thesis itself, so that examiners are clear about the framework within which they are being asked to comment.

It can be seen that the third paragraph focuses principally on clarity of design and expression. These are qualities of argumentation that have not, so far, been discussed in the book but which are essential for an explicit form of communication like argumentation. The comments concentrate on how the clarity could be improved and how well – and how elegantly – the various elements of the thesis fit together.

The final paragraph touches on various aspects of argumentation. There is, first, the question of analysis that in argumentational terms will be related to the appropriateness and design (including the provenance) of the analytical framework for the particular question that is to be answered and the kinds of data that have been collected. Second, there is attention to the structure, which will have provided the main architectural argument of the thesis itself.

Comments on the flagging up of that structure with summaries of the research along the way are indicative of a need for the thesis to be explicit but also, more pragmatically, of a need for signposts during the reading of a long text ('we have come so far on the journey of the argument; now we are heading in this direction; our compass bearing is reading due north' and so on). Third, mention of the bibliography indicates recognition of the scholarship that the student has brought to the enterprise; more important, this is scholarship *in the service of* argument in that the references provide support and counter-point, and orientation points, for the research and its expression.

The reservations expressed in that final paragraph also derive from concerns regarding argumentation. Criticality has been discussed previously in this book as closely related to argumentation (and additionally in the final chapter). The point about an excess of taxonomy suggests that the student has not quite got the balance right between categorization (paradigmatic analysis) on the one hand and the sequencing of ideas (syntagmatic analysis) on the other. Too much of the former makes for a weighty, scientific, or quasi-scientific approach to analysis; too much of the latter makes for momentum and narrative but not necessarily the clarity and sense of difference and differentiation that are needed for conceptual analysis.

In the following example (from a thesis in applied linguistics and gender studies), a different approach from the student toward argumentation requires a different response from the examiner. In this case, the topic itself and the means of communication are argument:

> This thesis examines the relationship between three social constructs: argumentation, gender and morality. It does so through a literature review of the fields from which each of the phenomena builds its identity in contemporary discourse, and through two kinds of empirical research: the analysis of features from *The Guardian*'s 'Head to Head' column, and from data gathered from two focus groups which discuss the topic of marriage.
>
> In terms of research paradigm, the thesis operates in an unconventional but consistent way. It poses six research questions and then proceeds to explore the issues generated by these questions. We are not, therefore, looking at a classic design of hypothesis and proof/disproof or even at a principal research question which a thesis attempts to answer. Rather, the range of research questions set out clearly at the beginning of the thesis provides a framework or series of points between which the researcher weaves her argument. What is produced is a network approach to the problems identified, where complementarity and mutual illumination is as important as claim and proof. The model of argument assumed is therefore one of consensus as much as conflict – and such an approach is reflected in the discussions recorded and transcribed via the focus groups.

> The thesis is aware of its approach, and sets out the justification for it in the conclusion as well as in the introduction. The limitations are made clear on p383. They *are* limitations, but understandable ones. From a conservative perspective, the scale of the empirical studies might be seen to be small and lightweight. However, the exploration of actual phenomena is thorough and the intention is to uncover and reveal interconnections between the main areas of study. The degree of scholarship as evidenced in the range of works literature review and also in the critical approach to the works examined is more than adequate; as is the detailed textual analysis of the transcripts.
>
> There is no doubting the originality of the enterprise. There are few studies which attempt to bring together gender, argumentation and morality. While not publishable it its present form, the thesis might provide material for a number of articles which focus on particular aspects of it. The contribution to knowledge largely rests in the juxtaposition of the three main areas of interest and in questions which are raised by such an act.
>
> Structurally, the thesis is sound. The structure is reinforced by excellent summaries throughout at the end of chapters, a subtle weaving together of the various themes, and much cross-referencing. The appendices are well presented and provide evidence of meticulous scholarship. Overall, the presentation is excellent.
>
> The thesis fulfils the criteria set out for the award of PhD in the guidance notes for the examination of research degrees.
>
> I look forward to a full discussion of some of the implications of the research; to discussion of the textual analysis and focus group methodology; and to exploration of the particular research paradigm in which the thesis positions itself. The network approach to the research questions has made for a thesis that is well-woven and coherent.

Referring back to the discussion of interdisciplinarity, earlier in the book, the types of argumentation implied by the subject focus are varied and complex. In this case, the informing fields are applied linguistics, gender studies, and ethics. More specifically, we could say that the disciplines behind these fields are linguistics, sociology, and philosophy. The candidate chose a methodology that involved making links between the various nodes of interest rather than a single proposition that required a set of evidence to interrogate it and/or support it. Indeed, the data set that appeared in the thesis was relatively small; the key to the success of the thesis, however, was its originality; its exploration of the issues of argumentation, gender, and ethics via the three disciplines and associated fields; and the use made of the data.

In this case, the second paragraph of the preliminary report sets out what is argumentational about the thesis. What is interesting, in reflecting on this feedback for the purposes of this book, is the way the argumentation is discovered and expressed: the phrase 'where complementarity and mutual illumination is as important as claim and proof' indicates that the argument paradigm that is operating in the thesis is different from an Aristotelian or Toulminian paradigm and, indeed, from most theories and models of argumentation that require 'statement and proof' in some form. Rather, the model of argumentation behind the thesis in question was one of tentative connection, of suggestion and inference, of the overall interconnecting network of links that made up a pattern that itself constituted a theoretical, argued model. It may be the case that, in hindsight, the thesis contributed to a clarification of thinking in the field and to the opening up of possibilities of connection that had not previously been imagined. What it did not do was prove a hypothesis.

One further point about this feedback: it notes, in paragraph five, that the structural clarity of the whole, reinforced or marked by the end-of-chapter summaries, is impressive and that the meticulous scholarship contributes to the overall quality of the work.

The Practical Dimension

Activity 10.1

Collect written feedback from lecturers on submitted and marked work by students. Examine it in detail to see what degree of attention is given to argumentation. Is there more than just an exhortation to argue more cogently, more coherently? If so, what forms does it take? Could there be attention to particular aspects of argumentation, like structure, position, or logical or quasi-logical sequence that would give the feedback more focus?

Activity 10.2

Examine the criteria for the assessment of work in your department and for the particular courses that you teach. Is argumentation mentioned? If so, is there any more-explicit or detailed account of what that means, to guide lecturers in how they should respond to students' work – and ultimately to help students produce work that is highly valued?

11
Methodological Issues in Researching Argumentation

Part of the problem in argumentation research is that it is informed by a number of disciplines, including sociology, linguistics, discourse studies, philosophy, and literature. Such a range of disciplines means that the underlying ideological assumptions and value systems are not stable or paradigmatic; the field is interdisciplinary. An added difficulty is that the phenomenon of argumentation is only evident in texts, images, codes, and the like; determining the nature of argued thought needs a range of approaches. This chapter draws on cutting-edge thinking on the questions of *how* to research the field. First, it deals with the question of what counts as evidence in the field of education; then it builds on a recent exploration of methodological issues in the investigation of argument and argumentation.

What Counts as Evidence?

The question of what counts as evidence is one that not only higher education needs to consider; it is also a key question for fields such as law, forensics, and scientific research. This part of the chapter focuses on the particular question of what counts as evidence in education research – an interdisciplinary field.

The twenty-first century, so far, has shown a marked preference for educational reform based on *evidence*, though it is not always clear what kind of evidence is called for, nor how to weigh it – nor, indeed, how it can be used to change policy and/or practice. The purpose of the following sections is to explore what counts as evidence in the field of educational studies.

Before embarking on such an exploration, it is necessary first to define the nature of evidence and which aspects of education are being referred to. Data, for example, are not necessarily evidence, and vice versa. Data can take various forms but are inert unless they are informed by a claim, thesis, or proposition. To use Toulmin's terminology (1958/2003), a claim is supported by grounds (evidence), the connection warranted by values and conventions within a field (e.g., a discipline). *Evidence*, therefore, is infused with ideas, assumptions, and values. Data, relatively speaking, are not.

Part of the problem addressed in this chapter is that education is not a discipline, such as history or biology. It is a *field of enquiry and practice* illuminated by various disciplines: most notably, sociology, psychology, philosophy, economics, and so on. As a result, there is no single theory or set of theories that can be said to underpin education. The Toulminian formula cannot, therefore, apply in the same way, as he acknowledged in the distinction between field-dependence and field-independence. What counts as evidence in this field will inevitably be more diverse than in disciplines, where set (or competing) theories and warrants (ways of connecting claims and evidence) are more established; indeed, they are the very fabric of disciplines. In such a wide and varied field, the kinds of evidence that can be called upon are going to vary according to purpose.

Existing Evidence

Often overlooked in the search for evidence is *existing* evidence. There are a number of different kinds of such evidence available, much of it under-used as researchers, policy makers, practitioners, and others feel the need for new empirical evidence to justify their actions. The drive for evidence-based or evidence-informed action has, however, given rise to a new infrastructure for managing and synthesizing evidence.

Research Reviews

In terms of a hierarchy of reliable research reviews, systematic reviews hold the highest position (see Torgerson, 2003). They might be better termed 'explicit' reviews in that all good reviews might claim to be systematic. The differences between so-called systematic reviews and other kinds are that (a) they are always undertaken by more than one person so that inter-rater reliability, if properly conducted, is a sine qua non; (b) they operate via explicit protocols, comprehensive search strategies, and transparent procedures, so are replicable; (c) they move through a series of stages, distilling the found studies down to the essence of what is required to satisfy the research question(s); and (d) they attempt to synthesize the results of the studies they review. All these stages are an attempt to minimize bias, and systematic reviews probably achieve such minimization better than any other kind of review. Two organizations that specialize in the commissioning, methodology and dissemination of systematic reviews are the American-based Campbell Collaboration and the United Kingdom-based Evidence for Policy and Practice Information and Coordinating Centre (EPPI-Centre). See http://www.campbellcollaboration.org/ for information on the Campbell Collaboration and http://eppi.ioe.ac.uk/reel for the EPPI-Centre's Research Evidence in Education Library.

Though both organizations are associated with positivist, effectiveness-based approaches that would seem to foreground the results of randomized controlled trial studies, both have undertaken a considerable amount of work with qualitatively derived data. The claim, then, that such reviews have fuelled a preference for experimental research as the only means of securing evidence about 'what works' is only partly true (see Biesta, 2007 for a critique of the 'what works' agenda). Randomized controlled trials (RCTs) can help determine what works, but they are not always successful (nor is it always possible to determine education outcomes precisely enough for RCTs to be valid and reliable), nor do they address *why* or *how* an intervention works. Furthermore, their underlying assumptions of causality, and of one-way effects or impact, are not always appropriate to the topic of the review. Such issues are critical when it comes to agreeing what counts as evidence in a particular field.

Lower down the hierarchy of reviews in terms of reliability are expert reviews (often undertaken as government reports, sometimes by a panel or committee supporting the expert); literature reviews by bodies that have an interest in a particular field (e.g., the excellent Futurelab series of reviews on new technologies and learning – see http://www.futurelab.org.uk/research/lit_reviews.htm, or reviews by the British Educational and Communication Technology Agency, such as Becta (2007); reviews by the Organization for Economic and Collaborative Development (OECD), or by the National Research and Development Centre for adult literacy and numeracy, such as Baynham, Macguire, and Morton, (2006); literature reviews in doctoral and masters theses (inevitably the work of one person and therefore more subject to bias, however comprehensive they may be or claim to be); and reviews incorporated into books (e.g., reference encyclopedias), reports, grant bids, or on websites such as wikipedia.com (this latter group may be undertaken by an individual or by a group).

None of the preceding can be considered a final word on a topic or research question, as even systematic reviews need to be updated (and rarely are). A sensible way to proceed, if existing evidence from reviews is to be a foundation for further work of a research, policy, and/or practice nature, is as follows. Whichever is the starting point (e.g., a Google search), it makes sense to establish first what is known in the field on the particular topic of enquiry. This is best done by examining the systematic reviews, then by looking at more recent expert reviews and specialist reviews, and then by investigating recent reports, dissertations, and newly published empirical studies.

Search Engines and Portals

What access to evidence do search engines and portals afford? And what kind of evidence for education is discovered via these routes?

First, more generally, search engines such as Google and Google Scholar give access to the whole range of websites. At the next level down are portals that provide entry to areas of interest in education, such as the Education Evidence Portal (http://www.eep.ac.uk), the British Education Index (http://www.leeds.ac.uk/bei/bei.htm), and the Teacher Training Resource Bank (www.ttrb.ac.uk), the remit of which is to use 'research and evidence to improve teaching and learning'. Academic libraries provide their own portals, such as the University of York's Educational Studies Information Sources facility (http://www.york.ac.uk/services/library/subjects/education.htm) or the Institute of Education's Information Services pages (http://ioewebserver.ioe.ac.uk/ioe/cms/get.asp?cid=10713). There are also a number of subscription-based research databases, such as Education Research Complete (http://web.ebscohost.com/ehost/), that provide access to online journals in the field (and PDF versions of printed journals). At a more specific level are sites devoted to particular aspects or sectors of education, each with their own research pages, such as the Higher Education Academy's site (www.heacademy.ac.uk).

The actual evidence that is elicited via these routes can range from material that is extensively peer-reviewed to material that is posted by individuals or groups on the Web and not at all peer reviewed. The sources of such evidence, therefore, need to be closely examined. It is not the case that just because an article or paper is peer-reviewed it is necessarily better in quality than material that has had no such review prior to publication. Questions need to be asked about the nature of peer review (When was it peer reviewed? How? By whom? With what degree of critique?). However, on balance, peer-reviewed material is likely to be more reliable than material that has not gone through such a process. Though it is often difficult to determine whether a piece has been peer reviewed, it is worth digging for this information as part of the scholarly process (and also getting as close to the primary sources as possible) to be as confident as possible about the foundation for evidence.

Existing Data and Secondary Data Analysis

An under-used source of data for evidence is secondary data analysis: the use, analysis, and application of data collected by someone else. Generally, secondary data analysis avoids many of the problems associated with primary data analysis: it is unobtrusive; it works with data in the public domain; its use is largely free of ethical considerations; it provides bases for comparison; and it has access to large bodies of data. An example of a dataset that is open to public access is available via OECD's PISA Web pages (2007); another is examination results.

There are various guides to accessing and analysing secondary data. For North American datasets, a useful one is provided by the Data and Information Services Center (DISC 2007) at the University of Wisconsin at Madison, which explains what data are, how to find them, how to access and use them, and which pitfalls to avoid. For United Kingdom-based social science, the journal *Social Research Update* provides clear accounts of data and evidence gathered for secondary analysis (e.g., Heaton, 1998, on secondary analysis of qualitative data). Secondary data analysis is of increasing interest to social and educational research, as evidenced in the recent call by the Economic and Social Research Council (ESRC) for research proposals on ethnicity:

> The ESRC is currently funding an initiative known as UPTAP, Understanding Population Trends and Processes. The primary aim of the initiative is to build capacity in secondary analysis, thereby promoting the use of the large-scale social science data sets.
>
> This [programme] offers a range of different opportunities and there are a number of major survey datasets that hold a significant amount of information on ethnicity both within the UK, such as the BHPS and Millennium Cohort, but also beyond, such as the European Social Survey which looks at attitudes, beliefs and behaviour patterns across Europe. Administrative datasets - the 2001 Census, for example - also contain valuable information on ethnicity at small area scales (ESRC, 2007).

See Gorard (2002) for further discussion of the value of secondary data analysis as part of a mixed methodological approach to any education research study.

New Evidence

First, it is worth exposing a couple of misconceptions about new evidence.

New evidence, as opposed to existing evidence, is often erroneously thought of as evidence gathered as part an empirical study. However, 'empirical' means data gathered via a trial or test. Evidence can be gained from sources much wider than the empirical in their nature and in their means of gathering data. Indeed, at one end of the spectrum of evidence, anything could be construed as or used as evidence: a photograph, an idea, a trace of blood, part of an e-mail, a sensation. The key aspect of evidence is, as stated earlier, its symbiotic but testable relationship with claims, theses, or propositions. The evidence does not have to be tangible. In the most abstract of the preceding examples, one can easily construct a statement such as 'the fact you have this idea about *x* is evidence of your imagination'. With abstract and intangible phenomena, however, there are philosophical and linguistic issues about whether a speech act (Austin, 1962; Searle, 1969) such as the foregoing fabricated quotation constitutes action in the world.

A more general point is that evidence for education can take shape in a number of different languages: numerical (generally quantitative data), verbal, or visual (generally qualitative data). The terms *quantitative* and *qualitative* are deliberately parenthesized: all too often, these terms are reified and erected as if they were methods ('qualitative methods') or data or results (e.g. 'quantitative results') when they are merely means of analysis that are broadly verbal or numerical. At worst, these two types of analysis of data are established as two sides in a 'paradigm war' in which much hot air is created and little light is shed on methodological problems; in such cases, they are used as smokescreens for anxiety about numbers on the part of the 'qualitatively inclined' or for the purposes of disparaging verbal and other kinds of data by the 'quantitatively inclined'. Such posturing has little to do with enlightenment through research.

The more interesting connection, as far as the present book is concerned, is Toulmin's question: what enables us to say that the data we have gathered is linked to the claims and propositions we have made? Toulmin (1958) terms the connecting agent the *warrant*, itself supported and informed by *backing* that comes from the particular social/epistemological context in which evidence is being sought and defined. Conventionally, an example of backing could be a discipline such as biology or history, wherein different *mores* and conventions determine what is possible in the connection between evidence and claims.

However, if education and educational studies do not constitute a discipline but are more like a field of enquiry informed by different disciplines, what are the key characteristics of the field? And can Toulmin's formulation be applied with any confidence in the field?

Fundamentally, education (and ultimately, educational studies) at personal and public levels is concerned with growth through transformation. The transformation could be minimal ('I now know how to spell "paranoia" ') to something more major ('I now understand paranoia'). It is not so much an established discipline with boundaries as a process of gaining (hopefully – not always the case in schooling) maximum learning through economical means. To compress what could be a lengthy exploration of the nature of the field, *evidence* for education might come in forms that support or challenge notions of means of bringing about such transformations. Evidence of *learning* will, besides the preceding, take into account Rogoff's (1991) notion that 'learning is an effect of community' and thus will need to account for how communities foster and enable learning.

What would evidence look like if it is part of an effect of community on the one hand and personal, social, and political transformation on the other? Just as in a discipline or field of enquiry, a community will have its *mores*, conventions, and values. The determination of evidence within a community will be a matter of what makes sense within the discourses of that community and what is validated by the warrants that connect claims and evidence. The transformational aspect of learning and education will be measured by *changes* in the state of knowledge within the individual (and the community). Within experimental studies, such changes are measured by pre-test and post-test devices, with delayed post-tests gauging the sustainability of the changes that are seen to take place as a result of interventions. In other kinds of study (e.g., a longitudinal case study), snapshots of the state of learning will take place at intervals. It is possible that we could actually see learning taking place if it were captured on film.

The *warrant* for a connection between claims and evidence, therefore, would be testable or definable against criteria that asked questions such as 'Does this supposed connection between claims and evidence hold?'; 'Is the connection theoretically elegant and coherent and does the connection work in practice?'; and 'What difference does it make to the learners in question?'

Once matters of the foregoing kind are settled, the choice of methods to elicit evidence is a secondary one. Remembering that any of the following can act as evidence, the methods and data can include the following:

- images, still and moving
- aural evidence
- interviews, in aural or transcribed form
- focus group discussions, in aural or transcribed form
- documents
- observations
- field notes
- data from think-aloud protocols
- anecdotes
- answers to questionnaires
- other.

To reinforce the preceding point about means of analysis, any of these could be analyzed qualitatively and/or quantitatively (the fact that some tend toward one kind of analysis is not the point).

There is no reason that the kinds of evidence listed earlier could not also apply to the study of e-learning. In Andrews and Haythornthwaite (2007), Caroline Haythornthwaite and I set out the parameters of the field of e-learning research, aiming to establish the underlying theories and methodological approaches (and thus the backings and warrants, in Toulmin's terms) that operate. However, it has to be said that the largely conventional methods for eliciting data, as set out earlier, can provide evidence of what is felt or thought *about* learning and e-learning; they cannot always get at the heart of what actual learning is taking place. To an extent, this is a problem in all education research; it is largely a matter, to quote Polonius in *Hamlet*, in which one has to 'by indirections find directions out'. Perhaps the closest we can get to learning's actually taking place in e-learning are the dialogic exchanges that occur on bulletin boards, in blogs and e-mail exchanges, and in more multimodal form via access grid and conferencing technologies. The distinctive difference between these kinds of (hopefully, transformational) exchanges is that the interaction itself *is* or is a *trace* of learning and is recorded as such, whereas, in conventional learning, although the same kinds of dynamic interchange are possible, any recording of them are a step removed from the learning itself. Another way of putting this is to say that e-learning is primarily textual (it can include visual and aural and verbal texts) and that the leaning is entirely mediated by those codes. We could thus say that the following types of data could become evidence of e-learning:

- bulletin board exchanges
- e-mail exchanges (these can be lengthy or brief)
- blogs
- adaptations of existing texts via annotation, editing, revising, re-publishing
- spoken interactions
- iconic and visual interactions
- combinations of the above.

Problems in researching e-learning are well documented (and to an extent solved) in recent doctoral theses (e.g., those by Ab Jalil, 2007, and Zhao, 2007). Ab Jalil's study uses traces of interactive exchanges on bulletin boards to come to tentative conclusions about the learning that is going on during a masters programme. The particular problem with such evidence, acknowledged by the researcher, is that it is only a partial trace of the interaction and is thus fairly wide open to interpretation. Zhao's study looks more directly at the problems in e-learning research and concludes that conventional research methods skirt around the edges of the learning itself.

Questions to Ask Regarding 'Evidence': A Provisional Checklist

In practical terms, it might help to set out in tabular form the questions to ask regarding evidence (Table 11.1). Such a table can act as a convenient checklist to use when reading arguments that purport to provide evidence.

Ultimately, what counts as evidence in education depends on what is being asked. If the (research) question is about effectiveness or direct impact, the best kind of evidence is going to result from experimental studies and trials (preferably randomized controlled trials to ensure fairness and reliability, assuming that validity can be established). If the question is about the nature of a problem or how some intervention works or how a naturally occurring process takes place, the best kind of evidence will be of a different nature. Essentially, the key to the kinds of evidence that count will be in the nature of the claim or proposition, which can be converted into a research question,

Table 11.1 Questions to ask regarding evidence

Key questions	*Further points to bear in mind*
What is being claimed or proposed? Does it take the form of a specific hypothesis to be proved/disproved, or question to be answered?	Is the claim clear, or is the paper unclear about what it is proposing, assuming that evidence can 'stand on its own' or 'count' without a claim to inform it?
What is the nature of the evidence in this case? What form does it take?	Does it take the form of numbers or words or some other mode?
Is there an explicit or implicit connection made between the claim and the evidence?	If so, how is the connection made?
If there is a connection made between the claim and the evidence?? is it made in the form of an explicit warrant?	This would be rare, as it is a technical device to link the claim to the evidence; but it might be mentioned in a research article or paper.
What internal and/or external checks are there on the validity and the value of this particular set of evidence?	Do we take the evidence at face value? Has it been validated or checked in some way?
What underlying 'backing' or set of values and/or conventions is there that makes the evidence count in this particular context?	Spelling out of the backing would be rare; it could be implicit – but then there is the danger of making assumptions or taking values and other conventions for granted.
Could there be other evidence that qualifies or counters the claim being made?	Does such evidence already exist? Could it be found? If it does not exist already, is it possible that it could exist?
In the light of the above, what *weight* do you accord to the evidence provided?	Weight of evidence will be determined by volume, quality, fitness for purpose and contingency.
In the light of the above, are you convinced by the evidence, and by the argument as a whole?	If not, why not?

hypothesis, or problem as appropriate (or all three if necessary) as a starting point for the research. Anyone with an interest in 'evidence', whether as a teacher, researcher, teacher-trainer, lecturer, policy maker, or student, needs to bear in mind the fact that evidence is always connected to a proposition of some kind and does not come unencumbered by that proposition. It cannot, therefore, be taken for granted that it is true. Even if the proposition that gives significance to the evidence is made clear, the reader still has to ask: how is the connection made possible? And what values, assumptions, and conventions are behind that kind of connection?

What Kinds of Methods can be Used to Investigate Argumentation?

Just as was suggested earlier in the book (Chapter 5) that evidence could take various forms in support of a claim or proposition as part of an argument, so too various methodologies and methods can be used to investigate argumentational practices. At the level of methodological approach – that is to say, the broader questions of research design that take their cue from but are not entirely determined by the epistemological basis of the investigation at hand – there is room for both large-scale surveys or experimental studies that compare one form of teaching argument to another on the one hand and, on the other hand, ethnographic, smaller-scale studies that look in depth at particular instances of argument. My own view is that the paradigm wars that characterize polarized debates about the virtue of one methodological approach over another (e.g., the so-called 'quantitative versus qualitative' debate) are a futile pursuit that appear to make a number of category errors. First, they assume that methodologies and methods in themselves are primary considerations and have some reified existence that is as important as the core research questions in hand. Second, they assume that *qualitative* and *quantitative* are terms that describe methods, whereas they are, more accurately, ways of describing approaches to the analysis of two broad kinds of data: verbal and numerical, respectively. Third, they assume that these approaches can be polarized so that one is diametrically opposed to, and has nothing in common with, the other. However, numerical data are usually abstractions or distillations from other kinds of data (sometimes verbal) that have been collected; they therefore have a relation to verbal or other data. On at least three grounds then, the distinction, when taken to the extremes of a paradigmatic opposition, is not only futile; it is a misrepresentation and a lost opportunity to explore the relationship between different kinds of data.

Having said that, this is a good opportunity to take forward some recent thinking about one particular method that colleagues and I undertook, published as Mitchell et al. (2008). The key point of that article was that questionnaires and interviews can be misleading or provide incomplete evidence, if the term *argument* is used in situations wherein the meaning may not be the same for the researcher as for the respondents – in this case students in biology. The issue raised again the one addressed in the early chapters of this book – that 'argument' may be too high a term for students who are learning the discourses of their disciplines and that proposing such a 'high' term may disenfranchise or confuse those who have yet to develop the meta-awareness, cognitive grasp, or meta-language to deal with such concepts. This is a valid criticism, especially if the term *argument* is seen as a general 'good thing' and expectation of academic courses, without being defined or set against other forms of discourse for comparison.

It is incontrovertibly true that not all discourses in academic disciplines are argumentational, and it would not be right in this book to suggest that they were. Nor is it the case that 'argument' is seen as a higher form of discourse than narrative, description, dialogue, or any other meta-genre. Although argument is often seen as a high-level discourse, it is because of the handling of abstractions; it is as if the metaphorical 'height' above the particular gets translated into a hierarchical position. I explored in an edited book, *Narrative and Argument* (Andrews, 1989), the interplay of the two meta-genres and how often narratives were able to carry arguments without any explicit reference to higher abstract levels and how, conversely, arguments could be couched in narrative form. It is thus useful to distinguish between argument as an abstract arrangement of concepts or phenomena that, collectively, establish or defend a position, and argument as discourse (identifiable in the tangible manifestations of the spoken and written word, image, sound, and the interplay between these modes of communication). Once we have made this distinction, we can see that there is often confusion between the two levels, with discourses being conflated with ideas and vice versa. Such confusion makes it difficult to separate the idea from the way in which it is expressed and, of course, sometimes that distinction is impossible to make.

More practically, disciplinary practices in courses at university will use a range of written genres to aid and channel communication. This range can include position papers, research papers, exploratory essays, timed essays, journal entries, logs, dissertations and theses, notes, and other written forms. Furthermore, this range of written forms can be informed by spoken genres and, in practice, can be prefaced by spoken interaction and/or followed by it. When we add the visual (still and moving images) and sound to the equation, the hybrid nature of what is possible and what is actually produced in higher education disciplines becomes evident. Some of these may have argumentational *intent* in that they are designed to form part of an argument in the discipline, and some will be explicitly argumentational. What would be helpful is for each discipline (in practice, each department) to identify the range of written and other discourses that take place in the business of their work and to explain to or explore with students the different weights that are attached to these genres.

A general methodological issue raised by this case is whether or to what degree a term should be tightly defined when undertaking an investigation. In the case of argument and argumentation, we have already made a distinction between the two, with the former being the more general term and the latter being reserved for the specific technical process of arguing in formal situations. The problem, as suggested by the Mitchell et al. article, is largely with the more general term. 'Argument' is asked to do a great deal of work as a term: it covers a wide range of written and spoken genres in the academy; it refers also to demotic, everyday arguments such as rows, quarrels, spats, and tiffs;

it is generally associated with challenge and aggression, and thus alienates many students, teachers, and lecturers who would prefer a more consensual and conciliatory approach to developing knowledge; it has a legacy from astronomical, navigational, and mathematical use, which generally refer to working out a third point from two given points – and thus can be off-putting to those of a less technically minded nature; it also brings with it associations of rhetoric and/or logic – such residual associations from the medieval *trivium* can be off-putting or seem irrelevant to contemporary concerns. All these associations can get in the way of its everyday use in academic contexts, even though each of them can also be turned to the positive as part of the history and application of the term.

Methodologically, it is probably best to approach research with a working definition that is neither so prescriptive as to delimit responses nor so loose as to make no comparisons between the responses reliable or valid. Such a working definition could start with something such as 'a series of propositions or claims, arrayed in a logical or quasi-logical sequence, and supported by evidence' and in the first stage of research explore and test that very working definition. When the first stage responses had been analyzed and synthesized, to make sure that what was understood by 'argument' by the researcher was close to what the respondents understood by it, investigation of the phenomenon itself could take place. Such negotiation is important: it helps explore and define concepts in any field, and it also guards against over- or under-determination and interpretation of responses. However, such negotiation is not always possible or desirable in the administering of a questionnaire, wherein the possibilities of misinterpretation are greater. The only way in which to address this problem – if, indeed, questionnaires are seen to be a useful approach with such research – is through piloting of the research instrument, with a focus group or response group being asked to reflect on the terms used in the draft questionnaire.

Finally, it can be said that the wide range of references for the term *argument* can be turned to advantage. To know that 'argument' can describe both an everyday altercation and a specialist academic approach is not necessarily a problem; it can be seen as advantageous to the development of argument in higher education if it does not lose touch with its demotic applications. The energy, dialogism, and passion of everyday arguments, however (seemingly) trivial some of their topics are, are part and parcel of the fabric of human communication and, in most cases, are means to a more consensual end. If some of that passion and energy can be carried over into academic argument, albeit within the more-formal, more-public domains of learning, the effect might be to enliven the practices of academic study and the development of thought.

Argumentation and Scientific Method

There have been examples of argumentation in action in science teaching/learning throughout the book, and especially in Chapter 8 on student views on argument. Here, in a chapter on methodologies in researching argumentation, the attention is on a more general topic: science in action.

Latour's book, *Science in Action* (1987), provides insight into how science, engineering, and technology actually work in social contexts. As we have seen in Chapter 8, it is not a simple matter of applying one 'scientific method' to all situations in science. The so-called classic approach of hypothesis and empirical proof as a means of progression in science, and thus also as a pedagogic principle for the construction of learning in science, does not give an adequate account of either progress in science or the didactics of science.

The model set out by Latour, grounded in the social contexts in which science operates and progresses, takes the form of a comic strip. Rather than reproduce it in the present book, here is the quotation at the heart of the conception, punctuated with comments as to how the model links to argumentation:

> …we start with a textbook sentence which is devoid of any trace of fabrication, construction or ownership; we then put it in quotation marks, surround it with a bubble, place it in the mouth of someone who speaks (p.15).

Latour's example is that of the discovery of the double helix structure of the DNA molecule by Watson and Crick. The 'textbook sentence' is something like 'The DNA molecule has the shape of a double helix'. Transferring it into speech (we will indicate that with double speech marks), "The DNA molecule has the shape of a double helix" makes it instantly part of a conversation, a statement made by a speaker in the form of a proposition. This transfer from detached, unvoiced, distant, 'given' truth into the words uttered by a person make it part of the everyday discourse, a hypothetical statement that is subject to interrogation *as discourse* rather than a hypothesis to be tested empirically. Latour continues:

> …then we add to this speaking character another character *to whom it* is speaking; then we place all of them in a specific situation, somewhere in time and space, surrounded by equipment, machines, colleagues (ibid.).

It is not necessary that the scientists are surrounded by the kind of equipment that one would find in a laboratory; they could equally be taking a walk in a field or be riding on a bus. The important thing is that the conversation – or to give it a more generic name that will link it to theoretical development – the *dialogue* takes place in a context at a particular time and in a particular place. There is no reason why the places could not be far apart and that the conversion could not take place electronically, via digital links, across the world. Whatever the context, the important point is that the conversation takes place in a particular context, embedded in a social, historical, and political nexus. It is thus subject to, and invites, ethnographic study. The point also being made by Latour is that 'theory' however grand, is born in local contexts.

So far the process described seems dialogic but not necessarily argumentational. However, the next stage moves the conversation to the level of argument:

> ...when the controversy heats up a bit we look at where the disputing people go and what sort of new elements they fetch, recruit or seduce in order to convince their colleagues; then, we see how the people being convinced stop discussing with one another; situations, localizations, even people start being slowly erased (ibid.).

When conversation becomes controversy, the dialogue is polarized to such an extent that it can no longer progress consensually in a mutually supportive matter. The declaration of position means that the ideas are at stake. We are in a situation of 'discussion with edge'. The metaphor used by Latour – that of a comic strip in which characters are recruited, elements fetched, people seduced to take a particular position – suggests that the process of establishing a new proposition is a complex one that involves much more than 'proving' or 'disproving' a hypothesis. It is a matter of establishing a new paradigm and involves social and rhetorical operations. To change the metaphor slightly for a moment: a flag is put up, a tent built to support it, a number of other tents are established nearby to create a camp of sorts, and soon a community is created that will argue – and possibly fight – to defend the new idea. The power of the new concept or proposition leads to the effects described by Latour: 'We see how the people being convinced stop discussing with one another; situations, localizations, even people start being slowly erased'. In other words, a paradigm shift has taken place in which people see the world differently from the new perspective. What does this adopting of a new perspective lead to?

> On the last picture we see a new sentence, without any quotation marks, written in a textbook similar to the one we started with in the first picture. This is the general movement of what we will study over and over again in the course of this book, penetrating science from the outside, following controversies and accompanying scientists up to the end, being slowly led out of science in the making (ibid.).

Although the translation from the French is awkward at the end, the general picture is clear. Conversation and dialogue, having done their job of providing a discourse space in which a new scientific concept or paradigm is established, now fade into time as the new proposition takes it place as received knowledge in the 'textbook'. It appears to be the incontrovertible truth but is actually the result of a complex process of human interaction. The complexity of this social interactivity is something most scientists, claims Latour, are unwilling to talk much about. They prefer the 'certain certainties' and orderly pattern of scientific method and rationality. They compress a complex process of discussion, interaction, supposition, and marshalling of support into a neat process of hypothesis and proof that is only the tip of the iceberg. In fact, the business of proof or disproof is a later, secondary matter. Latour is concerned primarily with the creation of hypotheses and their establishment as scientific fact without recourse to empirical testing.

The Practical Dimension

Activity 11.1

Visit the website www.ttrb.ac.uk or one of the other websites mentioned in the first part of the chapter to identify research in your field. What kind of evidence does it provide, if any? How is this evidence informed, or not, by a hypothesis or thesis?

Activity 11.2

If you are undertaking research on argumentation in your discipline, work out your research question(s), then what methodology (general approach) and methods (techniques) you will need for a pilot study, and then test these in the pilot study itself. Do the methods provide you with the kind of data you are looking for? If not, what others might you try to get closer to answering the question(s) you have set yourself? Does the question itself need revising in the light of your pilot work?

12
Conclusion and a Way Forward in Argumentation Studies in Education

Introduction

What don't we yet know about argumentation in higher education, and therefore what needs to be researched? Are there cross-cultural issues that need to be addressed, and if so, how are such studies to be conducted? What are the implications for research, policy and practice – and they way they inter-relate – from the present study?

The chapter looks back at the issue of whether argumentation is considered to be a generic skill at undergraduate level, and at some of the research and guides that have been published in the UK and USA to address the problem of argumentation at this level. Having covered the undergraduate levels for most of the book, it considers the importance of argument at (post)graduate level, and looks at a range of dissertations in Educational Studies and the different problems they uncover and solve. It is in this section in particular that cross-cultural issues are addressed.

It then moves to a consideration of a dissertation in a different discipline: engineering. The differences in modal selection, and the different ways in which the argument is carried, are investigated.

Common to all undergraduate and (post)graduate work is the question of criticality and its relation to argumentation. One of the most common complaints about student work is that it is not critical enough, and yet students are not often shown what that means in their own disciplines or in inter-disciplinary contexts. As criticality is an essential for the higher grades, the chapter argues that lecturers must make it clear what it means and help students to become more critical. The best way to do this is to encourage thinking and to aid its expression and articulation. Finally, the book returns to the issue of argumentation in the digital and/or multimodal age.

Looking Back

The educational tradition and context for assessment in higher education in England does not make argument (the product) or argumentation (the process of arguing) an explicit part of the undergraduate or postgraduate experience. Despite the fact that lecturers value argumentation highly and that it is the default genre of assessment in the humanities, social sciences, and some of the arts – especially from 16 years onwards through university – there is very little explicit attention paid to argument or argumentation in universities in England, even at undergraduate level. Current policy debates about postgraduate research student skills training in the United Kingdom (see the joint statement of the Research Councils'/Arts and Humanities Research Board skills training requirements for research students, 2001, and Diamond, 2003) develop a consistent line in insisting on the development of generic skills for postgraduate research students, but they fail to address one of the core academic generic 'skills' that underpins a good thesis or, more generally, a postgraduate education in a democratic society: argumentation.

Although the joint statement by the research councils makes it clear that its list of skills is not a set of criteria for research training, it nevertheless makes the research skills and techniques explicit. They are as follows:

1. the ability to recognize and validate problems;
2. original, independent, and critical thinking and the ability to develop theoretical concepts;
3. a knowledge of recent advances within one's field and in related areas;
4. an understanding of relevant research methodologies and techniques and their appropriate application within one's research field;
5. the ability to critically analyze and evaluate one's findings and those of others;
6. an ability to summarize, document, report, and reflect on progress.

It does include argumentation under the heading of communication skills: students will need to be able to 'construct coherent arguments and articulate ideas clearly to a range of audiences, formally and informally through a range of techniques'. The section of communications skills was one of those highlighted by Diamond (2003) in his letter to universities on behalf of the joint research councils, and accompanying funding is clearly intended 'for enhanced broadening skills rather than the discipline based scientific training that would normally be provided within the student's / researcher's department'.

It appears that argumentation, though mentioned as a communication skill, is not recognized as central to the shaping of discourses in a discipline, to systems of proposition/claim and grounds/evidence in disciplines, and how these elements of argument are validated and backed within disciplines and fields of enquiry. The invisibility or marginalizing of argument within the university system in England and Wales (less so in Scotland) is symptomatic of a more general myopia in this regard.

There have been various attempts to address the problem of argumentation in higher education in England and Wales. Mitchell and Andrews (2000) undertook a series of studies in the 1990s looking first at the transition from sixth-form to first-year undergraduate education, then at a range of disciplines in higher education itself (see also Andrews & Mitchell, 2001; Burwood, 1993; Costello & Mitchell, 1995; Mitchell, 1992, 1994a, 1997; Mitchell & Riddle, 2000). These studies have mostly been from the perspective of discourse in education, rather than, say, being informed by pragmatic-dialectical studies (the Amsterdam school, e.g., in the work of van Eemeren and Grootendorst and their followers: van Eemeren, 2001; van Eemeren, Grootendorst, & Snoeck Henckemans, 2002) or informal logic (the Canadian school, in the wake of Walton). The work of Mitchell, Andrews, and Riddle has taken Toulmin as a point of reference, adapting his 'model'. I have discussed the 'Toulmin model' along with other ways of conceiving of the problem and its solution in Andrews, 2005; and Andrews, Mitchell, and Prior (from the University of Illinois at Urbana-Champaign) began a study of first-year undergraduate argumentation, with Torgerson, for the Higher Education Academy, also in 2005. Neither the more general studies of writing in higher education such as Fairbairn and Winch (1996), Creme and Lea (2003), or Levin (2004) nor advances in writing research in academic disciplines (e.g., Jolliffe, 1988) address argumentation per se. The closest to a textbook in the field is probably Barnet and Bedau (1996), written very much for the North American market. In short, the best available theoretical field of the present article could be said to be post-Toulminian discourse studies in education. To date, there have been no specific studies of argumentation in postgraduate education in England or Wales.

In practice, on the one hand, the embeddedness of argument in the society and educational system is deep: the United Kingdom has a parliament that is arranged on an adversarial model, with the government on one side and the opposition on the other, assuming that 'truth emerges from the clash of opposites'. Democratic societies aim to operate via argumentation to explore and resolve differences at personal, local, regional, national and global levels...trying to reach consensus that is a basis for agreed action (Habermas, 1984). Argumentative capability is the hidden criterion in the assessment of student essays, research papers, critiques, and syntheses from about the age of 16 upward. Students who do well in the educational system are those who not only know their subject but can argue it well. In continental Europe at postgraduate level and in the research thesis or dissertation, students have a double responsibility: they not only have to write well on some topic in the field but they have to write *argumentatively*. The same is true for any postgraduate student in the United Kingdom, whether their dissertation is 15,000 words in length or they are studying for a PhD and have to submit a thesis of up to 100,000 words.

On the other hand, the emphasis on the substance of a discipline or subject in the English educational system from age 16 occurs at the expense of argument. Students are expected to be good at argument, but no one tells them how to be good at it or helps them to do it better. There are guides to writing essays that tend to focus on superficial features of the genre. In an elitist liberal system, it is assumed that immersion in a discipline will equip you with the argumentative skills and critical thought necessary to succeed in that discipline and, indeed, that the very nature of a discipline is that it is constructed around arguments, therefore there is no need to look at these explicitly. The relationship between thinking and expression in most disciplines is implicit: critical thinking is the desired dialectical *substratum*; argumentation is the process by which such thinking is manifested; and argument is the finished product (the essay, the dissertation). However, this assumption about how argument will be developed by osmosis in an elitist system is the nub of the problem facing higher education in the United Kingdom, the United States, and elsewhere: to what extent, and with what anticipated success, should we move to teaching argumentational skills in higher education?

The Distinctiveness of the English Argumentational Tradition at Postgraduate Level

The English tradition of argumentation in higher education is different from the European continental and North American traditions because of linguistic, cultural, and educational changes that took place in the nineteenth century. There are professors of rhetoric at Scottish universities but none in England. In the nineteenth century, the rise of English literature as a serious subject for study (through working-class extension classes and especially classes organized by women for evening and occasional study) resulted in the first degrees being offered in the subject at the University of Oxford in the 1880s (see Dixon, 1991b; Reid, 2004). By the 1920s, the study of literature had replaced classics as the central civilizing subject and discipline both in the school and the university curriculum (Newbolt, 1921). Rhetoric and argumentation have been relatively neglected in England and Wales for more than 100 years.

In Scotland, however, the tradition lived on. The rhetorical analysis of language and literature continued, was exported to North America and formed the backbone of the rhetoric and composition programs that form such an important part of undergraduate experience. The pragma-dialectical model (van Eemeren, 2002) that underpins academic programs in continental Europe operates in England in practice in the tutorial and seminar (by which I mean a 1:1 or very small group discussion with a tutor; and a group of up to 25 or so engaged in guided discussion with a lecturer or tutor) at undergraduate and postgraduate level, but on the whole it is not identified as such.

What is distinctive about the postgraduate experience in England and Wales? How do the differences from argumentation in other education systems reflect back on practices in these countries?

In England, at postgraduate level – especially in research degrees – the student is asked to work on his or her research topic from day one: devising and refining the research question, reading and reviewing the literature, and thinking of the methodology only after the research question has been established. Despite recent moves toward a year of postgraduate training in research methods prior to a doctorate (the '1+3' approach), the default approach does not see itself as 'training' the postgraduate workforce in skills and capabilities; rather, it sees itself as part of a liberal humanist tradition of educating and training the mind. To look at it another way, the emphasis is more on dialectic than rhetoric.

In such an approach, it is assumed that critical thought emerges from seminar or tutorial discussion wherein ideas are tried out, explored, challenged, and refined. What is discussed in the semi-public forum of the seminar or tutorial is assumed to change what is in the student's head (Britton, 1987; Vygotsky, 1986). That transformation then is demonstrated in the student's writing for assessment: usually in the form of the dissertation or thesis, which, along with the essay, are the default genres of postgraduate education in the arts, humanities, and social sciences.

Such practice, however, causes a problem: because there is no instruction in different written text-types such as the argumentational research paper, the critique, the synthesis, the thesis – nor in oral genres such as the persuasive speech – the student often has to guess how best to write down what they think and know. They probably know that the tutor will be looking for excellent argumentational skills, for knowledge of the subject, for lucid and eloquent expression of ideas and for critical verve, but they don't know exactly how a tutor will respond to their writing. Furthermore, no connection is made for the students between the oral forms of discussion and debate and speech on the one hand and the written forms of argument on the other. Often, the transfer from oral capability to written capability is poorly made. Trial and error will be one of the ways in which students learn to operate successfully in the system.

In such a system, it is assumed that something magical will happen in the student's mind and that it will be expressed in perfect argumentational form in writing submitted for assessment. The argumentation is assumed to inhere in the very nature of the discipline: that is to say, the way disciplines are constructed, with debates and inductive reasoning taking place in literature studies about, say, the treatment of Ophelia by Hamlet, is itself an organization of ideas that provides a model for the student. It is not coincidental that my example is from literary studies: literary studies are the cuckoo that pushed rhetoric out of the nest in the mid- to late-nineteenth century. Furthermore, *the dialectics of fiction* – a kind of inductive dialectic – as the central civilizing discipline of the twentieth century, has informed argumentational practice at school, college, and undergraduate and postgraduate levels through the study of literature.

What are the Principles of Argumentation as Manifested in Postgraduate Student Writing?

What do the argumentative text-types and genres used in the academy have in common? Whether we are talking about a short position paper, an argumentational research paper, a critique, a synthesis, a long essay (say 7,000 to 10,000 words), a short dissertation or thesis (15,000 to 35,000 words), or a long thesis (up to 100,000 words), the principles with regard to argumentational writing remain constant.

First, they all use a single authorial voice. This may seem obvious, but it is important when you consider that the talk and discussion that often prefigures the writing of an assignment is usually multi-voiced. Students often find it difficult to transfer the dialogic, multi-voiced nature of discussion and debate into the monologic form of the written argumentational assignment.

Second, they tread an interesting line between the 'personal' voice – represented by the use of 'I' in the written assignment ('I feel that…,' 'In the light of the evidence, I think that…') – and the impersonal voice ('Various critics have suggested that…,' 'It can be said that…'). This issue appears to be a secondary one, because it is possible write argumentatively and well both by using 'I' and by not using it.

Third, they require planning to ensure that they have a vertical, paradigmatic structure and organization and that they are more than an unstructured excursion, a 'loose sally of the mind' (Dr Johnson's definition of the 'essay'). Classification and categorization are fundamentals of scientific enquiry, and that influence shows itself in the arts, humanities, and social sciences through an emphasis on clarity of ideas, definitions, understanding of hierarchies of ideas, making distinctions between phenomena, and so on.

Fourth, they must have logical or quasi-logical structural momentum: one idea or paragraph must lead to another and have some clearly defined connection to it. The horizontal articulation of the written assignment must be as strong as the vertical programming of the ideas within it.

Fifth, they are usually explicit in the connections that are made vertically and horizontally. These connections are spelled out rather than implied. That is what makes these forms and text-types so readily assessable within the university. If you display and demonstrate your thoughts explicitly, the tutor can assess them and also differentiate between students. Such assessment is not so easy if the connections made in the written forms are implicit.

Sixth, there are aspects of the discourse of essay or paper writing that have to be understood for success in writing such assignments. Such aspects include the use of a certain kind of diction; the adoption of an academic tone; and the assumption that even if the piece is taking on a particular position to argue (rather than a balanced view, which is not always feasible), the academic nature of the assignment will mean that a detached, disinterested energy is brought to bear on the discussion. Evidence is important, whatever forms it takes (and evidence is differently weighed and valued according to the different disciplines and contexts). Feminist and post-structuralist critics, however, may not agree that detachment and disinterestedness are an integral part of argumentational writing, arguing instead that a committed, positioned stance might well eschew such distancing.

Seventh – and highly important – is that the written assignments must show evidence of critical thought. This is one of the most difficult aspects of writing in higher education for students to achieve or even understand. In some cultures, too, the critical dimension – which is a given part of academic discourse in the cross-cultural academy in Europe – is understood differently. Argumentation exists, in a range of cultures, in one form or another (see Berrill, 1996). Berrill and other contributors to her book point out that the range of argumentational forms and practices needs to be recognized so that students who move from one set of expectations to another can navigate these differences and, crucially, that tutors and lecturers who are the gatekeepers of student success (or otherwise) in their role as markers of written arguments are fully aware of different types of argumentation. For example, oral arguments can result in an 'agreement to differ' or in consensus or in compromise. In some cultures, the dissonance implied in the first outcome is not an acceptable outcome. Such oral genres can have a bearing on the way written arguments are framed, developed, and concluded.

Four Dissertations

To illustrate my point and also to provide some empirical grounds for the case I am building, let us look briefly at four masters dissertations completed within the past few years. These are not representative of all masters dissertations, let alone of those in the field of education and engineering. They do, however, illustrate generic qualities that shed light on the question of argumentation and criticality. Three of the dissertations are by Chinese students. As Watkins and Biggs (1996) suggest in their excellent book, *The Chinese Learner*, it is a myth reinforced by some in the 'West' that (a) Chinese students are significantly different in their learning styles and preferences from European/American students, (b) such students are 'unable to argue', and (c) the critical dimension is missing from such students' work. In taking the work of Chinese students who have recently studied in the United Kingdom, I wish to challenge all three false assumptions set out here but also to concentrate on the quality of argumentation across the aforementioned three dissertations.

Two of the dissertations in question were the final assignment, of between 15,000 and 20,000 words, in a 1-year full-time masters degree in educational studies. The third dissertation constituted the whole of the assessment for a masters degree in educational studies by research (25,000 to 30,000 words). Students chose their own topics for research, under the supervision of a lecturer.

Of the first two, Student A elected to study Chinese college students' perception of English teaching and learning in China. The study is a conventional one: a total of 87 students responded to questionnaires in Chongqing and York, and 10 of these were interviewed. Issues of motivation, pedagogy, and resource were explored, the conclusion being that what English education in China lacks most is training for communicative competence. The emphasis on the grammar-translation method of second language learning provides a solid foundation for learners' linguistic competence and reading comprehension skills but not for listening or speaking skills. The structure of this dissertation, too, is fairly conventional, moving from an introduction through chapters on the context of the study, the methodology, questionnaire findings, and interview findings and thus to a conclusion.

In argumentational terms, the dissertation is sound. It takes as a problem (an implied antithesis to its thesis) the fact that 'the predominant mode of instruction' – that of a traditional teacher-centred format 'with an emphasis upon grammar and reading and translation as measures of learning' – results in grammatical form taking precedence over meaningful communication. If there is a weakness in the argument, it is because the literature review is largely based on policy documents rather than on research from the 1970s to the present. There is also not much of a review of the research literature published in China. In a masters thesis, completed over 6 to 9 months, such a weakness is understandable. A full-scale review of the literature on grammar-translation method on the one hand, as opposed to the communicative approach in second language learning on the other, would be a gargantuan task. Needless to say, some indication of the theoretical underpinning to the argument and a quick review of the key protagonists in the field would have provided the ballast to set the empirical data and its analysis in context. It would have also provided more opportunity for critical comment: weighing evidence against claim, pointing out *lacunae* in the field, weighing one theorist against another. Overall, though, the dissertation passed because of its argumentational coherence, its scholarship, its elegant structure, and its critical perspective – and other qualities. All seven principles outlined earlier were embodied in the composition.

Student B's dissertation investigated the pedagogical similarities and differences between native and non-native teachers of English in Hong

Kong. Three research methods were used: 107 questionnaires of students, four interviews with teachers (two native, two non-native speakers), and four observations of classrooms. Structurally, the similarities/differences approach provides an underlying organizing principle; sequentially, the dissertation follows the conventional pattern of introduction, literature review, methodology, two chapters on findings (one on the questionnaires, one on the interviews and observations), a discussion, and a conclusion. It might be said that this particular structure offers more scope for argument and criticality than that of the previous student's dissertation. The inclusion of a substantial literature review maps out the 'backing' for the argument. Small advances in what is known – resulting from the empirical data and its analysis – can be gauged against the larger theoretical and research literature background. If there is a weakness, it is not so much to do with the argumentation of the dissertation or its critical dimension as with the assumption that methodological triangulation will increase content validity. As Gorard and Taylor (2004) have suggested, such triangulation may provide complementary perspectives on a common problem (assuming they have exactly the same focus) rather than determining a more precise and thus more valid account of the truth of a situation. Critical awareness of the limitations of such triangulation would have improved an already very good dissertation. Again, the seven principles are observed.

The third dissertation is different from the other two, not only in its length but because of its methodological approach and its topic. Student C chose to explore lifelong education systems in the United Kingdom and China. The study is investigative, qualitative, comparative, and exploratory in nature, using a single research method: the in-depth interview. Its intention might be said to undertake an overview of the grounds for comparison between lifelong learning/education systems in the two countries. Although it is slightly longer than the previous two dissertations, it goes into more depth as it tries to define the characteristics of the two systems. Part of the problem this dissertation was trying to solve is the unsystematic nature of lifelong learning structures, institutions, and qualification frameworks (at least in the United Kingdom) and the relatively embryonic nature of such provision in China. Because of the exploratory character of the dissertation and because of the complex and asymmetrical nature of the topic being researched, argumentation is hardly possible. Rather, the dissertation aims to classify and taxonomize the field. Its principal results are presented in a series of tables. If it does have an argument, it is couched in methodological, procedural terms – that there is a need for a methodology to deal with education systems in the light of the concept (or notion) of lifelong learning – and on such a basis the dissertation (excellently presented, as it was) warrants a pass. In terms of the seven principles set out earlier in the article, it fulfils the first three – a single authorial voice, a balance between the personal and impersonal (though in this case tending more to the impersonal than the first two dissertations), and a strong vertical, *classifying* structure – but because the fourth principle (that of a strong horizontal momentum) is more weakly applied, the fifth, sixth, and seventh are unable to establish themselves. I take each of these in turn, as they highlight the particular problems students encounter when they write *expositionally* rather than *argumentatively*.

To restate the problem: the student has a strong vertical, taxonomic structure in her work because that is the self-professed aim of her dissertation: to understand and make clear lifelong learning systems in Europe. Such an aim requires an interpretive approach rather than a critical or argumentational one. The horizontal axis of the work is not brought to the fore because logical or sequential links between different elements of the exposition are not sought out. The spirit of the work is one of discovery and presentation, not of a 'connected set of ideas' that is at the heart of argument. It follows that being explicit (the fifth of the principles set out earlier) is hardly necessary, because there is little in the way of personal, critical stance or development to be explicit about. Only if the student is able to stand back from the emerging exposition of the categories in the field and apply some degree of critical perspective (e.g., to suggest a different taxonomy or critique the existing ones) will discussions of the explicit nature of the argument occur.

The source of the problem of an under-argued dissertation or other argumentational text-type appears to be a misunderstanding about the sixth principle: that of the nature of the discourse in academia. If students do not fully understand the framework within which they are operating, with its political, social, conventional aspects informing the textual elements, then they are unlikely to be able to fulfil the requirements of the genre. Such understanding is not so much of the surface features of dissertation and essay writing as of the deeper assumptions that underpin the genre, like the expectation on the part of the lecturer/tutor/supervisor that the work will be argued, that the student will conduct his or her own research, that there will be a degree of originality in the work, and the like.

Last, the critical dimension is diminished if there is no scope for argument. Exposition is rarely critical; its very function is to make clear, to re-present, to interpret. If there is no linking of one idea to another and no questioning about the nature of those links, the work is likely to remain at the expositional and uncritical level.

The best of these dissertations (by student B) has the edge because it builds in a second layer of analysis from the start; its questions invite the organization of ideas and the conventional structuring of the writing. It is, thus, able to draw on a body of existing literature and to critique existing work. It is not so much that it draws on more theory than the other two dissertations; rather, it is able to move between one set of organizing ideas (similarities/differences) and another (the 'horizontal' momentum of the writing itself) and, thus, has more options for critical comment. Though the other two dissertations were more than satisfactory, the dissertation by student B was closer to the very good/distinguished standard.

Argument in Engineering: The Case of a Dissertation

In contrast to the three dissertations from educational studies, we now move on to look at a particular case in point – an undergraduate dissertation in engineering – before returning to the wider questions of criticality and argumentation.

Andrews (2007) is a 60-page final-year dissertation written as part of a degree course in general engineering at an English university. The four-year course leads to a masters degree; students then graduate and look for work while they move toward certification as graduate engineers. This particular project had as its aim the development of a piece of software for use with gear design; it would also act as a learning aid for future students at the university, and serve as a research tool to aid the stress analysis of gear teeth.

It is interesting to look, first, at the overall structure of the dissertation as it reveals the shape of what the discipline expects in terms of accounting for and discussing the practical project of designing the software. The main sections of the dissertation are introduction, gear transmission theory, software development, software capabilities, testing, discussions, conclusions, and further work. This, the main body of the text, is framed at the beginning by lists of figures (of which there are 61), a summary, a project plan, and a nomenclature or glossary and at the end by references, a bibliography, and seven appendices.

The relative length of the different sections is indicated in the following:

List of figures	1 page
Summary	One-third of a page
Project plan	3 pages
Nomenclature	1 page
Introduction	5 pages
Gear transmission theory	14 pages
Software development	5 pages
Software capabilities	5 pages
Testing	6 pages
Discussions	2 pages
Conclusions and further work	1 page
References	1 page
Bibliography	1 page
Appendices	18 pages

It has to be remembered that the page length includes an average of one table or diagram per page.

First, the structure of the main body of the dissertation is not dissimilar to a dissertation in the humanities or social sciences, or, indeed some of the arts.

The Introduction contains immediate contextual material, setting the scene for the project. It discusses the scope for the stress analysis program as a research tool, thus preparing the reader for part of the rationale for the project. It also looks at existing design software – a section, with a critical evaluation of existing programs, that one might find in a literature review in a humanities or social sciences dissertation. There is no proposition or claim in this introduction, nor any research question. The argument operates on the basis that there is 'scope' for a new software product. That scope is briefly charted. The product, then, is underway, as it were, and needs little justification. The argument will inhere in how the product is developed and how theory is applied to create something new and useful. It is as if the product itself is persuasive and carries much of the burden of argument that words in a different discipline would carry. The relatively small number of words in the engineering dissertation (about 6,000) does not carry the main burden of the argument; that weight is also carried by the 60+ diagrams and tables and by the product itself, which is appended in a CD–ROM.

The second chapter, on gear transmission theory, is the longest in the dissertation. It concerns simple gear trains, epicyclic (more complex) gear trains, gear meshing, tooth profiles, contact points, curves, and stress points. Each is dealt with in some detail, with explanatory illustrations. The relationship between the diagrams, tables, and verbal text is complex: sometimes the words carry the burden of the argument, and sometimes the illustrations do. In each case, the other mode is used to complement, explain, justify – rarely just to illustrate or provide an example. There is a good deal of mathematical calculation and the summoning up of equations in this chapter, as the engineering theory is underpinned by mathematical formulae. This chapter does not so much set out the problems as the *issues* to be borne in mind during the software development phase and, in particular, issues to do with gearing. The chapter is engineering-focused rather than computer software–focused; it is concerned with content and with making sure that all the right formulae and considerations are in place before the design work begins. In Toulminian terms, the groundwork on engineering might be characterized as the 'backing' needed for innovative work in software design for engineering purposes.

The next chapter deals with software development and is largely technical. What might appear to be principally descriptive writing contains, on closer examination, justifications for the choice of software structure to get particular 'views' on different parts of the gearing systems. This brief chapter is followed by one on software capabilities. The capabilities of the software are, basically, what it can do in terms of displaying information, checking the progress of the learner through the stages of understanding gearing, how it can gauge stress, and so on. These two chapters are short and straightforward, but they are backed up by pages of calculations that are collected in the appendices. These calculations, and the software design and development as a whole, took up a great deal of time prior to the writing of the dissertation and must be considered as a key part of the argument as a whole.

Testing, as part of the software development, plays the role of providing the grounds or evidence for the claim that is being made. The actual testing itself is driven by a warrant that says, in effect, 'if we can work out a way of gauging student response to the new gearing software, and show that it is more effective than not having the software, then the product is effective'. Methods used are a simple questionnaire, discussions with the respondents, and provision of formal feedback from the respondents. The aim of the testing is not only to see whether the product works but to improve it. Part of the testing, too, is to weigh the advantages of the new software against existing software, in terms of both design and accuracy.

The discussion and conclusion sections are relatively brief but condensed. Purely in words, they cite the advantages of the created software and point out where it could be improved. They discuss the usability of the software, its value as a learning aid, and its potential as a research tool. Ultimately, these chapters suggest that further features could be added but that they 'would require extensive re-programming of the code, and would be...something that would most likely be developed in a subsequent release of the software'. As in most academic dissertations, there was no further release or development of the software; it was an academic exercise designed to convince the tutors of the course that the student could be admitted to the degree of master in engineering. Its argument is simple and elegant and is underpinned by complex calculations and reasoning.

Before we leave discussion of this engineering dissertation, what does the ancillary material add to the argument, if anything? Most of it provides further supporting evidence of calculations behind the design and execution of the software; in a sense, it is the base of the iceberg. Most of the preliminary material is indicative (list of figures, nomenclature) of the content of the main body or acts as a summary of the project. The project plan is interesting in that it records how the project was planned and delivered. References and bibliography fulfil their usual functions. The really significant extra material – not even listed in the contents – is the program software itself. As a colleague at the Institute of Education in London suggested, some of the most significant material in contemporary dissertations and theses appears as an annex or attachment. In many ways, this material should be central to the dissertation and appear centrally. With a different format for the dissertation – for example, a non-linear, multimodal website – the software could appear the centre and be surrounded by the verbal/textual material.

The Critical Dimension

When it comes to assessing student assignments (whatever the marking scale), one of the key dividing lines is between those that are graded as excellent or very good and those that are marked good or satisfactory. The dividing line is important to students and to employers; you need to be very good or above, for example, to continue studies at the masters or doctoral level. All work at the masters level and above *has* to be critical.

The key qualities of work above the line are that it is argumentational as opposed to merely expositional and that it possesses a critical dimension. How are these two essential qualities related? What does it take to make a piece of writing critical? How can thinking best be manifested in the production of an assignment for assessment? How can the quality of argumentation be improved?

I have discussed the question of the critical dimension to academic writing with many of my students, some of them from the Confucian-heritage cultures of East Asia for whom exposition and clarity is a highly prized quality; yet, when they come to Europe to further their education, sometimes they find it difficult to adjust to the particular cultural demands for a critical dimension in their work. One of the important aspects of being a student in this Confucian tradition is deference to teachers and lecturers, in which criticism can be construed as being disrespectful; but what Confucius actually taught and what students come to learn is that positive critical energy is not only a part of learning at the highest level; it is so closely woven into the European and Confucian-heritage traditions that it would seem hard to imagine a university education without it. This is because the European tradition is heavily influenced by dialogic thinkers such as Socrates, Hegel, Kant, Bakhtin, Habermas, and others and because, in the Confucian-heritage tradition, critique is valued once the field has been 'mastered'. The difference is that in the latter tradition, more emphasis is placed on working from particularities to generalities, rather than backward and forward between particularities and generalities, and/or on the weighing up of competing and complementary generalities, as tends to be the European approach.

It is also worth commenting at this point on the question of 'power' in critical discourse in postgraduate education. To be critical is to take on a powerful position. Such a position, or disposition, assumes scepticism toward given truths; reserves the right to develop its own position; weighs up different claims to the truth against the evidence, and/or via logical operations; and assumes a certain degree of knowledge in the field on the basis of which a critical position can be established. Suspension or recognition of power relations between a supervisor and his or her supervisees is essential if the critical spirit is to flower for the student. The issue of critical *space* is thus important to cultivate, allowing the student to take over critical responsibility in due course for the position that is developed.

What are the Actual Ingredients of a Critical Approach?

One aspect of being critical is being able to weigh up one source against another. If a student is referring to one writer to support his or her argument, and then another, which of them is closest to what he or she is trying to say? Do they each approach the problem that is being addressed from a different angle? In which case, what are those angles, and how do they relate to each other?

Another aspect is recognizing that some points of view that have already been expressed by existing writers are *in contrast to* the points that are being made. A sentence or paragraph might start, 'Whereas X suggest that…, it seems to me that….' In other words, sources are being used to define a position. The American writers about composition and argument (Kaufer & Geisler, 1991) have an interesting and useful model that acknowledges how important this kind of criticism is in the undergraduate and postgraduate essay, which they call the 'faulty path' model (which we discuss in Chapter 3).

Third, there is the general attitude toward reading and thinking that the French philosopher Ricoeur (1970) calls a 'vow of suspicion'. That is to say, when we read critically, we read with scepticism: we do not necessarily believe what we read. This is the opposite to a 'vow of obedience' in which, to use Coleridge's phrase, we suspend disbelief and accept what we are told. In argument, we adopt a vow of suspicion; in narrative, a vow of obedience. An argumentative *disposition*, then, is an asset in being critical.

Last, critical thinking in argument is, to some degree, detached. It is not always disinterested, because critical argument can be fiercely partisan and committed to a particular cause or cool, distanced, and impartial.

Does the Thesis or Dissertation Encourage Critical Thinking?

It might be accepted that argumentation as a process encourages critical thinking, but do the essay, the argumentational research paper, the position paper, and the thesis or dissertation as text types used in universities encourage critical thinking?

On the one hand, it is the dialogic and dialectical nature of argument that encourages critical thinking. Argument explores difference; it likes to make distinctions between things and between ideas. It thrives best where, in a democratic society, there is a chance to challenge ideas; to understand, appreciate, and resolve differences and to develop an extended argument, whether in speech or writing. It could be said, as Michael Billig (1996) argues in *Arguing and Thinking: A Rhetorical Approach to Social Psychology* – a book that owes much to Vygotsky – that arguing as a social practice is internalized as thinking. In other words, thinking (critical thinking, or thinking with 'edge' and which challenges received ideas) is arguing with oneself.

On the other hand, if the essence of critical thinking is dialogic and if argument is not just discussion but 'discussion with edge', to what extent do the written forms of argument in higher education encourage that kind of thinking? Dissertations or theses are cases in point. They begin with a research question, problem, or hypothesis (sometimes with all three). This very first step is important. Some questions are better than others at providing the opportunity to argue and to think.

The criteria for judging whether a dissertation or thesis is successful vary from institution to institution, but essentially they come down to the following:

- scholarship
- independent critical thought
- an original contribution to public knowledge, and therefore 'publishable'
- argumentative coherence
- conventions of presentation.

A dissertation/thesis will not be truly argumentational until it has (a) worked out its theoretical position, (b) reviewed the literature, (c) designed an appropriate empirical study (if it is that kind of study), (d) gathered the evidence, (e) arrayed the evidence into categories, and (f) found its own position in relation to those categories, arranging them in a sequence that carries the argument of the piece as a whole. Many students deal only with the middle elements: they undertake a review, sort the evidence (sources, quotations, facts, hypotheses) into categories, and then write. What they write is *exposition*. It is not argument, and it is not critical, and it does not involve much thought: that is why it may or may not pass, according to the criteria for a pass in any particular course of study. The last stage – finding a position in relation to the material that has been researched – is not easy. It involves wide reading and research; the weighing up of evidence and sources from the Internet, from books, from journals; the development of a position; and then the sequencing of the thoughts and material into a coherent, logical, or quasi-logical sequence. It involves being modest about claims that are unsupported by evidence; being able to see that the most carefully formulated arguments are open to criticism from other positions; and being prepared to change ideas in the light of new evidence. This is where Kaufer and Geisler's model is helpful: it suggests the identification of a line of argument at the macro-level.

There are two further difficulties facing students and the general demands of argumentational writing set out earlier. They are, first, that written forms such as the dissertation or thesis are monologic forms (in a single voice) that are trying to bring together multiple voices from different sources. There may have been excellent discussion leading up to the writing of a chapter that somehow does not seem to manifest itself in the chapter itself. Some students will be in the fortunate position of having instruction and practice in public speaking: ideas are explored and arranged in sequences, persuasive presentations are made, and debate (both informal and formal) is engaged. However, many students find it difficult to transfer the liveliness of dialogic and critical thinking in speech (or what Bakhtin, 1986, calls the 'speech genres') to the written genres of the academy: the essay, the research paper, the position paper.

Second, written argumentational forms are *demonstrations* of argumentational ability in a field rather than actual new arguments in a field. A student might have made a major breakthrough in a field, and it could be as simple as πr^2 or an equation for the speed of light or an insight into the relationship between Greek classical syllabic metre in poetry and twentieth-century free verse rhythms, but if he or she cannot set out the argument and demonstrate it to a supervisor and examiners in written form, he or she will not get the success deserved.

Does this ritual justify the effort on the part of postgraduate students? I would suggest that argumentational lines of enquiry are the golden thread that runs through a good thesis or dissertation. It is not easy to make the thread visible through 25,000 to 35,000 words, let alone 85,000 to 100,000 words. The visibility of the argument, made manifest in explicit rhetorical signposting, is based on the arrangement – the *dispositio* – of the thesis. The arrangement, in turn, is based on the theoretical orientation and the momentum of the piece. If the student can manage to keep the whole in mind and at the same time weave a strong argument chapter by chapter, paragraph by paragraph, sentence by sentence, he or she will have created/composed a written thesis that will stand up to any critique by an examiner.

The advantage of using the Toulmin model *after* the writing of a first draft is that his theory of argumentation was designed to test the *soundness* of arguments, not as a scaffold for the composition of arguments. The model is not dynamic in the way that Kaufer and Geisler's is. However, its proposed link (the 'warrant') between the grounds and the claim of an argument; its underpinning of the warrant with 'backing' or the value systems and beliefs that give credence to the warrant within a particular context; and its positioning of the rebuttal, questioning the soundness of the link between grounds (evidence) and claim (proposition), and thus either strengthening or weakening that link: all these elements are useful in developing a strong argument and in *testing* it before it is submitted.

This kind of planning and structuring, plus the weighing up of evidence against claims and propositions, the considerations of faulty paths, and the rebutting of opposing views, all provide a strong theoretical framework for writing at the postgraduate level.

Interim Conclusion

This chapter has concentrated, so far, on the dissertation as a form of argumentation common in postgraduate experience. Its basic structures have been discussed, and three dissertations were examined to test the degree to which they embodied argumentation and criticality. It has been argued that the critical dimension is not exclusive to 'Western' thinking in the Greek classical, Hegelian, or dialectical traditions. A particular dimension was explored as part of the chapter: to what extent does the genre of dissertation or thesis encourage, support, and/or inhibit what has come to be known as 'critical thinking': thinking that is aware of its relativity, has 'edge', and is aware of itself as a process? More broadly, is the dissertation or thesis the best genre for the development of thinking and the furtherance of private and public research in the arts, humanities, and social sciences?

The conventional dissertation format *is* conducive to argumentation and critique *if* the opportunities offered by the form are taken up. The presence of a substantial literature review ought to provide ballast to the dissertation as a whole, providing a basis from which the student can build and a foundation on which new discoveries – however small – can be established. Such multi-levelled shaping in a dissertation are reflected in the 'Toulmin model', where the literature review acts as a backing to the argument as a whole, setting out the main theoretical issues to be addressed and the parameters and paradigms within which the new discoveries are to be judged (or claiming that there is no such theoretical underpinning to the question in hand). The warrant, or the means by which the evidence or grounds may be connected to the propositions or claims in the argument, is also important and could form part of the methodology chapter in a dissertation. This is not to say that the Toulmin model provides a template for writing a dissertation; rather, as originally intended, it provides a means for testing the soundness of the argument at the end of the thinking and composition process. The architecture (or, if we are digging to find hidden structures, the archaeology) of an argument allows space for critical reflection and comment, because the structures of argument can be imagined otherwise; the relationship between evidence and propositions can be examined; the writer can stand outside the constructed building and appraise its qualities; one method can be compared with another; and so on.

When dissertations fail or scrape through in the assessment process, it is usually because the lack of argumentational power and clarity allows little scope for critical commentary. If they fail to foreground argument and argumentation, guidelines on postgraduate student skills appear to underplay a key element in development at this level and to miss an opportunity to relate cognitive and intellectual processes to communicative ones.

The Dissertation in the Digital Age

Whether a dissertation is undergraduate or (post)graduate, some common issues apply with regard to how argumentation operates in the digital age.

First, it must be re-stated that the conventional verbal and printed dissertation or thesis (the term *dissertation* is used here, as *thesis* tends to be reserved for doctoral level work) continues and will continue to be an excellent format for the presentation of extended work in a number of disciplines. The expression in words (the verbal mode) and realization in a printed soft- or hard-bound dissertation (the medium) has been the default form of expression for dissertation since the Renaissance. Its linear structure supports a particular kind of argumentation that has horizontal momentum (i.e., points, paragraphs, and sections follow each other in sequence). There may be strong vertical or hierarchical patterning in the argument too, but the horizontal drive is crucial.

What happens to the argument of dissertations when they take advantage of affordances and possibilities offered by the digital age? What is meant by this is as follows: digitization, because of its ubiquity in electronic media, enables the putting together of images, sounds, and words in what used to be called 'multimedia' applications. A more accurate term for this contiguity is 'multimodality' (i.e., the multiple presences of different modes or 'languages' or sign systems of communication). Such modes are combined in different media. For example, television (as a medium) includes moving image, sound, and verbal language, usually in speech but sometimes in print; computers can do the same.

In terms of the dissertation, multimodal and electronic affordances allow the inclusion of images and sound and the written language. It was always possible to include still images in a conventional verbal and printed dissertation, but moving image and sound were not possible (the latter only via transcription). That means that a website could now be submitted as the whole or part of a submission for examination, depending on the regulations of the university in question.

An example of such regulations are in the set below, approved in 2008 by the Institute of Education, London:

> If appropriate to the field of study, and subject to approval by the Head of Department at the start of the programme, a candidate may submit, in lieu of a thesis, **a portfolio of original artistic or technological work** undertaken during his/her period of registration. The work may take the form of, for example, **objects, images, films, performances, musical compositions, webpages or software**, but must be documented

> or recorded in the portfolio by means appropriate for the purposes of examination and eventual deposit in the Institute of Education library. **The portfolio must include written commentary on each item of artistic or technological work and either an extended analysis of one item or a dissertation on a related theme**.

These particular regulations apply to the doctoral thesis, but there is no reason at all why they could not also be applied to the undergraduate or masters dissertation.

I have highlighted the main points in this alternative to the conventional dissertation. First, instead of a dissertation, a 'portfolio of original artistic or technological work' can be submitted. In arts departments, this could take the form of an exhibition, so that the 'portfolio' is not so much a physical object as a metaphor for a range of work. For example, if the British artist Andy Goldsworthy were to submit his work for examination, he would have trouble: his works are environmentally-based, ephemeral, subject to transformation by wind, rain, and sun. They could be captured in photographs and exhibited in a room and in a portfolio, but they wouldn't be quite the same. To give another, more manageable example: software designs for a new computer program could be submitted as 'original… technological work', and these could be contained on a CD–ROM, conventionally bound as an appendix into the back of a printed dissertation. The important move that is taking place is that much material that has, to date, been appended to conventional dissertations is now making its way into the main body of the text, or – more accurately – *as* the main body of the text.

Second, the list of examples of what might constitute the portfolio includes films, objects, performances, and musical compositions. No further comment is needed there, but this list reinforces the expanded nature of the 'portfolio'.

Third, 'the portfolio must include written commentary on each item of artistic or technological work and either an extended analysis of one item or a dissertation on a related theme'. This is where the written word re-asserts its centrality in the process of the demonstration of independent critical *thought* and the development of *explicit* argumentation in the service of the dissertation as a whole. It is interesting that the words must comment individually on each item in the portfolio, plus include an extended analysis of one item or a dissertation on a related theme. These written commentaries and analysis must together (for a doctoral thesis) 'be no more than 40,000 words' (i.e., no more than half the length of a conventionally framed thesis). For an undergraduate or masters dissertation, the length would need to be scaled down accordingly.

In the last paragraph, in commenting on the Institute of Education regulations, I italicized 'explicit argumentation'. This is somewhat different from the distinction between deductive and inductive argumentation discussed earlier in the book, but it could be couched as simply as that (i.e., deductive argument is explicit in that it states its propositions or claims and works 'down' to evidence and grounds from those explicit claims). It is the most common form of argumentation in academic dissertations in the West. Inductive argumentation, conversely, works 'up' from perceptions, data, and other kinds of evidence toward emerging propositions and claims. It has some of the characteristics of grounded theory approaches in that assumptions are not made; they emerge as the phenomena that are observed give them shape and identity – and are continually tested by new data and phenomena.

Explicit argumentation, which tends to be the modus operandi of the academy, needs to be contrasted to implicit argumentation. Explicit argumentation usually takes the forms of discourses in words *about* phenomena that are being discussed: it deals with ideas, propositions, claims, notions – in short, abstractions. It thrives on the linearity of the conventional written and printed dissertation, and it needs the two dimensions of verticality (categorization, hierarchy) and horizontality (logic, *post hoc ergo propter hoc*) to operate fully. In explicit argumentation, the proposition or 'thesis' (to use the term in the sense of the main proposition of the assignment) is stated up front, and its clarity and exposition are much to do with how the assignment is judged and how persuasive the assignment is. Most of the present book is not only about explicit argumentation but about how to make its processes *more* explicit to student and lecturers/professors.

Implicit argumentation, conversely, is more mysterious; less open to public challenge; more open to multiple interpretation; equally persuasive, perhaps, but in a more subtle and indirect way. It is suggestive of arguments rather than a direct presentation of them. Artworks operate in this way: they may have an explicit argument in mind, but they do not state it explicitly. Rather, they embody, in whatever modes and media they use for expression, the essence of their argument within their physical presence. There is more room for subjectivity (and more room for intersubjectivity in their appraisal) and more of a studio culture than a classroom culture in terms of their context and setting.

A dissertation, then, that is multimodal and implicit might have these qualities of implicit argumentation if it somehow embodies the original artwork and/or presents it for examination in a portfolio (the implication here is that the portfolio is a manageable, transportable device for collecting – in no necessary order or sequence – the works to be examined). We should remember, too, that the portfolio might be a virtual portfolio; that 'portfolio' (with its etymology from the carrying of leaves [of paper!]) is both a metaphor and a physical *portmanteau*. There remains, however, the question of how the implicit and the explicit dimensions of argumentation are balanced or reconciled in the examination.

In the Institute of Education regulations and those of many similar such sets of rules, a written counterpart to the contents of the portfolio is requested to make explicit what holds the portfolio together, what its explicit argumentation is, what the sequence (if any) of the collection is, and so on. Such a compromise allows both the presentation of creative artwork for examination and having the conventional, largely written critique to accompany it.

Perhaps the spectrum of possibilities can be best depicted as in Table 12.1.

Multimodality and Argumentation

I now return to a theme that has been addressed twice in the book so far: in Chapter 2 and Chapter 6.

Studies in argument (the product) and argumentation (the process) have only recently and partially begun to address the question of multimodality via the International Society for the Study of Argumentation (ISSA) conferences, though there is yet to be a strand at those conferences that addresses multimodality directly. Since the turn of the century, *visual argumentation* has become a well-established strand of enquiry and, in 2006, *argumentation in education* was also established with about 20 papers devoted to this aspect of argumentation. Because the ISSA conferences come from a tradition of pragma-dialectical argumentation, it is not surprising that their mode of communication has been principally verbal. Nevertheless, the recent emphasis on visual argumentation and on learning/education suggests that there is interest in what multimodality has to offer to argumentation in the field of education. That interest was certainly manifested in a seminar at the Open University in early 2008, wherein still and moving images were discussed as were verbal texts with regard to argumentation, and in a conference on multimodality and learning in London in the summer of that year.

From a multimodality point of view, argumentation appeared explicitly in only two papers at the 2008 conference: the one that forms this section of the chapter, and Petr Kaderka's 'Common-sense knowledge and argumentation in multimodal discourse'. It is likely, however, that interest in argumentation from the multimodal standpoint will grow, for a number of reasons. First, argumentation or persuasion is implicit in many of the other locations of multimodal enquiry: literacies, learning environments, the arts, social interactions, and the like. Second, explicit argumentation has always involved multimodality to some extent, and the early twenty-first-century environment of multimodal communication makes it impossible to consider argumentation without a dimension of multimodality. Third, the need for good and communicable argumentation in a world where democracy (whose life-blood is argumentation) is a matter of almost constant vigilance and debate means that multimodal argumentation must be understood and practiced, both in and outside formal educational contexts. It is possible that new rhetorical theory might provide some help here.

Table 12.1 From implicit to explicit argumentation in dissertations

Totally Implicit	*Principally implicit*	*Balanced between implicit and explicit*	*Principally explicit*	*Totally explicit*
In such a presentation, there is no attempt to explain or make explicit the intention of the piece; it 'speaks for itself'	Here, the artwork carries most of the burden, but there is some allowance for verbal interpretation (e.g. in plaques on a wall, or short statements by the artist)	In a dissertation or exhibition catalogue, for example, a balance is struck between the artwork itself and its exegesis in the verbal form	A conventionally verbal and printed dissertation, for example, might include illustrations or examples of work that operates more implicitly	More like a conventional dissertation, with an explicit up-front claim or proposition, supported by written and other evidence.

Argument is Not The Same as Persuasion

A single image can *persuade*, but it doesn't necessarily *argue*. Take the example of the image of a particular brand of jam beside the selection of jams in your local supermarket – especially if that image is accompanied by a sign saying that the cost of the jam is reduced or that there is a special offer of '2 for 1'. This sign is highly persuasive, but it doesn't argue. You could say that it becomes an element in an argumentational chain of reasoning if the shopper begins to weigh up his or her usual brand of jam versus the one on offer. Then the shopper has two claims to decide between and evidence underpinning both to consider. However, the argument does not inhere inside the sign advertising the particular kind of jam, though it might be implicit. Persuasion can also take other forms besides the visual and verbal.

An argument, conversely, usually consists of a claim/proposition or series of propositions; evidence or grounds to support the proposition; a warrant validating the connection between the proposition and its grounds; and some sort of backing that provides an agreed set of values, parameters, and common discourses as a foundation for argument. It may also contain a rebuttal in opposition to the proposition and/or to its connection with the evidence. That rebuttal could bring about a qualification of the argument. The conceptual framework I have used to describe argument here is again that of Toulmin (1958/2003). There is a linearity to such a model of argument, plus a clear delineation between an abstract claim/proposition at one level and the particular grounds or evidence for it at another. The model is not necessarily dynamic: it is not a model for composition but for the testing of sound arguments.

In What Sense can Argument be Multimodal?

Toulmin's model is stretched when it comes to multimodal presentation. An advertisement on the Web for Swift Freight uses a montage of images of means of transport to show the 'multimodal' (i.e., multi-modes of transport) solutions available to the shipper of goods around the world. On the website, the montage stands alongside the words:

> A leader in multimodal solutions, Swift Freight pioneered sea-air combined transportation in the Middle East and is today the largest sea-air operator into Europe via the United Arab Emirates. This uniquely cost effective and time sensitive solution connects the corners of the world and bridges the gap between sea and air freight. For the European sector, Swift is the exclusive handling agent for S.A.T. Sea-Air Transport of Germany. Swift also provides sea-air solutions for a number of regions in Africa, executing special projects and offering innovative and customized solutions to suit any requirement.
>
> (http://www.swiftfreight.com/Multimodal_Transportation.htm)

Here, the claim or proposition is absent (it has to be something like 'You should use Swift Freight'; such a basic proposition operates in all advertisements), but the image is balanced with the words so that each supports the other. The image is an illustration of the verbal text, but the text is also an elaboration of the image. When the proposition is absent, as in this case, it can be assumed to be either implicit or to be embodied in the message. Such conflation of propositions and evidence makes for a range of possible avenues that one can travel (the link to 'sea-air solutions' is one such avenue) under the broad canopy of the macro-proposition.

With such close juxtaposition, the possibilities for comparison and tension are foregrounded. The chance to compare and contrast not only the images but the verbal texts and the particular combinations of image and text in each case is made evident, and it is no surprise to know that such comparisons are the basis of much educational work (such comparisons are typical of essay questions, especially in examination contexts). Such comparisons between the nature and affordances of different modes, and of their combination, make for clearer articulations of their qualities and of the means and effects of communication. There is more chance for argument. Artists such as Barbara Kruger use the juxtaposition of word and image to good effect, generating argument via the friction between the two modes.

Moving Image

The basis of the moving image is one image followed by another. There is thus more than one image in play and some degree of contiguity. Because there is contiguity, there is the possibility of argument. The principle behind the notion that moving image can be argumentational is, again, that of *post hoc propter hoc*. So moving image has the capacity for, or perhaps suggests, argumentation. Narrative and causality come together in this suggestive relationship.

Clearly there is a spectrum of possibility in this relationship, from the barely suggestive to fully fledged, explicit, and conceptual argumentation. A 'purely' narrative or descriptive film (e.g., in the latter case, an evocation of a place) will hardly argue unless there is the presentation of some tension or conflict, some sense of contrast or opposition within it. A photo-essay or documentary film, conversely, is more evidently argumentational, with the structures of argument (propositions, sequence of ideas, evidence, and the like) more obviously to the fore than the structures of narrative or description.

Film, in itself, is multimodal in that it operates in space and time with a range of modes – moving image, speech, sound, music. In what may be an interesting path for multimodality studies to pursue, there will be some foregrounding of one or two modes – and backgrounding of others – at particular points in the film. Such movement, variation, and balancing set up rhythms within the artwork that could be said to constitute an argument, just as in a piece of music or choreography. In these senses, argument is similar to the creation of a pattern in the course of a time-based work of art; it is internal to the artwork itself. It may not argue in the sense of making a case, intervening in the public discourse of positioning, taking a stand, and so on.

Further Discussion

Argument can thus be seen to take place where there is difference at play. Such difference might be between modes, with one or two foregrounding themselves and others providing a background (part of the 'backing', to use Toulmin's term). The difference always has to carry some degree of abstraction from particularity, so that one level of phenomena can be interpreted and given meaning by a higher level. Once such levels of significance are established, there is the space for criticality and argumentation. The levels can be created inductively, from the bottom upward, or they can be created deductively, from the top downward. However, there is rarely a case when argumentation is not possible. Such would be the case if, theoretically, the discourse moved on a level plane without reaching above or below itself to create some degree of significance or meaning.

Modes of communication have levels of significance. However, besides the hierarchical, vertical operation of levels of meaning, there is also a horizontal drive. Where there is horizontal movement, even in the complementarities of an image and a verbal text, between two images or between other modes of communication, there is the possibility of argument.

There are, thus, implications for both argumentation theory and multimodality theory in the bringing together of the fields of argument and multimodality. For argumentation, there is a need to move beyond visual argumentation and mono-modal (largely verbal) theories of how argument operates, to a wider conception of multimodal operations. For multimodality, there is an opportunity to take what is a meta-modal and multimodal perspective and apply it in the field of argumentation, wherein rationality, rhetoric, some degree of logic and the movement toward consensus or accepting difference have predominated.

In Chapter 8, after the presentation of an interview with a second-year chemistry student, the following discussion took place:

> If we wished to unravel what is assumed by the phase 'a series of facts used to prove a point' in Chemistry, we could so do with an elaboration: 'a [logical or quasi-logical] series of [generally accepted common truths, which were once hypotheses, and are now known as] facts used to prove a point [which, in turn, is a proposition or claim that posits some new position, new knowledge]'. It can be seen, then, that the progress of knowledge in Chemistry is a matter of the positing of new hypotheses, some of which becomes reified as 'facts' which, for a

time provide support for claims/propositions and a stable relationship between theories and facts. The driving force here is new ideas...and thus a new theory of the nature of knowledge and learning, to be taken up and discussed in the final chapter of this book.

Let us take this argument further.

There is, from the point of view of the beginnings of a new theory of argument, no such thing as a certain fact. All is contestable, and knowledge progresses through the continued challenge to accepted view of how the world works. The driving force of learning is this well-spring of inquiry, which questions existing facts and common sense understandings of the world. 'Facts', from this point of view, are the dead husks of learning, left behind for those who wish to use them to prove that something happened or something was the case. However, they can be no more than husks, and anyone using them in this way to decipher the lineaments of knowledge or learning is using evidence that remains after the event: picking through the embers. To understand the event itself – the moving spirit and fire of learning as it happens, and knowledge as it is created – requires a willingness to enter the fire, to get to the centre of intellectual inquiry. That is where argument operates.

References and Bibliography

Ab Jalil, H. (2007). Role of assistance in computer-mediated communication in higher education. Unpublished PhD thesis. Bristol: University of Bristol, School of Education.

Andrews, D. (2007). Gear design software. Unpublished final year MEng project. Durham: Durham University, Department of Engineering.

Andrews, R. (ed.). (1989). *Narrative and argument.* Milton Keynes: Open University Press.

Andrews, R. (1992). An exploration of structural relationships in narrative and argumentative writing, with particular reference to the work of year 8 students. Unpublished PhD thesis. Hull: University of Hull, School of Education.

Andrews, R. (ed.) (1992). *Rebirth of rhetoric: essays in language, culture and education.* London: Routledge.

Andrews, R. (1993a). Developing argument. *The English and Media Magazine, 28,* Summer 1993, 34–38.

Andrews, R. (1993b). Argument in schools: the value of a generic approach. *Cambridge Journal of Education, 23*(2), 277–285.

Andrews, R. (1994). Democracy and the teaching of argument. *English Journal, 83*(6), 62–69.

Andrews, R. (1995). *Teaching and learning argument.* London: Cassell.

Andrews, R. (1997a). Learning to argue. In Riddle, M. (ed.), *The quality of argument: a colloquium on issues of teaching and learning in higher education.* Middlesex University: School of Lifelong Learning & Education, 9–12.

Andrews, R. (1997b). Reconceiving argument. *Educational Review, 49*(3), 259–69.

Andrews, R. (2000). Introduction: Learning to argue in higher education. In Mitchell, S., and Andrews, R. (eds), *Learning to argue in higher education.* Portsmouth, NH: Heinemann/Boynton-Cook, 1–11.

Andrews, R. & Mitchell, S. (2001). *Essays in argument* (Research in Education series). London: Middlesex University Press.

Andrews, R. (2002). Argumentation in education: issues arising from undergraduate students' work. In van Eemeren, F. H., Blair, J. A., Willard, C. A., and Henkemans, F. S. (eds), *Proceedings of the fifth conference of the International Society for the Study of Argumentation.* Amsterdam: SicSat (International Center for the Study of Argumentation), 17–22.

Andrews, R. (2003a). The end of the essay? *Teaching in Higher Education, 8*(1), 117–28.

Andrews, R. (2003b) *Research questions.* London: Continuum.

Andrews, R. (2005). Models of argumentation in educational discourse *and* Response to Paul Prior. *Text, 25*(1), 107–27, 145–147.

Andrews, R. (2007). Argumentation, critical thinking and the postgraduate dissertation. *Educational Review, 59*(1), 1–18.

Andrews, R. (2008) What counts as evidence in education? Published online on *Teacher Training Resource Bank* at www.ttrb.ac.uk (July 28, 2008) – article ID 14608.

Andrews, R. (2009). *The importance of argument in education* [professorial lecture]. London: Institute of Education Publications.

Andrews, R., and Costello, P. (1992). *Improving the quality of argument 7–16: interim report.* Hull: University of Hull, Centre for Studies in Rhetoric, 122 pp.

Andrews, R., Costello, P., and Clarke, S. (1993). *Improving the quality of argument, 5–16: final report.* Hull: University of Hull, Centre for Studies in Rhetoric, 247 pp.

Andrews, R., and Gibson, H. (1993). A critique of the 'chronological/non-chronological' distinction in the National Curriculum for English. *Educational Review, 45*(3), 239–49.

Andrews, R., and Mitchell, S. (2001). *Essays in argument.* London: Middlesex University Press.

Andrews, R., Torgerson, C., Low, G., McGuinn, N., and Robinson, A. (2006a). *Teaching argumentative non-fiction writing to 7–14 year olds: a systematic review of the evidence of successful practice.* Report. In *Research Evidence in Education Library*. London: EPPI-Centre, Social Science Research Unit, Institute of Education, University of London (http://eppi.ioe.ac.uk/reel).

Andrews, R., Torgerson, C., Robinson, A, See, B-H., Mitchell, S., Peake, K., et al. (2006b). *Argumentative skills in first year undergraduates: a pilot study.* York: Higher Education Academy, 70 pp.

Andrews, R., and Haythornthwaite, C. (eds). (2007). *The handbook of e-learning research.* London: Sage.

Andrews, R., Torgerson, C., Low, G and McGuinn, N. (2009) Teaching argument writing to 7-14 year olds: an international review of the evidence of successful practice, *Cambridge Journal of Education,* Autumn 2009.

Anon. (2003). What is the range of marks made on paper by a five year old boy? How do these marks demonstrate a development in written literacy? Unpublished BA dissertation. York: University of York, Department of Educational Studies.

Applebee, A. (1978). *The child's concept of story.* Chicago: Chicago University Press.

Assessment of Performance Unit (1998). *Language performance in schools: review of APU language monitoring 1979–1983.* London: Her Majesty's Stationery Office.

Austin, J. L. (1962). *How to do things with words.* London: Oxford University Press.

Bakhtin, M. M. (1981). *The dialogic imagination: four essays by M .M. Bakhtin.* ed. M. Holquist, trans. C. Emerson and M. Holquist. Austin, TX: University of Texas Press.

Bakhtin, M. (1986). *Speech genres and other late essays.* Austin, TX: University of Texas Press.

Barnes, D., Britton, J., and Rosen, H. (1969). *Language, the learner and the school.* Harmondsworth: Pelican.

Barnet, H., and Bedau, H. (1996). *Critical thinking, reading and writing: a brief guide to argument* (2nd ed). Boston Bedford Books of St Martin's Press.

Bazerman, C. (1988). *Shaping written knowledge: the genre and activity of the experimental article in science.* Madison: The University of Wisconsin Press.

Baynham, M., Macguire, T., and Morton, T. (2006). *A literature review of research on teacher education on adult literacy, numeracy and ESOL.* London: National Research and Development Centre.

Becta (2007). Impact of ICT in schools: a landscape review. Coventry: British Educational and Communication Technology Agency.

Berrill, D. (ed.) (1996). *Perspectives on written argument.* Cresskill, NJ: Hampton Press.

Biesta, G. (2007). Why 'what works' won't work: evidence-based practice and the democratic deficit in educational research. *Educational Theory, 57*(1), 1–22.

Billig, M. (1996) *Arguing and thinking: a rhetorical approach to social psychology,* revised edition. Cambridge: Cambridge University Press

Black, P., and Muecke, S. (1992) A moment in fashion. In Andrews, R. (ed), *Rebirth of rhetoric: essays in language, culture and education.* London: Routledge.

Blair, J. A. (2002). The relationships among logic, dialectic and rhetoric. In van Eemeren et al. (eds), *Proceedings of the fifth conference of the International Society for the Study of Argumentation.* Amsterdam: SicSat, 125–131.

Britton, J. (1987) Vygotsky's contribution to pedagogical theory . *English in Education,* 21:3, 22ff

Burke, K. (1969). *A rhetoric of motives.* Berkeley: University of California Press.

Burkhalter, N. (1994). Applying Vygotsky: teaching preformal-operational children a formal-operational task. Unpublished research report. University of Wyoming. ERIC document ED379208.

Burkhalter, N. (1995). A Vygotsky-based curriculum for teaching persuasive writing in the elementary grades. *Language Arts, 72,* 192–199.

Burwood, S. (1993). *Essay writing: an introduction.* Hull: University of Hull, Department of Philosophy.

Campbell Collaboration. (2007). Retrieved April 11, 2007, from http://www.campbellcollaboration.org/

Cockcroft, R., & Cockcroft, S. M. (1992). *Persuading people: an introduction to rhetoric.* London: Macmillan.

Coffin, C. (2004). Arguing about how the world is or how the world should be: the role of argument in IELTS tests. *Journal of English for Academic Purposes,* 3(2), 229–246.

Coffin, C. (2007). *The language and discourse of argumentation in computer conferencing and essays: full research report*. ESRC end of award report. Swindon: Economic and Social Research Council
Coffin. C., and Hewings, A. (2005). Engaging electronically: using CMC to develop students' argumentation skills in higher education. *Language and Education, 19*(2), 32–49.
Coffin, C., Painter, C., and Hewings, A. (2005). Argumentation in a multi-party asynchronous computer mediated conference: a generic analysis [special edition]. *Australian Review of Applied Linguistics 26,* 41–63.
Coffin, C., North, S., and Martin, D. (2009). Exchanging and countering points of view: a linguistic perspective on school students' use of electronic conferencing. Available online at http://www3.interscience.wiley.com/cgi-bin/fulltext/120121863/PDFSTART
Cohen, L and Manion, L. (1994) *Research methods in education* London: Routledge
Copeland, S., Siddhartha, S., and McMillan, G. (2007). *Electronic theses and dissertations: pragmatic issues and practical solutions*. Oxford: Chandos.
Corbett, E. P. J. (1965). *Classical rhetoric for the modern student*. New York: Oxford University Press.
Corbett, E. P. J., and Connors, R .J. (1999). *Classical rhetoric for the modern student* (4th edn). New York: Oxford University Press.
Costello, P. J. M. (2000), *Thinking skills and early childhood education*. London: David Fulton.
Costello, P. J. M., and Mitchell, S. (eds). (1995). *Competing and consensual voices: the theory and practice of argument*. Clevedon: Multilingual Matters.
Creme, P., and Lea, M. R. (2003). *Writing at university: a guide for students*. Maidenhead: Open University Press.
DfES. (2007). Retrieved April 11, 2007, from http://www.standards.dfes.gov.uk/research/
Diamond, I. (2003). Implementation of the Roberts Report on the supply of scientists and engineers in the UK [letter to Vice-Chancellors and Principals of UK Higher Education Institutions, July 10, 2003].
DISC. (2007). Retrieved April 20, 2007, from http://www.disc.wisc.edu/types/secondary.htm
Dixon, J. (1991a). A schooling in English. *English in Education, 25*(3), 10–17.
Dixon, J. (1991b). *A schooling in English: critical episodes in the struggle to shape literary and cultural studies*. Milton Keynes: Open University Press.
Driver, R., Newton, P., and Osborne, J. (2000). Establishing the norms of scientific argumentation in classrooms. *Science Education, 84*(3): 297–312.
Education Evidence Portal. (2007). Retrieved April 11, 2007, from http://www.eep.ac.uk
Entwistle, N., Nisbet, J., and Bromage, A. (2004). Teaching-learning environments and student learning in electronic engineering. Paper presented at Third Workshop of the European Network on Powerful Learning Environments, Bruges, September 30 to October 2, 2004 and Economic and Social Research Council: Teaching and Learning Research Project (Enhancing Teaching-Learning Environments in Undergraduate Courses).
EPPI-Centre. (2007). Retrieved April 11, 2007, from http://eppi.ioe.ac.uk/reel
ESRC (2007). Retrieved April 20, 2007, from http://www.esrcsocietytoday.ac.uk/ESRCInfoCentre/opportunities/current_funding_opportunities/index27.aspx,
Fahnestock, J., and Secor, M. (2004). *A rhetoric of argument* (3rd ed). New York: McGraw-Hill.
Fairbairn, G., and Winch, C. (1996). *Reading, writing and reasoning: a guide for students*. Maidenhead: Open University Press.
Freedman, A., and Pringle, I. (1980). Writing in the college years. *College Composition and Communication 30*, October 1980, 311–324.
Freedman, A., and Medway, P. (eds). (1994). *Genre and the new rhetoric*. London: Taylor and Francis.
Fulkerson, R. (1996). *Teaching the argument in writing*. Urbana, IL: National Council for the Teaching of English.
Futurelab. (2007). Retrieved April 11, 2007, from http://www.futurelab.org.uk/research/lit_reviews.htm
Gage, J. T. (1996). The reasoned thesis. In Emmel, B., Resch, P., and Tenney, D. (eds), *Argument revisited; argument redefined*. Thousand Oaks, CA: Sage.
Gan, L. (2002). Chinese college students' perception of English teaching and learning in China. Unpublished MA dissertation. York: University of York.
Gee, J. P., Hull, G., and Lankshear, C. (1997). *The new work order*. St Leonards NSW: Allen and Unwin.
Giere, R. N. (1991). *Understanding scientific reasoning* (3rd ed). Fort Worth, TX: Holt, Reinhart & Winston.

Giltrow, J. (2000). 'Argument' as a term in student talk about writing. In Mitchell, S., and Andrews, R. (eds), *Learning to argue in higher education*. Portsmouth, NH: Boynton/Cook, 129–145.

Google. (2007). Retrieved April 11, 2007, from www.google.com

Gorard, S. (2002). The role of secondary data in combining methodological approaches. *Educational Review, 54*(3), 231–237.

Gorard, S., and Taylor, C. (2004). What is 'triangulation'? In *Building research capacity*. Cardiff: Cardiff University, Cardiff School of Social Sciences, 7, 7–9.

Govier, T. (1988). Are there two sides to every question? In Govier, T. (ed.), *Selected issues in logic and communication*. Belmont, CA: Wadsworth, 43–54.

Graves, D. (1983). *Writing: teachers and children at work*. Portsmouth, NH: Heinemann.

Grimshaw, J. (1990). *Argument structure*. Cambridge, MA: MIT Press.

Gross, J. (ed.). (1991). *The Oxford book of essays*. Oxford: Oxford University Press.

Habermas, J. (1984). *The theory of communicative action: vol 1 Reason and the rationalization of society* (McCarthy, T., trans) [originally published in 1981 by Suhrkamp Verlag, Frankfurt]. Boston: Beacon Press; London: Heinemann.

Hammann, L. A., and Stevens, R. J. (2003). Instructional approaches to improving students' writing of compare-contrast essays: an experimental study. *Journal of Literacy Research, 35*, 731–756.

Heaton, J. (1998). Secondary analysis of qualitative data. *Social Research Update* no 22. Retrieved April 20, 2007, from http://sru.soc.surrey.ac.uk/SRU22.html

Hegelund, S., and Kock, C. (2000). Macro-Toulmin: the argument model as structural guideline in academic writing. In Tindale, C., Hansen, H.V., and Sveda, E. (2000). *Argumentation at the century's turn*. Peterborough, Ontario: The Ontario Society for the Study of Argumentation (CDRom, proceedings from the OSSA 1999 conference).

Heilker, P. (1996) *The essay: theory and pedagogy for an active form*. Urbana, IL: National Council of Teachers of English.

Hewings, A., and Coffin. C. (2007). Writing in multi-party computer conferences and single-authored assignments. *Journal of English for Academic Purposes, 6*(2), 126–142.

Hewings, A., Coffin, C., and North, S. (2007). Supporting undergraduate students' acquisition of academic argumentation strategies through computer conferencing. Higher Education Academy Research Report. York: Higher Education Academy. Accessible from http://www.heacademy.ac.uk/ourwork/research

Hidi, S., Berndorff, D., and Ainley, M. (2002). Children's argument writing, interest and self-efficacy: an intervention study. *Learning and Instruction. 12*, 429–446.

Higher Education Academy. (2007). Retrieved April 11, 2007, from www.heacademy.ac.uk

Hill, C. A. (1995). Thinking through controversy: evaluating written arguments. In Costello, P., and Mitchell, S. (eds), *Competing and consensual voices: the theory and practice of argument*. Clevedon: Multilingual Matters, 160–171.

Honderich, T. (1995). *The Oxford companion to philosophy*. Oxford: Oxford University Press.

Hounsell, D., and McCune, V. (2004). The development of students' ways of thinking and practising in three final-year biology courses. Paper given at Northumbria/EARLI Second Biannual Assessment Conference, Bergen, 23–25 June 2004 and ESRC: Teaching and Learning Research Project (Enhancing Teaching-Learning Environments in Undergraduate Courses).

Index to Theses. (2008). Retrieved September 23, 2008, from www.theses.com

Institute of Education. (2007). Retrieved April 11, 2007, from http://ioewebserver.ioe.ac.uk/ioe/cms/get.asp?cid=10713

JISC. (2008). *Electronic theses*. Retrieved September 23, 2008, from *http://www.jisc.ac.uk/whatwedo/programmes/programme_fair/project_rgu_etd.aspx*

Jolliffe, D. A. (1988). *Advances in writing research: writing in academic disciplines*. Norwood, NJ: Ablex.

Kaufer, D., and Geisler, C. (1991). A scheme for representing academic argument. *The Journal of Advanced Composition, 11*, 107–122.

Kellogg, R. (1970). Understanding children's art. In Cramer, P. (ed.), *Readings in developmental psychology today*. Delmar, CA: CRM.

Key Services Ltd and UCL Library Services. (2006). *Evaluation of options for a UK electronic thesis service: findings from a study of EthOS*.

Kinneavy, J. (1971/1980). *A theory of discourse*. New York: W.W. Norton.

Knudson, R. E. (1992). *An analysis of persuasive discourse: learning how to take a stand*. Paper presented at the Annual Meeting of the National Reading Conference, San Antonio, TX. ERIC document ED353581.

Kress, G. (1989). Texture and meaning. In Andrews, R. (ed.), *Narrative and argument.* Milton Keynes: Open University Press.
Kroll, B. (ed.). (1990). *Second language writing: research insights for the classroom.* Cambridge: Cambridge University Press.
Kuhn, D. (1991). *The skills of argument.* Cambridge: Cambridge University Press.
Lamb, C. (1991). Beyond argument in feminist composition. *College Composition and Communication, 42.*
Lamb, C. (1996) Other voices, different parties: feminist responses. In Berrill. P. (ed.), *Perspectives on Written Argument* Cresskill NJ: Hampton Press, 257-69
Larson, M., Britt, M. A., and Larson, A. (2004). Disfluencies in comprehending argumentative texts. *Reading Psychology, 25*(3), 205–224.
Latour, B. (1987). *Science in action: how to follow scientists and engineers through society.* Cambridge, MA: Harvard University Press.
Leith, R., and Myerson, G. (1989). *The power of address: explorations in rhetoric.* London: Routledge.
Levin, P. (2004). *Write great essays!* Maidenhead: Open University Press.
Lillis, T., and Scott, M. (2008). Defining academic literacies research: issues of epistemology, ideology and strategy. *Journal of Applied Linguistics, 4*(1), 5–32.
Lindeman, E. (1982/2001). *A rhetoric for writing teachers* (4th ed.). New York: Oxford University Press.
Lipman, M. (1976). *Philosophy for children.* Oxford: Basil Blackwell.
Litosseliti, L. (2002). The discursive construction of morality and gender: investigating public and private arguments. In Benor, S., Rose, M., Sharma, D., Sweetland, J., and Zhang, Q. (eds), *Gendered practices in language.* Stanford, CA: Stanford University.
Lok, B. (2002). Pedagogical differences between native and non-native English teachers in Hong Kong secondary schools. Unpublished MA dissertation. York: University of York.
Lunsford, K. (2002). Contextualizing Toulmin's model in the writing classroom: a case study. *Written Communication, 19*(1), 109–174.
MacColl, J. (2002). *Electronic theses and dissertations: a strategy for the UK. Ariadne, 32,* (July 2002).
Martin, D., Coffin, C., and North, S. (2007). What's your claim? Developing pupils' historical argument skills using asynchronous text-based computer conferencing. *Teaching History, 126,* 32–7.
Medway, P. (1986). *What counts as English: selections from language in a school subject at the twelve-year-old level.* Unpublished PhD thesis. Leeds: University of Leeds.
Meyer, S. L. (1993). Refusing to play the confidence game: the illusion of mastery in the reading/writing of texts. *College English, 55*(2), 46–63.
Miller, C. (1984). Genre as social action. *Quarterly Journal of Speech, 70,* 151–167.
Mitchell, S. (1992). *The teaching and learning of argument in sixth forms and higher education: interim report.* Hull: University of Hull, Centre for Studies in Rhetoric.
Mitchell, S. (1994a). *The teaching and learning of argument in sixth forms and higher education: final report.* Hull: University of Hull, Centre for Studies in Rhetoric.
Mitchell, S. (1994b). English A Level and beyond: a case study. *English in Education, 28*(2), 36–47.
Mitchell, S. (1997). *Improving the quality of argument in higher education: interim report.* London: Middlesex University, School of Lifelong Learning and Education.
Mitchell, S. (2000). *Improving the quality of argument in higher education: trial materials.* London: Middlesex University, School of Lifelong Learning and Education.
Mitchell, S., and Andrews, R. (1994a). Learning to operate successfully in advanced level History. In Freedman, A., and Medway, P. (eds), *Teaching and learning genre.* Portsmouth, NH: Heinemann-Boynton/Cook, 81–104.
Mitchell, S., and Andrews, R. (1994b). The development of argument in English and Politics in 16–18 year old students. *Literacy Learning: Secondary Thoughts, 1*(2), 8–16.
Mitchell, S., and Andrews, R. (eds). (2000). *Learning to argue in higher education.* Portsmouth, NH: Heinemann-Boynton/Cook.
Mitchell, S., and Riddle, M. (2000). *Improving the quality of argument in higher education: final report.* London: Middlesex University, School of Lifelong Learning and Education.
Mitchell, S., Prior.P., Bilbro, R., Peake, K., See, B-H., and Andrews, R. (2008). A reflexive approach to interview data in an investigation of argument [special issue]. *International Journal of Research and Method in Education, 31*(3), 229–241.
Moffett, J. (1968). *Teaching the universe of discourse.* Boston: Houghton Mifflin.

Myerson, G. (1992). *The argumentative imagination: Wordsworth, Dryden, religious dialogues*. Manchester: Manchester University Press.
Myerson, G. (1994). *Rhetoric, reason and society: rationality as dialogue*. London: Sage.
Newbolt, H. (1921). *The teaching of English in England*. London: Her Majesty's Stationery Office.
Newkirk, T. (1989). *Critical thinking and writing: reclaiming the essay*. Urbana, IL: National Council of Teachers of English.
Networked Digital Library of Theses and Dissertations. (2008). Retrieved September 23, 2008, from www.ntltd.org
North, S. P., Coffin, C .J., and Hewings, A. (2008). Using exchange structure analysis to explore argument in text-based computer conferences. *International Journal of Research and Method in Education, 31*(3), 257–276.
OECD/PISA. (2007). Retrieved April 16, 2007, from http://www.oecd.org/department/0,2688, en_2649_35845621_1_1_1_1_1,00.html
Painter, C., Coffin, C., and Hewings, A. (2003). Impacts of direct tutorial activities in computer conferencing: a case study. *Distance Education, 24*(2), 159–174.
Prior, P. (2005). Towards the ethnography of argumentation: a response to Richard Andrews' 'Models of argumentation in educational discourse'. *Text, 25*(1), 129–144.
Reid, I. (2004). *Wordsworth and the formation of English studies*. Aldershot: Ashgate.
Research Councils UK. (2001). Joint statement of the Research Councils'/Arts and Humanities Research Board's skills training requirements for research students. London: Author.
Ricoeur, P. (1970). *Freud and philosophy: an essay on interpretation*. New Haven: Yale University Press.
Riddle, M. (2000). Improving argument by parts. In Mitchell, S., and Andrews, R. (eds), *Learning to argue in higher education*. Portsmouth, NH: Heinemann/Boynton-Cook, 53–64.
Rogoff, B. (1991). *Apprenticeship in thinking: cognitive development in social context*. New York: Oxford University Press.
Schön, D. A. (1983). *The reflective practitioner: how professionals think in action*. New York: Basic Books.
Schön, D. A. (1990). *Educating the reflective practitioner: toward a new design for teaching and learning*. San Francisco: Jossey-Bass.
Searle, J. (1969). *Speech acts*. Cambridge: Cambridge University Press.
Sheeran, Y., and Barnes, D. (1991). *School writing*. Milton Keynes: Open University Press.
Storey, W. K. (2009). *Writing history: a guide for students* (3rd ed). New York: Oxford University Press.
Strickland, S. (2008). *Engladesh*. Final masters presentation. London: City University. Available at: www.engladesh.com.
Swales, J. (1990). *Genre analysis: English in academic and research settings*. Cambridge: Cambridge University Press.
Swift. (2008). Retrieved June, 2008, from www.swiftfreight.com/Multimodal_Transportation.htm.
Tannen, D. (1991). *You just don't understand: women and men in conversation*. London: Virago.
Tannen, D. (1999). *The argument culture: changing the way we argue and debate*. London: Virago.
Tarnay, L. (2002). The conceptual basis of visual argumentation: a case for arguing in and through moving images. In van Eemeren, F. et al. (eds), *Proceedings of the fifth conference of the International Society for the Study of Argumentation*. Amsterdam: SicSat, 1001–1005.
Teacher Training Resource Bank. (2008). Retrieved July 29, 2008, from www.ttrb.ac.uk
Tindale, C., Hansen, H.V., and Sveda, E. (2000). *Argumentation at the century's turn*. Peterborough, Ontario: The Ontario Society for the Study of Argumentation (CDRom, proceedings from the OSSA 1999 conference).
Topoi. (2008). Retrieved September 30, 2008, from http://www.springer.com/philosophy/journal/11245 -
Torgerson, C. (2003). *Systematic reviews*. London: Continuum.
Torgerson, C., Andrews, R., Low, G., McGuinn, N., and Robinson, A. (2006). *Improving argumentative skills in undergraduates: a systematic review*. York: Higher Education Academy, 80 pp.
Toulmin, S. (1958/2003). *The uses of argument*. Cambridge: Cambridge University Press.
Toulmin, S., Rieke, R., and Janik, A. (1984). *An introduction to reasoning* (2nd ed). London: Collier Macmillan.
Troia, G. A., and Graham, S. (2002). The effectiveness of a highly explicit, teacher-directed strategy instruction routine: changing the writing performance of students with learning disabilities. *Journal of Learning Disabilities, 35*, 290–305.

UNESCO. (2008). *The guide to electronic theses and dissertations*. Retrieved September 23, 2008, from http://www.etdguide.org/
University of York. (2007). Retrieved April 11, 2007, from http://www.york.ac.uk/services/library/subjects/education.htm
van Eemeren, F. (ed.). (2001). *Crucial concepts in argumentation theory*. Amsterdam: Amsterdam University Press.
van Eemeren, F. (ed.). (2002). *Advances in pragma-dialectics*. Amsterdam: SicSat, and Newport News, VA: Vale Press.
van Eemeren, F. H., Grootendorst, R., and Snoeck Henkemans, F. (2002). *Argumentation*. Mahwah, NJ: Lawrence Erlbaum.
van Eemeren, F., Blair, J. A., Willard, C., and Snoeck Henkemans, A. F. (eds). (2002). *Proceedings of the fifth conference of the International Society for the Study of Argumentation*. Amsterdam: SicSat.
VanTassel-Baska, J., Johnson, D. T., Hughes, C. E., and Boyce, L. N. (1996). A study of language arts curriculum effectiveness with gifted learners. *Journal for the Education of the Gifted*, *19*, 461–480.
VanTassel-Baska, J., Zuo, L., Avery, L. D., and Little, C. A. (2002). A curriculum study of gifted-student learning in the language arts. *Gifted Child Quarterly*, *46*, 30–44.
Vygotsky, L. (1986). *Thought and language*. Cambridge, MA: MIT Press.
Vygotsky, L. (1991). Genesis of the higher mental functions. In Light, P., et al. (eds), *Learning to think*. London: Routledge, 32–41.
Walton, D. (1989). *Informal logic: a handbook for critical argumentation*. Cambridge: Cambridge University Press.
Watkins, D. A., and Biggs, J. B. (eds). (1996). *The Chinese learner: cultural, psychological and contextual influences*. Hong Kong: University of Hong Kong, Comparative Education Research Centre.
Wenzel, J. (1980). Perspectives on argument. In Rhodes, J., and Newell, S. (eds), *Proceedings of the 1979 summer conference on argumentation*. SC: Falls Church.
Wilkinson, A., Barnsley, G., Hanna, P and Swan, M. (1980) *Assessing language development* Oxford: Oxford University Press.
Womack, P. (1993). What are essays for? *English in Education*, *27*(2), 42–59.
Yeh, S. S. (1998). Empowering education: teaching argumentative writing to cultural minority middle-school students. *Research in the Teaching of English*, *33*, 49–83.
Yoshimi, J. (2004). Mapping the structure of debate. *Informal Logic*, *24*(2), 1–21.
Zhao, Y. (2007). The impact of computer technology on teaching and learning English listening and speaking as a second language in UK higher education. Unpublished PhD thesis. York: University of York, Department of Educational Studies.

Index

References to tables and figures are indexed as, respectively, 116t and 116f.

23996956R00138

Printed in Great Britain
by Amazon